THE
USBORNE
BOOK OF
WORLD
HISTORY
DATES

Jane Chisholm

Designed by Melissa Alaverdy, Robin Farrow and Julia Rheam
History consultants - Dr. Anne Millard and Malcolm Falkus

Illustrated by Susanna Addario, Philip Argent, Gary Bines, Simone Boni, Stephen Conlin,
David Cuzik, Peter Dennis, Richard Draper, Luigi Galante, Jeremy Gower, Nicholas Hewetson,
Ian Jackson, Colin King, John Lawrence, Joseph McEwan, Radhi Parekh, Justine Peek,
Evie Safarewicz, Claudia Saraceni, Ross Watton, Gerald Wood and David Wright

Map illustrations by Jeremy Gower

Picture researcher - Ruth King   Editorial assistant - Rachael Swann
Artwork co-ordinators - Ruth King and Cathy Lowe
Managing designer - Amanda Barlow

Contents

ABOUT THIS BOOK

This book is divided into eight periods, marked with a tag at the top of each right-hand page. Each section contains features on important topics, as well as date charts, arranged in columns according to geographical areas.

This means you can follow what was happening in different parts of the world at the same time.

Dates that appear in brackets after a person's name, such as Isaac Newton (**1642-1727**), refer to his or her life. In the case of kings, queens and emperors, such as Maria Theresa (**1740-1780**), the dates of the reign are shown instead.

Historians often disagree about dates in very early history, so you may find that some dates vary slightly from those in other books.

ABBREVIATIONS

A number of abbreviations have been used in this book.

c. stands for *circa*, the Latin for "about". Early dates often begin with **c.** as experts have only been able to find an approximate date.

AD stands for *Anno Domini* (meaning "year of the Lord" in Latin). It applies to all the years after the birth of Jesus Christ.

BC stands for "Before Christ". **BC** dates are counted back from **AD0**. However, many experts believe that, due to a miscalculation, Christ's birth was probably in **c.5BC**, rather than the year **0**.

AD and **BC** have been used in the first section of the book, in the features, in the first entry of each column of the dates charts, and where dates change from **BC** to **AD**.

The first farmers

The earliest people lived as nomads, moving from place to place, hunting wild animals and gathering wild plants.

Hunters left rock paintings of themselves, and the animals that they ate and used for tools, shelters and clothing.

Nomadic people made camps, like this one, but only stayed there as long as there were enough wild animals and plants to feed them.

Gradually, people learned how to farm and changed to a more settled way of life. This happened in different places at different times, but it probably began in about **9000BC**, in an area of the Middle East known as the Fertile Crescent (see the map on page 6).

THE FIRST TOWNS

As people adopted farming, they began to build permanent places to live. One of the best known is Jericho, in Jordan, which had about 2,000 people by **8000BC**. It was destroyed in **7000BC** and later rebuilt.

By **6000BC**, Çatal Hüyük, in Turkey, was a flourishing town of 5,000-6,000 people. They made pottery and textiles, and traded widely, particularly in cloth and obsidian (a volcanic rock used for making tools).

THE MIGRATION OF PEOPLES

Between **3000-2000BC**, there were movements of peoples across Asia and Europe. Many belonged to one of two main language groups: Semitic and Indo-European.

Semitic languages include Arabic and Hebrew, as well as languages that have died out, such as Babylonian. By **c.3000BC**, the Semites were spreading out all over the Middle East.

The Indo-Europeans may have originally come from southern Russia. But after **2000BC**, many of them began to move into new areas. Most modern European languages, as well as Armenian, Latin, Sanskrit and some Hindu dialects, are descended from a common Indo-European language.

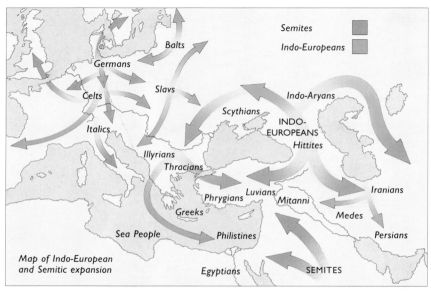

Map of Indo-European and Semitic expansion

Semites
Indo-Europeans

Balts
Germans
Celts
Slavs
Italics
Illyrians
Thracians
Phrygians
Greeks
Sea People
Philistines
Egyptians
Scythians
Indo-Aryans
INDO-EUROPEANS
Hittites
Luvians
Mitanni
Iranians
Medes
Persians
SEMITES

Çatal Hüyük consisted of small houses joined one to another. People entered through holes in the roofs.

The ladders that led to the roofs could be pulled up if the town was attacked.

Crete

The earliest known European civilization developed in Crete between **c.3000-2000BC**.

Rich Minoan women wore elaborate costumes

Crete had well-planned towns, skilled craftsmen, a form of writing (picture writing and an early script known as Linear A), and flourishing trade. We call this civilization Minoan, after the legendary King Minos.

Crete's golden age, known as the First and Second Palace Periods, lasted from **c.2000-1450BC**. The Minoans built a series of large and splendid palaces, including Knossos, Phaistos and Mallia, and developed trading links with Greece, Egypt and the eastern Mediterranean.

KNOSSOS DECLINES

In about **1450BC**, all the Cretan palaces were destroyed. This may have been linked to the eruption of a volcano on the island of Thera. At about the same time, people called Mycenaeans from the Greek mainland took over the island. Knossos was destroyed again in **c.1380BC**, possibly due to an earthquake, a local rebellion, or an attack by rival Mycenaeans. By **c.1100BC**, Crete had declined.

Craftsmen produced and sold goods such as this decorated pottery jar.

Statue of a bull, an animal sacred to the Minoans

Stylised bull's horns, in a repeated pattern, were used as a rooftop decoration.

Fresco from a Minoan palace showing young people leaping over bulls as part of a ritual

The Palace of Knossos was rebuilt several times between c.1900BC and 1450BC. At one stage it covered around 20,000m² (215,000 ft²).

Probable throne room

The queen's bedroom, decorated with frescos

As many as 30,000 people may have lived in the palace and surrounding area.

Food, oil and wine were stored in huge earthenware jars, some taller than a fully grown man.

Europe

c.35,000-18,000BC
Caves are painted in France and Spain.

Cave painting of a bison found at Lascaux, Dordogne, France

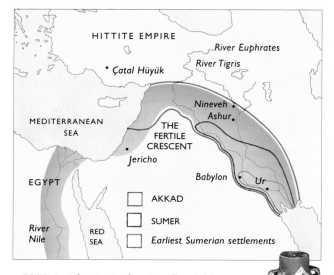

The first farmers grew vegetables and cereal crops and kept sheep.

c.6000 Groups of farmers, possibly from Turkey, reach Crete, mainland Greece and the Aegean islands.

c.5200-2000 Farming spreads throughout northern and western Europe.

c.4000-1500 Building of megaliths, large stone monuments such as temples, tombs and henges (circular areas, often made of stones), in Malta, Brittany, the Iberian peninsula (Spain and Portugal) and the British Isles.

Stonehenge, the most spectacular of many megaliths in Britain

c.4000 Copper is being worked in the Balkans.

c.3000 Olives, vines and cereals are being cultivated in the Aegean islands. Some trading contacts abroad.

Olives and wheat could both be stored in winter.

c.2500 Bronze, obsidian (a kind of volcanic glass) and flint are traded.

Grapes could be made into wine which people traded because it lasted a long time.

Bronze Age farm c.2100BC. A cone shaped construction was the simplest way of making a rainproof shelter.

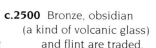

Beaker Ware

Corded Ware

c.2500-2000 Corded Ware and Beaker cultures spread in northern Europe.

The Middle East

c.9000BC Agriculture is under way in the Fertile Crescent (see map).

Wild goat *Domesticated goat*

Map:
- HITTITE EMPIRE
- River Euphrates
- River Tigris
- Çatal Hüyük
- Nineveh
- Ashur
- MEDITERRANEAN SEA
- THE FERTILE CRESCENT
- Jericho
- Babylon
- Ur
- EGYPT
- River Nile
- RED SEA
- ☐ AKKAD
- ☐ SUMER
- ☐ Earliest Sumerian settlements

c.8000 Jericho, in Jordan, is a flourishing town of about 2,000 people.

c.7000 Pottery, spinning, weaving and hammering metal are all in use.

c.6000 Çatal Hüyük, in Turkey, is a town of about 5,000-6,000 people.

Pot from Turkey c.5700BC

c.5000 First farmers in Sumer in Mesopotamia. Towns appear from about **4000BC** (see page 8).

c.4000 The technique of copper and gold smelting is discovered.

Necklaces of gold and semi-precious stones

Treasures from the royal Sumerian tombs at Ur c.2500BC

Gold dagger and sheath

Copper bowl

c.3400 The wheel is invented in Sumer.

c.3300 The Sumerians develop writing.

c.2371-2230 The kingdom of Akkad is established (see page 8).

Bronze head of Sargon, King of Akkad

Clay tablets with Sumerian cuneiform writing

Africa

c.5000BC The Sahara Desert, which had once been green, is still fertile in parts and there is evidence of cattle herders. As the Sahara continues to dry out, many people migrate to the Nile Valley.

Rock painting from this period found in the Sahara region

c.5000 Farming begins in Egypt. The Egyptians also develop pottery, linen making and, later, metal working.

c.3300 Hieroglyphic writing develops in Egypt.

An early Egyptian village

c.3118 King Menes unites Upper and Lower Egypt.

c.2686-2181 Old Kingdom in Egypt: dynasties III to VI. The pyramids are built.

Egyptian hieroglyphs

Pyramids and Sphinx at Giza, Egypt

c.2181-2040 First Intermediate Period in Egypt: dynasties VII-X.

c.2133-1633 Middle Kingdom in Egypt: dynasties XI-XIII.

Asia

Early Asian horse

c.5000BC Gradual adoption of farming in China. The Yangshao culture grows up around the Huang Ho River. Farmers grow millet, fruit, nuts and vegetables and keep pigs and dogs.

c.4000 Farming develops along the Yangtze River in China. Beginning of the cultivation of rice.

Yangshao village

c.4000 Farming communities settle in the Indus Valley in India.

c.3000 Hunter gatherers living on Japanese islands. Use of pottery.

c.2500 Longshan period in China. Farmers are better organized and keep chickens, cattle, sheep, goats, and buffalo.

c.2500-1800 The Indus Valley Civilization flourishes in India, based on agriculture, with contacts as far west as Mesopotamia. The Indus Valley people have large cities, with public buildings and good sanitation. They also have a form of writing. The best known sites are Mohenjo-Daro and Harappa.

Urban based civilizations c.2000BC

c.2500-1500 Bronze Age culture in Bactria, in Central Asia.

c.2205 Traditional earliest date of Xia (or Hsia) dynasty in China.

The Americas

By **c.15,000BC** First people arrive in North America, crossing over from Asia via a bridge of land and ice.

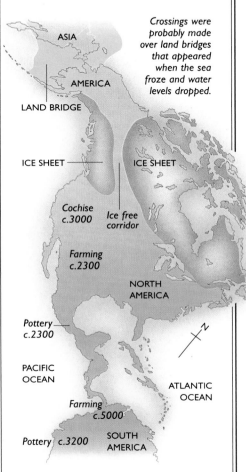

Crossings were probably made over land bridges that appeared when the sea froze and water levels dropped.

c.5000 The farming of corn develops in Central America.

c.3500 The llama is first used as a pack animal in Peru.

c.3200 Pottery in use in Ecuador.

c.3000 Pottery in use in Colombia.

c.3000 Hunter gatherers known as Cochise are living in the southwest of North America.

c.2300 Farming leads to settlement in permanent villages in Mexico.

c.2300 Use of pottery spreads to Mexico and Guatemala.

Mesopotamia

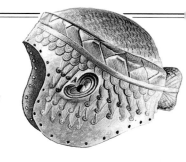

Gold and silver helmet, from Ur

SUMER AND AKKAD

By **c.3100-2800BC**, city states such as Ur, Eridu and Uruk had been established in Sumer, in southern Mesopotamia. Each state was ruled by a king, with power shifting between the different cities.

A ziggurat, or terraced temple, built c.2100BC at Ur

The fertile land bordering the great rivers Tigris and Euphrates, in the Middle East, was the heart of one of the earliest civilizations in the world. Historians call it Mesopotamia. Cities developed there from about **4000BC**, with impressive public buildings and organized political and legal systems. The wheel was invented in southern Mesopotamia in **c.3400BC**, and a form of writing, known as cuneiform, in **c.3300BC**.

A Semitic tribe rose to power in the nearby state of Akkad, and set up a dynasty under King Sargon (**c.2371-2361BC**). He conquered Sumer and united all of Mesopotamia under his rule. As a result, the city-states lost much of their importance.

In **c.2230BC**, Akkad was invaded and taken over by people called Gutians from the Zagros mountains. Sumer regained its independence, in **c.2100BC**, under Ur-Nammu, who founded Dynasty III at Ur and united Sumer. The city was destroyed in **c.2000BC**, after invasions by a people called the Elamites.

The Battle Standard of Ur

A Sumerian village

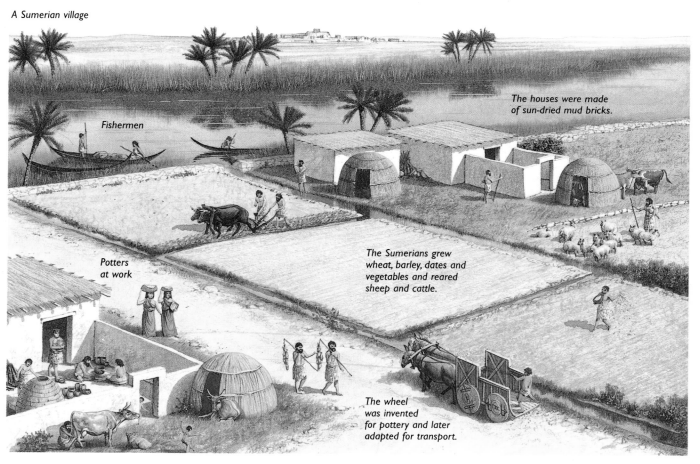

Fishermen

The houses were made of sun-dried mud bricks.

Potters at work

The Sumerians grew wheat, barley, dates and vegetables and reared sheep and cattle.

The wheel was invented for pottery and later adapted for transport.

BABYLONIA

The Amorites were a Semitic people, who set up kingdoms based around the old city-states. Two of these - Babylonia and Assyria - grew into great empires.

Babylonia expanded from the city of Babylon and conquered Akkad in **c.1894BC**. Later, under Hammurabi (**c.1792-1750BC**), all of Sumer and Akkad was absorbed into the Babylonian kingdom. He defeated the Gutians, and took territory from the Elamites and Assyrians. Hammurabi was also a clever administrator and diplomat, and was concerned with law and order and the welfare of his people.

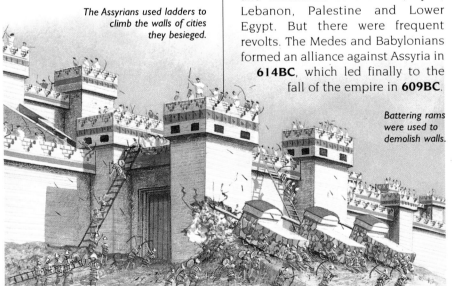

Stone slab which records Hammurabi's system of laws

Unrest followed Hammurabi's death, and parts of the kingdom broke away. In **c.1595BC**, Babylonia was invaded by Kassites from the Zagros mountains. They were ousted by Elamites (**c.1174BC**), but in **c.1158BC**, Babylonian rule was re-established, reaching its peak under Nebuchadnezzar I (**1126-1105BC**). Babylon fell to Assyrians in **689BC**.

The Assyrians used ladders to climb the walls of cities they besieged.

THE ASSYRIANS

The Assyrians were Semites who settled around the cities of Ashur and Nineveh. They became an aggressive, militaristic people.

An Assyrian king receiving prisoners after a battle

The First Assyrian empire (**1814-1754BC**) was built up by Shamshi-Adad and his son, Ishme-Dagan. It was smashed by the Babylonians and passed under the control of the Mitanni people in **c.1450BC**.

The Assyrians regained their independence to form the Middle Assyrian empire (**c.1375-1047BC**). King Tiglathpileser I (**1115-1077BC**), conquered more territory, exacting tribute payments from his subjects. But the empire fell apart with the arrival of Aramaeans in **c.1047BC**.

The New Assyrian empire (**c.911-609BC**) dominated the Middle East. At its peak, it covered Mesopotamia and mountains to the east, Syria, Lebanon, Palestine and Lower Egypt. But there were frequent revolts. The Medes and Babylonians formed an alliance against Assyria in **614BC**, which led finally to the fall of the empire in **609BC**.

Battering rams were used to demolish walls.

THE NEO BABYLONIAN EMPIRE

With the help of the Medes, the Babylonians defeated the Assyrians and, in **627BC**, they formed the Neo (New) Babylonian empire. It lasted until **539BC**, when it was invaded by Persians and became part of the Persian empire. Babylonia was conquered by Alexander the Great in **331BC**, and in **301BC** passed to the Seleucid empire. This came under the control of the Parthians in **126BC**. By **AD200**, Babylon was a deserted ruin.

The Ishtar Gate at the north entrance to Babylon

THE HITTITES

The Hittites were Indo-Europeans who arrived in Anatolia, in Turkey, in **c.2000BC,** and set up small rival states. They were united by King Labarnas, who founded the Old Kingdom (**c.1650-1450BC**). The Hittites spread into north Syria and overran Babylon in **c.1595BC**. In the Empire Period (**c.1450-1200BC**), their territory stretched from the Mediterranean to the Persian Gulf, but it collapsed with the advance of a people known as the Sea Peoples in **c.1200BC**.

The Hittite city of Hattusas

Europe

c.2000BC Horses and wheeled vehicles used in Eastern Europe.

c.2000-1700 First Palace Period on Crete (see page 5).

Bronze model of a sun chariot from Trundholm, Denmark c.1500

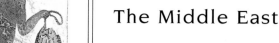

Cretan wall painting

c.2000-1500 Wessex culture in southern Britain.

c.1900-1200 Civilization of Mycenae (see page 16).

Mycenaean gold cup

c.1700-1450 Second Palace Period on Crete. Writing known as Linear A is in use. Linear B, an early form of the Greek language, is introduced **c.1400**.

A tablet engraved with Cretan writing known as Linear A

c.1450 Volcanic eruption on Thera (an island near Crete).

c1400-1200 Mycenae is at its height.

c.1380 Fall of Knossos on Crete.

c.1300 Urnfield culture in central Europe.

Greek terracotta figure of a mythical creature called a centaur

c.1250 The Trojan Wars, between the Mycenaeans and the Trojans (from Troy in Turkey), lead to the destruction of Troy.

c.1050-750 The Dark Ages in Greece.

The Mycenaeans tricked the Trojans by presenting them with a wooden horse full of soldiers as a gift.

The Middle East

c.2000BC The Hittites (see page 9) set up states in Anatolia (Turkey).

c.2000 Rise of Babylon.

c.1814-1754 First Assyrian empire.

c.1792-1750 Reign of King Hammurabi of Babylon.

c.1650-1450 Hittite Old Kingdom.

Assyrian stone relief

c.1595 Hittites sack and burn Babylon.

Statue of a Mitannian king

c.1500 Indo-Europeans, or Aryans, settle in the land now named after them, Iran.

c.1450 Assyrian empire is controlled by the Mitanni, an Indo-European people.

c.1450-1200 Hittite New Kingdom.

c.1400 First mention in Egyptian records of raiders known as Sea Peoples. They comprise several groups from the Mediterranean islands, the Turkish coast and Greece.

c.1380-1340 Shuppululiumash, King of the Hittites, destroys the Mitannian kingdom and causes the break-up of the northern part of the Egyptian empire.

c.1375-1047 Middle Assyrian empire.

Ramesses II was a great warrior and builder.

c.1269 Treaty between King Hattusilis II of the Hittites and Ramesses II of Egypt.

c.1200 Migration of the Sea Peoples, who conquer Cyprus and many Middle Eastern cities and destroy most of the Hittite empire.

c.1200 Arrival of Hebrews in Canaan, led by Moses and Joshua.

c.1200-1000 Rise to power of the Phoenicians in Lebanon. They found colonies on the southern and western shores of the Mediterranean, with cities at Byblos, Sidon, Beirut and Tyre. Their alphabet forms the basis for Greek, Latin and modern Roman scripts.

The Phoenician letter Aleph, which developed into Alpha, the first letter of the ancient Greek and modern Roman alphabets

c.1190 Ramesses III of Egypt defeats the Sea Peoples. One group, the Peleset (or Philistines), settle in Canaan, which becomes known as Palestine after them.

c.1010-926 United Jewish kingdom of Israel.

Philistine pottery was considered the finest in the region.

Africa

c.1674-1567BC Second Intermediate Period in Egypt: dynasties XIV-XVII.

Tomb models from the First Intermediate Period

1567-1085 New Kingdom in Egypt: dynasties XVIII-XX.

Earrings were introduced in the New Kingdom

c.1500 Cattle and goats are domesticated in West Africa.

1490-1468 Reign of Hatshepsut, female pharaoh of Egypt.

Statue of Hatshepsut, wearing a false beard

c.1450 The Egyptian empire reaches its greatest extent.

1364-1347 Egypt: reign of Akhenaten. He tries to impose the worship of one god, but fails.

Bust of Akhenaten's wife, Nefertiti

1190 Ramesses III of Egypt defeats the Sea Peoples.

c.1085 Nubia and Kush (modern Sudan) regain their independence from Egypt.

1085-656 Third Intermediate Period in Egypt: dynasties XXI-XXV. Egypt begins to decline.

Gold objects from the royal burials of dynasty XXI at Tanis

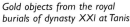

Asia

c.1800BC Decline of the Indus Valley Civilization, partly due to the arrival of Indo-Europeans, or Aryans, from the northwest, and partly to the flooding of the Indus, which destroys cities already in decline. Aryan control spreads as far east as the Ganges.

Baked clay figure of an Indus Valley goddess

This statue may be of an Indus Valley ruler or priest.

c.1765-1027 Shang dynasty in China: a feudal state with walled cities and temples, ruled by priest-kings. First examples of Chinese writing.

The Bronze Age in China began with the Shang dynasty. Elaborate containers like this were used in religious ceremonies.

The earliest known Chinese writing shown on an oracle bone - a scorched bone that was thought to reveal messages about the future.

c.1500-600 Vedic Period in India. The Hindu religion is gradually established. Scriptures called the *Vedas* are composed, and the Hindu caste system develops.

c.1028-771 Chou dynasty in China.

A chariot ornament found in a grave near Loyang, the Chou capital

The Americas

c.2000BC First evidence of metal working in Peru.

c.2000-1500 Pottery spreads among farmers in Peru.

c.2000-1000 The beginning of Mayan culture in Mesoamerica (Central America). This is known as the Early Pre-Classical Period. Farmers begin to settle in villages.

c.1800-900 The Initial Period in Peru. People settle in permanent villages, and there is evidence of social and religious organization. Pottery spreads.

c.1500 North America: agriculture reaches the southeast and, rather later, the midwest.

Giant basalt head made by the Olmecs

c.1500-AD200 Rise of the Olmec culture on the coast of the Gulf of Mexico. The Olmecs use hieroglyphics (picture writing) and calendars. They build ceremonial architecture at La Venta and other sites, and carve huge heads from basalt (stone) and small baby-faced jade figures.

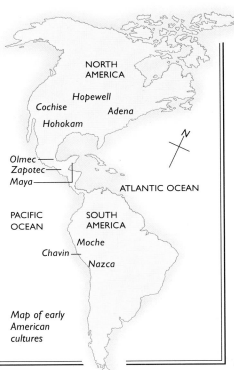

NORTH AMERICA

Hopewell
Cochise
Adena
Hohokam

Olmec
Zapotec
Maya

ATLANTIC OCEAN

PACIFIC OCEAN

SOUTH AMERICA

Chavin
Moche
Nazca

Map of early American cultures

Ancient Egypt

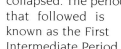

Pyramids and Sphinx (statue of king with lion's body) at Giza

Beaded collar and bracelets from New Kingdom tombs

Ancient Egypt was one of the earliest and greatest civilizations in the world. The Egyptians produced fine works of art and architecture and, in the construction of the pyramids, demonstrated extraordinary feats of engineering. They also invented a form of writing, called hieroglyphics.

Hieroglyphs spelling out the name of the Ptolemaic Period Egyptian queen, Cleopatra

THE PREDYNASTIC AND ARCHAIC PERIODS

Farming communities grew up along Egypt's great river, the Nile, before **5000BC**. By **c.3300BC**, they were organized into two kingdoms: Upper Egypt (the Nile Valley) and Lower Egypt (the Delta).

Archaic Period carving, found at Sakkara, near Memphis

The kingdoms were united in **c.3118BC** by King Menes, who built a capital at Memphis.

Carving of Narmer of Upper Egypt, thought to be Menes, triumphing over a Lower Egyptian prince

THE OLD KINGDOM

Under the Old Kingdom (**c.2686BC-2181BC**), there was a great flowering of Egyptian culture. This was the time when the pyramids were built as tombs for their kings. Trade flourished as far afield as Lebanon and Punt (Somalia), and the army defended frontiers and trade routes.

Craftsmen made fine works of art, and scholars standardized writing, and studied astronomy, medicine and mathematics. By the end of the period, however, the power of the nomarchs (provincial governors) was growing, and central government collapsed. The period that followed is known as the First Intermediate Period.

EGYPTIAN PERIODS

Archaic	c.3100-2686BC
Old Kingdom	c.2686-2181BC
1st Intermediate	c.2181-2040BC
Middle Kingdom	c.2133-1633BC
2nd Intermediate	c.1674-1567BC
New Kingdom	c.1567-1085BC
3rd Intermediate	c.1085-656BC
Late Period	664-332BC
Macedonian kings	332-305BC
The Ptolemies	305-30BC

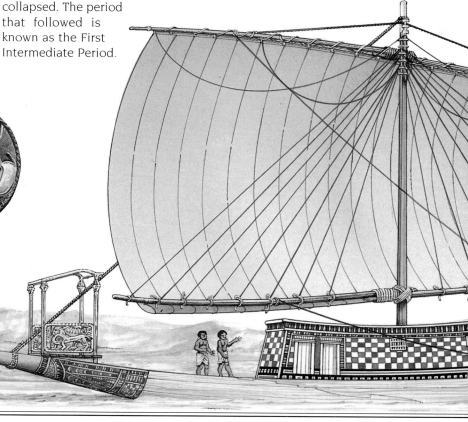

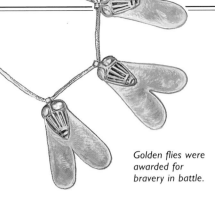

THE MIDDLE KINGDOM

Princes from Thebes rose to power and reunited the country under the Middle Kingdom (**c.2133-1633BC**). During this period, Egypt conquered part of Nubia (Sudan) and built large forts to defend its frontier.

Wall painting of Nubians bringing gifts

Then came invasions of people called Hyksos, who conquered the Nile Delta. They also forced much of Middle Egypt to pay tribute. Only the far south remained independent.

The Hyksos were the first to bring horses and chariots to Egypt.

Golden flies were awarded for bravery in battle.

THE NEW KINGDOM

Eventually, Theban princes drove out the Hyksos and reunited Egypt under the New Kingdom (**1567-1085BC**). The New Kingdom was the great age of warrior kings, known as pharaohs, when Egyptian power was at its height. The army was radically reorganized and conquered a vast empire, from the fourth Cataract of the Nile as far as Mesopotamia.

Most of what we know about Ancient Egypt dates from the New Kingdom. The kings were no longer buried in pyramids, but in tombs cut deep inside cliffs, in a remote valley, called the Valley of the Kings. The tombs were brightly painted, and filled with furniture and jewels.

Among the most famous rulers were Hatshepsut (**1490-1468BC**), the female pharaoh; Amenhotep IV, or Akhenaten, (**1364-1347BC**), who introduced the worship of one god; Tuthmosis III (**1468-1436BC**), the greatest of the warrior kings; and Ramesses II (**1289-1224BC**), a great warrior, who reigned for 65 years.

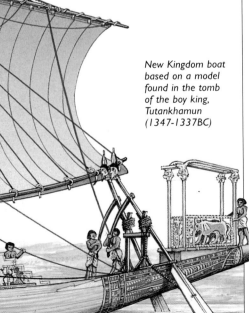

New Kingdom boat based on a model found in the tomb of the boy king, Tutankhamun (1347-1337BC)

The Egyptians preserved, or mummified, the bodies of royalty and rich people. New Kingdom mummies were put in a nest of coffins, inlaid with gold and semi-precious stones

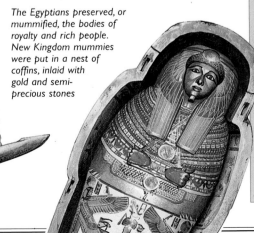

THE LATE PERIOD

From **c.1085BC**, Egypt's power declined. At various times, Egypt was conquered by Nubians and Persians. It became part of the empire of Alexander the Great in **332BC**, and passed into the Roman empire from **30BC**.

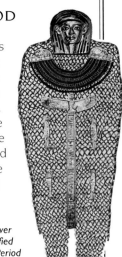

Beaded mummy cover (right) and mummified cat from the Late Period

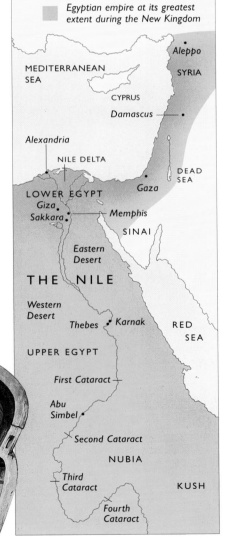

Egyptian empire at its greatest extent during the New Kingdom

MEDITERRANEAN SEA

Aleppo

SYRIA

CYPRUS

Damascus

Alexandria

NILE DELTA

DEAD SEA

Gaza

LOWER EGYPT

Giza

Sakkara

Memphis

SINAI

Eastern Desert

THE NILE

Western Desert

Thebes • Karnak

RED SEA

UPPER EGYPT

First Cataract

Abu Simbel

Second Cataract

NUBIA

Third Cataract

KUSH

Fourth Cataract

Europe

c.900BC The Etruscans are established in northern Italy. They are skilled at working in metal.

Mounted archer from an Etruscan bronze bowl

800 Homer composes the *Iliad* and the *Odyssey*: Greek epic poems describing the Trojan Wars.

776 Traditional date for the first Olympic Games in Greece.

Olympic athletes taking part in a pentathlon, from a Greek vase

753 Traditional date for the founding of Rome.

c.750 The Greek city-states begin to found colonies.

c.700-500 Culture named after Hallstatt in Austria, with evidence of salt mining and iron working.

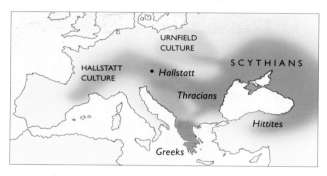

(map) URNFIELD CULTURE / HALLSTATT CULTURE / •Hallstatt / SCYTHIANS / Thracians / Hittites / Greeks

c.700 An Indo-European people called the Scythians spread from Central Asia to Eastern Europe.

Gold pieces made for the Scythians by Greek craftsmen

683 Athens replaces its hereditary kings with nine archons (chief magistrates), chosen yearly by the nobles.

c.600-500 The Archaic Period in Greek art.

594 Solon is made sole archon of Athens. He introduces government reforms.

510-509 Rome becomes a republic, governed by the Senate, composed of 100 men, called senators, from the most important families.

A Roman senator wearing a purple edged toga, a sign of his status

509-507 Cleisthenes introduces reforms which lead to democracy in Athens.

The Middle East

926BC Israel splits into Israel and Judah.

Assyrian gold

Reconstruction of an Assyrian city

c.911-609 New Assyrian empire.

874 First mention of people called Nabataeans in Arabia.

835 Rise of the kingdom of the Medes.

835-825 Sarduri I founds the kingdom of Urartu (or Ararat) around Lake Van, Turkey, an important base for trading in iron and copper. It is conquered by Assyrians (**721-715**), then the Scythians and the Medes (**610**).

800 Kingdom of Phrygia is established.

722-705 Reign of Sargon II: the height of Assyria's military power. He conquers Israel and sacks Babylon.

c.700-600 Phrygia falls under the Cimmerians. Lydia rises to prominence. The Lydians are first to develop coins.

668-631 Reign of King Ashurbanipal of Assyria.

653-583 Reign of Cyaxeres of the Medes.

Painting of an Assyrian official

627-539 The Neo Babylonian empire.

615-609 Medes and Babylonians ally against Assyrians, causing the collapse of their empire.

605-560 Lydia rises in power under King Alyattes.

586-538 Nebuchadnezzar II of Babylon (**605-561**) destroys Jerusalem, taking Jews captive.

560-546 Croesus of Lydia subdues most Greek colonies.

550 Persian empire founded by Cyrus II. He conquers Assyria (**550**), Lydia and Greek cities in Turkey (**546**), and Babylonia (**539**).

The Hanging Gardens and the Ishtar Gate, Babylon

Africa

814BC Founding of Carthage in North Africa by the Phoenician princess, Elissa of Tyre.

750-656BC Egypt is ruled by kings from Kush (dynasty XXV), who are later driven back south, where they set up the kingdom of Meroë.

A pyramid at Meroë   *King Taharka of Kush (690-664BC)*

c.700 Cattle and sheep are domesticated in West Africa.

671 Egypt is conquered by the Assyrians.

664-332 Late Period in Egypt: dynasties XXVI-XXX. The country is reunited by princes of Saïs.

Necho II, a prince of Saïs, sent an expedition down the Red Sea and around Africa, returning to Egypt by the Straits of Gibraltar.

663 The use of iron tools and weapons spreads in North Africa.

c.650 Carthage builds up a fleet to protect her colonies.

525-404 Egypt is conquered and occupied by Persia.

510 First of several treaties between Carthage and Rome, ensuring Carthage's trade monopoly in the western Mediterranean.

Asia

c.800BC Hindu religion spreads into southern India.

Hindu symbol known as the wheel of life, representing the cycle of life, death and rebirth

660 Legendary date for the founding of Japan under Emperor Jimmu. Japan was probably not united under a monarchy until **c.120**.

c.650 Iron smelting begins in China.

c.600 Probable date for the introduction of the religion and philosophy of Taoism, by the Chinese philosopher Lao-tze.

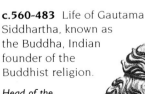

Taoist symbol representing the harmony between the two opposing forces of the Universe, known as yin (female) and yang (male)

c.560-483 Life of Gautama Siddhartha, known as the Buddha, Indian founder of the Buddhist religion.

Head of the Buddha from Gandhara, India

c.551-479 Life of Kung Fu-tze, also known as Confucius, the Chinese philosopher. He lived in a period of warfare and believed that peace could only be restored if people obeyed a strict code of conduct.

Portrait of Confucius

512 Indian provinces of Sind and Gandhara become part of the Persian empire.

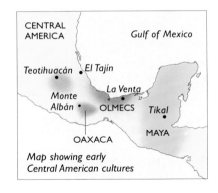

The Americas

c.900BC Mexico: the Olmecs build the first ball court at La Venta, for use during religious festivals.

c.900-200 The Chavín culture flourishes in Peru, producing work in gold and silver.

Chavin gold mask

c.700 Founding of Monte Albán, the sacred city of the Olmecs, in Oaxaca, Mexico.

c.600 Oaxaca becomes the base for Olmec culture.

Olmec jade scuplture

c.600-200 The Adena people are based around the Ohio River Valley in North America. They live in small groups, farming corn and beans. They also construct burial mounds and earthworks for ceremonial buildings.

Snake-shaped Adena burial mound

CENTRAL AMERICA   Gulf of Mexico

Teotihuacán • • El Tajín

La Venta

Monte Albán •   OLMECS   Tikal •

OAXACA   MAYA

Map showing early Central American cultures

15

Ancient Greece

By about **2500-1900BC**, groups of Indo-Europeans who spoke an early form of Greek were settled on the Greek mainland. They built a series of strongholds, each ruled by a king.

THE MYCENAEANS

From **c.1600-1200BC**, the mainland was dominated by a people we call Mycenaeans, after Mycenae, the site where remains of their culture were first discovered. The Mycenaeans invaded Crete, Rhodes and Cyprus, taking over the prosperous trade that the Minoans had built up. They also developed Linear B, an early form of Greek writing.

A Mycenaean wall painting, possibly of the goddess Demeter

However, by **c.1250BC**, Mycenaean society was disrupted by famine and warfare, and by **1050BC** their civilization had collapsed. The old cities were destroyed, the art of writing forgotten and people dispersed. This period is sometimes described as the Dark Ages. Trade was taken over by the Phoenicians from the eastern Mediterranean.

A Mycenaean king's gold burial mask

THE CITY-STATES

From **c.750BC**, trade revived. A new alphabet was adopted in **c.725BC**, based on the Phoenician one. Small city-states grew up around the old strongholds - the most important of which were Corinth, Sparta and Athens.

Bronze figure of a Spartan warrior

In many states, kings were replaced as rulers by an aristocracy (a group of nobles), an oligarchy (a small group) or a tyrant, later followed in some cases by a democracy (the rule of the people).

The Athenian fleet defeating the Persians, off the island of Salamis in 480BC

THE CLASSICAL AGE

The 5th century BC was the great age of Greek civilization, especially in Athens, which became the focus for a thriving commercial and cultural life. The foundations of European civilization are based on ideas about art, architecture, literature, drama, politics, philosophy, science and history which developed at this time.

THE WARS WITH PERSIA

The Greeks founded colonies in Turkey and the Aegean islands, but they were threatened by the expanding Persian empire, which took over the colonies in **546BC**. The Greek colonists tried to rebel against the Persians in **500-494BC**, but they were unsuccessful. Then, Athens, Sparta and other states banded together and defeated the Persians, after several major battles (Marathon **490BC**, Salamis **480BC** and Plataea **479BC**).

Map showing important Greek battles ⚔

PELOPONNESIAN WAR

Rivalry between Sparta and Athens, and resentment of Athenian power, led to the Peloponnesian War (**431-404BC**), which tore the Greek world apart. Sparta won in **404BC**, supported by a league of states in the Peloponnese (the southern part of Greece), but was later defeated by Thebes at Leuctra in **371BC**.

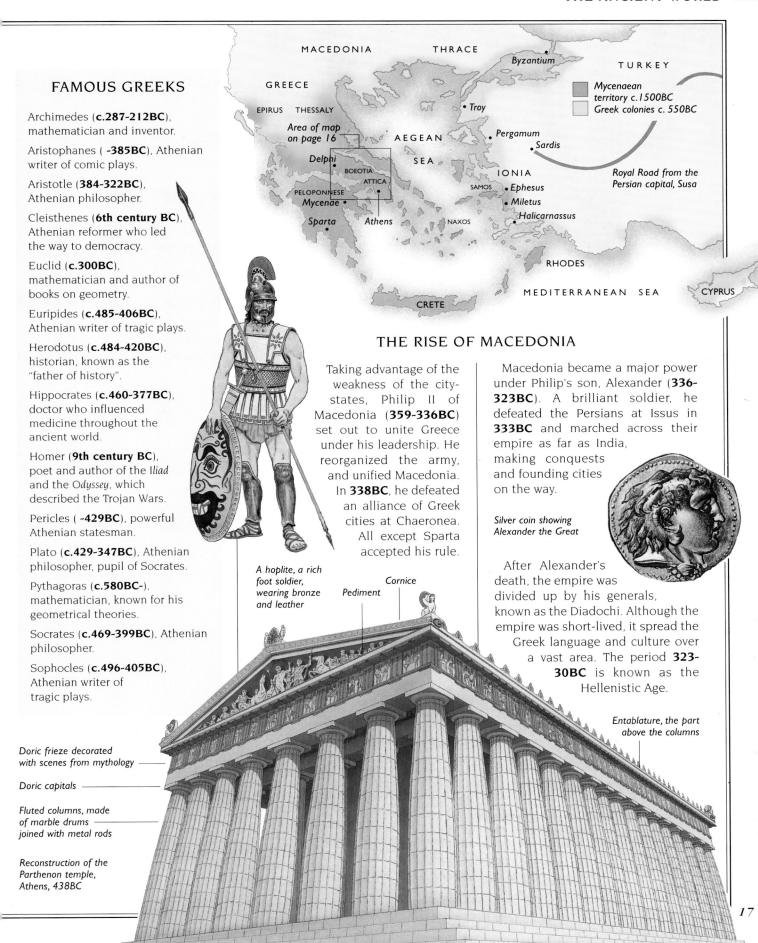

FAMOUS GREEKS

Archimedes (**c.287-212BC**), mathematician and inventor.

Aristophanes (**-385BC**), Athenian writer of comic plays.

Aristotle (**384-322BC**), Athenian philosopher.

Cleisthenes (**6th century BC**), Athenian reformer who led the way to democracy.

Euclid (**c.300BC**), mathematician and author of books on geometry.

Euripides (**c.485-406BC**), Athenian writer of tragic plays.

Herodotus (**c.484-420BC**), historian, known as the "father of history".

Hippocrates (**c.460-377BC**), doctor who influenced medicine throughout the ancient world.

Homer (**9th century BC**), poet and author of the *Iliad* and the *Odyssey*, which described the Trojan Wars.

Pericles (**-429BC**), powerful Athenian statesman.

Plato (**c.429-347BC**), Athenian philosopher, pupil of Socrates.

Pythagoras (**c.580BC-**), mathematician, known for his geometrical theories.

Socrates (**c.469-399BC**), Athenian philosopher.

Sophocles (**c.496-405BC**), Athenian writer of tragic plays.

MACEDONIA THRACE

Byzantium

TURKEY

GREECE

EPIRUS THESSALY

Area of map on page 16

Mycenaean territory c.1500BC

Greek colonies c. 550BC

Troy

AEGEAN

Delphi

BOEOTIA

ATTICA

SEA

Pergamum

Sardis

IONIA

SAMOS *Ephesus*

Miletus

Halicarnassus

Royal Road from the Persian capital, Susa

PELOPONNESE

Mycenae

Sparta *Athens*

NAXOS

RHODES

MEDITERRANEAN SEA

CYPRUS

CRETE

THE RISE OF MACEDONIA

Taking advantage of the weakness of the city-states, Philip II of Macedonia (**359-336BC**) set out to unite Greece under his leadership. He reorganized the army, and unified Macedonia. In **338BC**, he defeated an alliance of Greek cities at Chaeronea. All except Sparta accepted his rule.

Macedonia became a major power under Philip's son, Alexander (**336-323BC**). A brilliant soldier, he defeated the Persians at Issus in **333BC** and marched across their empire as far as India, making conquests and founding cities on the way.

Silver coin showing Alexander the Great

After Alexander's death, the empire was divided up by his generals, known as the Diadochi. Although the empire was short-lived, it spread the Greek language and culture over a vast area. The period **323-30BC** is known as the Hellenistic Age.

A hoplite, a rich foot soldier, wearing bronze and leather

Cornice

Pediment

Entablature, the part above the columns

Doric frieze decorated with scenes from mythology

Doric capitals

Fluted columns, made of marble drums joined with metal rods

Reconstruction of the Parthenon temple, Athens, 438BC

Europe

c.500-338BC Classical Period in Greek art.

461-429 Pericles plays a leading role in Athenian politics.

Bust of Pericles

Classical Greek vase

c.450 Celtic culture, named after site at La Tène in France.

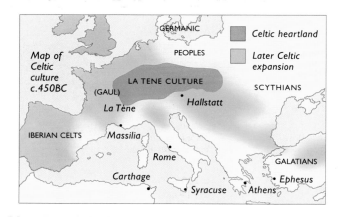

Map of Celtic culture c.450BC

GERMANIC PEOPLES

Celtic heartland

Later Celtic expansion

LA TENE CULTURE

(GAUL)

La Tène

Hallstatt

SCYTHIANS

IBERIAN CELTS

Massilia

Rome

Carthage

Syracuse

Athens

GALATIANS

Ephesus

431-404 Peloponnesian War in Greece.

395-387 Athens, Thebes, Corinth and Argos fight Sparta.

387 Rome is sacked by Gauls, a Celtic tribe.

338 Philip II conquers Greek cities at Chaeronea.

336-323 Reign of Alexander the Great (see page 17).

280-168 Antigonid dynasty in Macedonia.

261-241 1st Punic War.

218-201 2nd Punic War: Hannibal of Carthage invades Italy.

Hannibal's army crossing the Alps with his war elephants

215-205, **200-197** and **171-163** Wars between Rome and Macedonia end in the partition of Macedonia.

149-146 3rd Punic war between Rome and Carthage.

102-101 Roman General Marius defeats invading Germanic tribes.

82 Sulla becomes dictator of Rome.

58-51 Julius Caesar conquers Gaul (France).

49-45 Julius Caesar becomes dictator. He is assassinated in **44**, and civil war follows.

31 Battle of Actium: Octavian defeats Antony and Cleopatra and becomes ruler of Rome.

Emperor Augustus

27BC-AD14 Octavian becomes Emperor, taking the title Augustus.

The Middle East

490 and **480-479BC** Persian wars with Greece.

4th century BC Nabataeans build a city in rock at Petra, Jordan. They dominate the rich trade in goods from as far as India.

333 Alexander the Great conquers the Persian empire.

Ruins of the city of Petra

304-64 Seleucid empire controls Asia Minor, Persia, Mesopotamia and India, but is gradually reduced in size.

c.280-47 Kingdom of Pontus, founded by Mithridates I.

279 Celts establish kingdom of Galatia in Turkey.

279-74 Kingdom of Bithynia is established.

263-133 Kingdom of Pergamum, founded by Eumenes I.

247BC-AD277 Parthian kingdom founded. Mithridates I (**171-138BC**) extends control in Persia and Mesopotamia.

Map of the Hellenistic world c.200BC

MACEDONIA

GALATIA

BITHYNIA

PONTUS

ARMENIA

CAPPADOCIA

MEDIA ATROPATENE

PERGAMUM

Antioch

PARTHIA

SELEUCID

Seleucia

EMPIRE

INDEPENDENT GREEK STATES

Alexandria

Petra

EGYPT

168 Judas Maccabeus leads Jews against the Seleucids.

133 Last king of Pergamum bequeathes kingdom to Rome.

88-64 Kingdom of Pontus is reduced after war with Rome.

74 Kingdom of Bithynia passes under Roman rule.

64 Palestine becomes the Roman province of Judea.

47 Battle of Zela: Julius Caesar conquers the kingdom of Pontus.

37-4 Rule of Herod the Great, King of Judea.

c.5 Birth of Jesus Christ in Bethlehem, Judea.

Jesus's mother Mary on her way to Bethlehem

Africa

c.500BC-AD400 Nubian kings move their capital south to Meroë. A new phase of cultural development follows, with the building of towns, temples, palaces and pyramids, all showing Egyptian influence.

c.500BC-AD200 Nok civilization in Nigeria.

343-332 Egypt is conquered and occupied by Persia.

332 Egypt is conquered by Alexander the Great.

Mosaic of Alexander defeating the Persians at the Battle of Issus, 333

323-30 The Ptolemaic dynasty (descended from Ptolemy, one of Alexander's generals) rules Egypt from Alexandria. It becomes an important base for learning and invention, and the largest city in the Greek world.

Alexandria lighthouse, one of the wonders of the ancient world

203 Romans defeat the Carthaginians at Tunis, North Africa.

202 Romans destroy the Carthaginian army at Zama, Tunisia.

146 Carthage is destroyed and becomes a Roman province.

111-105 Jugurtha of Numidia, North Africa, is defeated by Marius, and his kingdom absorbed by Rome.

30 Egypt is a Roman province.

Asia

327-325BC Alexander the Great campaigns in India.

321-185 Maurya dynasty in India.

300BC-AD300 Yayoi culture in Japan is influenced by

Capital of a column erected by Indian King Asoka

people who come from China and Korea with bronze making skills.

272-231 Reign of King Asoka in India. He builds an empire uniting northern and central India and becomes a Buddhist.

221-206 Qin (Ch'in) dynasty unites China. The Great Wall of China is built to keep out the Hsiung-Nu (Huns) in **214**.

The Great Wall of China being attacked by Huns

206BC-AD222 Han dynasty rules China. China grows in size and prosperity.

c.200 Three kingdoms are established in South India.

c.200 India is invaded by Bactrians and Parthians. Small Greek states are set up in the Punjab from **c.170**.

c.150BC-AD50 Bronze age culture in North Vietnam, named after the village of Dong-son.

140-87 China expands under Emperor Wu-ti to include Korea and North Vietnam. He develops an efficient civil service, reduces the power of the nobles, and builds a network of roads and canals.

Emperor Wu-ti

c.100s North India is invaded by Greeks and nomadic tribes.

The Americas

c.300BC Gradual decline of the Olmec culture in Mexico. Rise of Zapotec culture in Oaxaca.

c.300BC-250AD Rise of the Maya in Central America: the Late Pre-Classical Period. Important political and religious bases develop around cities such as Monte Albán, Teotihuacán and El Tajín.

Part of a Mayan calendar. Dots, dashes and curved lines indicate dates.

c.300 North America: the Hopewell people displace the Adenas. They are great mound builders and traders.

c.200BC-AD200 Paracas Necropolis culture flourishes in Peru. Brilliant embroidered textiles have been found in a cemetery from this period.

c.200BC-AD600 Peru: regional development and technological experiments among the Moche people of the north coast and the Nazca people of the south coast.

Nazca pottery

c.200BC-AD700 The rise of the culture of Teotihuacán in Mexico.

c.100BC North America: Hohokam people in the southeast build ditches and dykes to irrigate their crops. They also build platform mounds and ball courts.

The Persian empire

In about **1500BC**, Indo-Europeans began moving into the area now called Iran. One tribe, the Medes, emerged as the dominant group. By **670BC**, they had united under one kingdom, Media, with their capital at Ecbatana. In the reign of Cyaxeres, the Medes allied with the Babylonians and crushed the Assyrians (see page 9). In about **700BC**, another tribe, called the Persians, set up the rival kingdom of Parsa, or Persia, ruled by the Achaemenid family.

An image of one of the 10,000 bowmen, known as "Immortals", who guarded the Achaemenid kings

In **550BC**, the Persian King Cyrus II (**559-529BC**) united the two kingdoms after he defeated his grandfather, Astyages of Media. He took over Lydia in **547-546BC**, other Greek cities in Asia Minor in **545BC**, and then Babylon in **539BC**. In **525BC**, his son Cambyses (**529-522BC**) conquered Egypt too.

THE REIGN OF DARIUS

Probably the greatest of all the Persian rulers was Darius I (**522-485BC**). He extended the empire and established a fair and efficient administrative and legal system. Under him, the empire was divided into 20 provinces, called satrapies, each run by a satrap (governor).

Darius also built roads to link Persia to its far-flung provinces, and to enable soldiers and messengers to travel quickly and easily. Officials went on regular tours of inspection and subject peoples had to pay tribute (a form of tax) and to provide soldiers and ships for the army and navy.

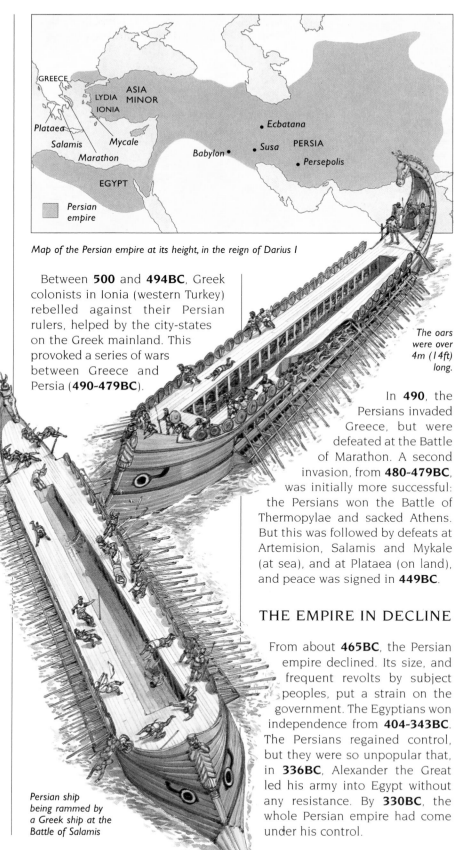

Map of the Persian empire at its height, in the reign of Darius I

The oars were over 4m (14ft) long.

Persian ship being rammed by a Greek ship at the Battle of Salamis

Between **500** and **494BC**, Greek colonists in Ionia (western Turkey) rebelled against their Persian rulers, helped by the city-states on the Greek mainland. This provoked a series of wars between Greece and Persia (**490-479BC**).

In **490**, the Persians invaded Greece, but were defeated at the Battle of Marathon. A second invasion, from **480-479BC**, was initially more successful: the Persians won the Battle of Thermopylae and sacked Athens. But this was followed by defeats at Artemision, Salamis and Mykale (at sea), and at Plataea (on land), and peace was signed in **449BC**.

THE EMPIRE IN DECLINE

From about **465BC**, the Persian empire declined. Its size, and frequent revolts by subject peoples, put a strain on the government. The Egyptians won independence from **404-343BC**. The Persians regained control, but they were so unpopular that, in **336BC**, Alexander the Great led his army into Egypt without any resistance. By **330BC**, the whole Persian empire had come under his control.

Early India

The earliest civilization in India seems to have grown out of small communities that had settled in the Indus Valley by about **3000BC**. They made a living from farming, and later from trade. The ruins of over 100 cities have been found, the most impressive of which are at Mohenjo-Daro and Harappa.

The cities were laid out on a grid pattern, with good roads and drainage, and a high walled area, where the ruler may have lived. The houses were built of mud bricks and many had two floors. Although we know very little about their system of government or religion, the Indus Valley people had a form of writing, which is found carved on many objects, including baked clay seals.

Indus Valley pot

Baked clay figure from Indus Valley

THE ARRIVAL OF THE ARYANS

From about **1800BC**, the Indus Valley civilization declined. No one is sure why, but there appear to have been frequent floods and overgrazing of the land. In about **1500BC**, Indo-Europeans, calling themselves Aryans, occupied the area. By **c.1000BC**, they began to drift east as far as the Ganges.

Much of what we know about the Aryans comes from religious poems, called *Vedas*, composed by priests and passed on by word of mouth. These became the basis for the Hindu religion.

The Aryans set up several kingdoms, each ruled by a *rajah*. Society was divided into four classes: priests, warriors, farmers and traders, and Dravidians (the original non-Aryan inhabitants). This was the origin of the Indian caste system.

Hindu god Shiva

BUDDHISM

The Aryans believed that after death a person's soul passed into a new body. So how a person behaved in one life would affect the next. Holy men gave up their possessions and lived in poverty, preaching and meditating. These ideas influenced the founding of a new religion, Buddhism, by an Indian prince, Gautama Siddhartha (**c.560-483BC**). He became the Buddha (which means "the Enlightened One") and his teachings spread rapidly through the Far East.

Siddhartha (above) and the Buddhist wheel of life (right)

Statue of Buddha

River Indus *Harappa*

Mohenjo-Daro

Ganges Delta

Indus Valley civilization

Empire of Chandragupta 297BC

Expansion to 232BC under Asoka

Map showing early Indian empires

THE MAURYA EMPIRE

The first Indian empire was founded in northern India by Chandragupta Maurya (**c.381-185BC**). He seized the kingdom of Magadha and then took control of much of Pakistan and Afghanistan, which had been part of the empire of Alexander the Great.

His grandson, Asoka (**c.272-231BC**), conquered most of the subcontinent. He ruled India well, and built a good network of roads. Despite his early reputation as a warrior, Asoka later converted to Buddhism and abandoned military conquests. He introduced laws to reduce poverty and improve social conditions, which were engraved on pillars and rocks all over India.

The empire was divided after his death, and the Mauryas declined in power. In the 2nd century BC, India was invaded by Greeks and nomadic tribes from Central Asia.

Column on which Asoka's laws were carved

Europe

AD43 The Romans conquer Britain.

61 Queen Boudicca of the Iceni, a British tribe, leads a revolt against the Romans in East Anglia.

98-117 Reign of Emperor Trajan: the Roman empire reaches its greatest extent.

122-127 Hadrian's Wall is built to mark the northern frontier of the Roman empire in Britain.

Head of the Emperor Hadrian

c.200 Germanic tribes attack the frontiers of the Roman empire.

284-305 Emperor Diocletian splits the Roman empire into two.

313 Edict of Milan: Christians allowed to worship in Roman empire.

324-337 Reign of Constantine the Great.

c.370 Huns invade Europe.

378 Battle of Adrianople. Emperor Valens is killed by Goths.

Germanic or Gothic warrior

391 Emperor Theodosius makes Christianity the state religion.

395 Roman empire becomes permanently split into east and west.

401-413 Visigoths invade Italy and sack Rome. Roman capital is moved to Ravenna.

415 Visigoths found kingdom of Toulouse.

416-711 Visigoth kingdom in Spain.

443-534 Burgundian kingdom is set up in Rhône-Saône area of France.

449 Angles, Saxons and Jutes invade England.

451 Battle of Châlons, France: Romans and Franks halt the invasions of Huns.

455 Vandals sack Rome.

457 Anglo-Saxons establish seven kingdoms in Britain.

476 The end of the Western Roman empire.

481-511 Reign of Clovis, King of the Franks.

493 Italian kingdom of Theodoric the Ostrogoth.

496 Clovis the Frank converts to Christianity.

Clovis and his queen Clotilda, at Notre Dame de Corbeil, France

The Arch of Titus, commemorating the capture of Jerusalem by Rome in AD70

The Middle East

AD26-36 Pontius Pilate is governor of Judea.

c.29 Jesus Christ is crucified.

45-48, 49-52, 54-58 Paul of Tarsus makes missionary journeys around the eastern Mediterranean, spreading Christianity.

70 Romans sack Jerusalem during the Jewish revolt of **66-73**.

73 Romans destroy Jewish stronghold of Masada.

Plan and sideview of Masada

106 The Nabataean kingdom is reduced to a Roman province by Emperor Trajan.

115-117 Uprisings of Jews in Egypt, Cyrenaica and Cyprus.

131-135 Unsuccessful Jewish revolt, led by Bar Cochba. Jerusalem is destroyed.

227 The Sassanid dynasty is established in Persia by Ardashir I.

260 Shapur I of Persia defeats the Romans and captures Emperor Valerian.

268-272 Queen Zenobia of Palmyra conquers Syria, Mesopotamia and parts of Egypt.

Roman ruins at Palmyra in Syria

Statue of a noblewoman from Palmyra

310-379 Reign of Shapur II of Persia.

324 Constantine rebuilds Byzantium and renames it Constantinople. It becomes the capital of the Roman empire.

325 First Council of the Christian Church meets at Nicaea in Anatolia.

484 The Persian empire is attacked by Huns and the emperor is killed.

The Huns were armed horsemen, using stirrups, then unknown to the Indo-Europeans.

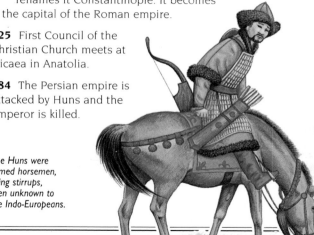

Africa

AD44 Mauretania (Morocco) is conquered by Rome.

70 Christianity reaches Alexandria. Starts spreading south from **c.180**.

100-800 Civilization of Axum (Ethiopia): a trading state which derives its wealth from maritime trade and the export of ivory.

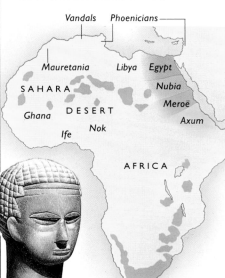

193-211 A Libyan, Septimius Severus, becomes Roman emperor.

238 Revolt begins in North Africa against Roman rule.

c.285 Monastic life starts in Egypt.

c.333 The state of Axum converts to Christianity.

c.350 Axum conquers Meroë and becomes the dominant power in the Red Sea area.

Obelisk from Axum

c.350-600 The X-group culture flourishes in Nubia.

c.400 The first towns appear south of the Sahara Desert.

c.400 The use of iron spreads in East Africa.

429 Vandal kingdom of North Africa is set up.

Sandstone sculpture from Meroë

Areas where rock paintings have been found

Asia

AD8-25 Hsin dynasty in China.

25-222 Han dynasty is restored: a new age of Chinese culture.

c.50 Nomadic tribes from Bactria, Central Asia, establish the Kushan empire in northern India.

91 The Chinese defeat the Huns in Mongolia.

c.100 Paper is invented in China.

c.100 Buddhism reaches China.

Flying horse bronze statue from Kansu, China

c.180 Tribes start to unite in Japan.

c.195-405 Parthians control northern India.

222-265 Han dynasty in China is replaced by three separate states.

265-316 Small states in China.

c.285 Traditional date for the introduction of writing to Japan.

c.300 Yamato government in Japan. Society is organized into clans, who follow the Shinto religion.

A torii, an archway to a Shinto shrine

304 Huns break through the Great Wall in northern China.

316 Japan invades Korea.

316-589 Rival dynasties in north and south China.

320-535 Gupta empire in India is founded by Chandragupta II. The Classical Age in India.

430-470 The Gupta empire breaks up after invasions by Huns.

Statue of the god Vishnu from the Gupta period

The Americas

c.AD50 Central America: city of Teotihuacán is built, including the Great Pyramid of the Sun.

Pyramid of the Sun, Teotihuacán

c.200-600 Growth of civilization around the city of Tiahuanaco, near Lake Titicaca in Bolivia.

Carving from Tiahuanaco

c.250-850 Classical Period of Mayan civilization in Central America: their artistic and intellectual peak. They use hieroglyphics (picture writing) and astronomers develop advanced mathematical skills.

The Maya played a ball game as part of a religious ceremony.

c.250-750 The Classical Period of the Zapotec culture.

c.500 Basket makers culture in the southwest of North America.

Ancient Rome

From about **1000BC**, a new wave of Indo-Europeans, skilled in working with iron, settled in Italy among the Bronze Age farmers. One group, the Latins, built a cluster of villages on the edges of the River Tiber. These grew into the city of Rome, the heart of a great civilization which lasted nearly a thousand years. The traditional date for the founding of Rome is **753BC**, but it may have been earlier. The early Romans were influenced by a people called Etruscans, who lived in northwest Italy.

Bronze statue of an Etruscan warrior

Romans building an aqueduct, a pipeline for carrying water

The Romans produced many great works of engineering and architecture (see right), as well as literature, politics, philosophy and law.

Some Roman gods and goddesses

Roman glass

THE ROMAN REPUBLIC

The Romans were ruled by kings until **510-509BC**, when a republic was set up. By about **250BC**, most of Italy was under Roman influence. Clashes with Carthage in North Africa led to a series of wars: **264-241BC**, **218-210BC** and **149-146BC**. Carthage was destroyed and Rome gained an empire. By **44BC**, the Romans controlled most of the Mediterranean.

The expansion of the overseas empire and the political ambitions of the military commanders put the constitution under strain. There was a period of civil war and rule by strong military leaders: Marius **88-86BC**, Sulla **82-79BC**, Pompey **52-46BC** and Julius Caesar **45-44BC**, ending with the victory of Caesar's heir, Octavian, in **31BC**. He took the title Augustus and became the first Roman emperor from **27BC-AD14**. This began the Empire Period.

Head of Emperor Trajan

THE ROMAN EMPIRE

The Roman empire reached its greatest extent under emperors Trajan (**98-117**) and Hadrian (**117-138**). From **c.200**, the frontiers were attacked by Persians, Moors and Berbers (from North Africa) and barbarian tribes (see opposite). Economic recession, civil wars, and a succession of weak and corrupt emperors, led to the collapse of Roman government in **235**.

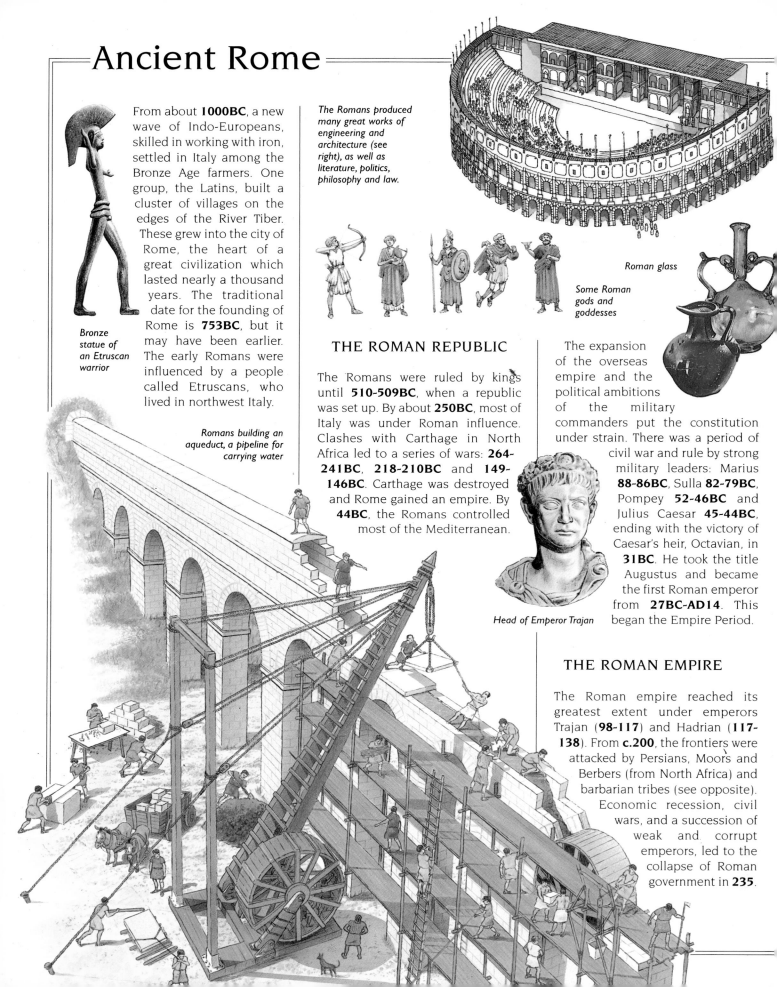

THE DECLINE OF ROME

Diocletian (**284-305**) attempted to make the empire easier to govern by dividing it in two. It was reunited by Constantine (**306-337**), who moved the capital to Byzantium, renaming it Constantinople. But, by **395,** the empire had permanently split, with the western half ruled from Rome. Outlying provinces fell to barbarians, and Rome itself was sacked by Goths in **410** and Vandals in **455**. The western empire came to an end in **476**.

Coin with the head of Constantine

THE BARBARIAN INVASIONS

As early as **230-200BC**, nomadic tribes of Indo-European origin, later known as Germani, began migrating south from Scandinavia and the Baltic to the northeastern borders of the Roman empire. Some were allowed to settle on the frontiers as *foedorati* (confederate states), while others were recruited into the Roman army.

In **c.AD370**, the Huns, a nomadic people from the Altai region of Mongolia, began arriving in eastern Europe. They pushed many of the Germanic tribes farther west, into conflict with the Romans. When a tribe of Goths invaded Italy in **402**, it frightened the emperor, Honorius, into moving the capital to Ravenna, in northern Italy. Gradually, the western empire was overrun. When it fell in **476**, it was replaced by different Germanic kingdoms. In **493**, Italy itself came under the control of Theodoric, chief of the Ostrogoths, who ruled from Ravenna until his death in **526**.

Germanic warrior's shield, helmet and spear

Germanic warrior

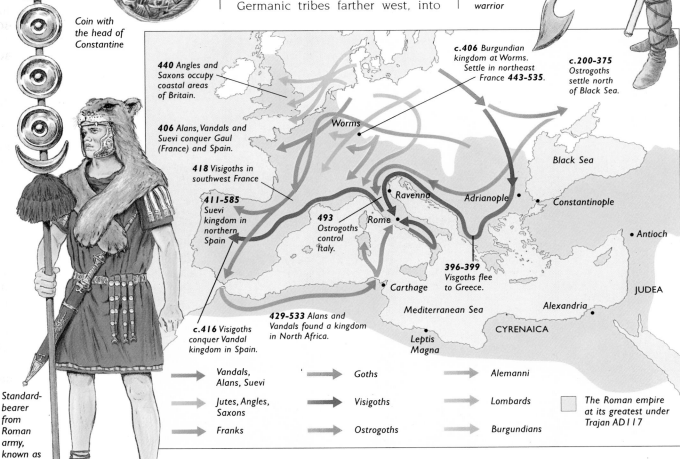

Map of the Roman empire and barbarian kingdoms

Standard-bearer from Roman army, known as a signifer

Judaism and Christianity

The Hebrews, later known as Jews, were Semitic tribes united by a belief in one God. In **c.1200BC**, they were led by Moses to Canaan (also known as Palestine). Under pressure from other tribes in the area, they united under one king, Saul, in about **1010BC**.

Early Egyptian painting of Semitic people

In the reign of King David (**c.1000-966BC**), they defeated the Philistines and set up the kingdom of Israel, based around Jerusalem. Israel flourished under David's son, Solomon (**c.966-926BC**), who built a temple in Jerusalem.

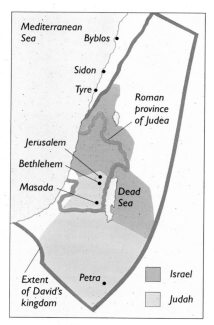

Map of Palestine

Mediterranean Sea · Byblos · Sidon · Tyre · Roman province of Judea · Jerusalem · Bethlehem · Masada · Dead Sea · Petra · Extent of David's kingdom · Israel · Judah

After King Solomon's death, his kingdom was split into Israel and Judah. Israel was destroyed by the Assyrians in **722BC**, and Judah by Babylonians in **587BC**. Thousands of Jews were held captive in Babylon from **586-538BC**, but when Persia conquered Babylon in **539BC**, the Jews were allowed to return to Jerusalem. In **332BC**, they were conquered by Alexander the Great, and passed under the control of the Ptolemies in **301BC**, then the Seleucids in **198BC**.

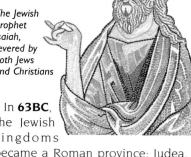

The Jewish prophet Isaiah, revered by both Jews and Christians

In **63BC**, the Jewish kingdoms became a Roman province: Judea. Tensions grew, and there were uprisings in **AD66-70** and **AD132**. Jerusalem was finally destroyed, and many Jews went into exile.

THE EARLY CHRISTIAN CHURCH

The Christian religion began in Judea with a Jew named Jesus of Nazareth (**c.5BC-AD29**), later known as Jesus Christ. He upset the Jewish religious authorities and the Romans, who were afraid his ideas might lead to political unrest. Jesus was arrested and crucified (nailed to a cross to die).

Icon of Christ on the cross

After his death, the faith was spread by his followers, known as disciples, especially by Paul of Tarsus, who made missionary journeys by ship around the Eastern Mediterranean in **45-48**, **49-52** and **54-58**. Jesus's followers claimed he was the Son of God and had risen from the dead. Some wrote gospels, stories about his life, to convert people to Christianity. At first the teachings were directed mainly at Jews, but when few converted, it was preached to gentiles (non-Jews) instead.

Christianity spread rapidly throughout the Roman empire, especially among the poor, despite severe repression and persecution of Christians by the Roman authorities. By the 4th century, the Church was organized into areas called dioceses, each under the control of a bishop. The most important of these were Alexandria, Antioch and Rome. Emperor Constantine made Christianity legal in **312**, and in **391** it became the official religion of the Roman empire.

Saint Mark writing a gospel

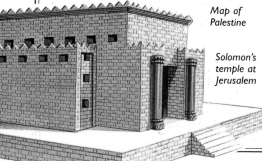

Solomon's temple at Jerusalem

A 5th century mosaic from Ravenna, Italy, showing Jesus Christ as a shepherd

The rise of Islam

Mohammed (**c.AD570-632**), the founder of Islam, was born in Mecca, Arabia - a place of pilgrimage for Arabs who came to worship at the Kaaba, a black meteoric stone. In **610**, he began preaching that there was only one God, Allah. He won many converts, but aroused the hostility of the local aristocracy.

A Muslim reading the Koran, the Holy Book of Mohammed's teachings

In **622**, Mohammed was forced to flee to Medina, where he organized his followers into a community. He defeated the people of Mecca at al Badr in **624**, and in **630** captured Mecca itself, making it a base for the new faith.

By the time of his death, Islam had spread through most of Arabia, both by conquest and conversion. Mohammed was succeeded by a series of elected caliphs, who defeated the tribes of southern Arabia. By **711**, the Arabs had conquered Persia, North Africa and Spain, and occupied the Oxus and Indus regions. In **751**, they beat the Chinese at Talas River.

A mosque, a Muslim place of worship

Map showing the spread of Islam:

SPAIN 711
Omayyads 750-1031
Carthage 698
Kairouan 670
Almoravids 1061-1163
Almohads 1135-1269
EGYPT 642
Fatimids 969-1171
Black Sea
Damascus 635
Baghdad
Jerusalem 638
Balkh 651
Herat 651
Kabul 664
SIND 712
Medina
ARABIA
Mecca
Arabian Sea

Expansion under Mohammed
Expansion of Islam to c.750
Expansion of Islam c.750-850
Abbasid caliphate at its peak

Map showing the spread of Islam in the centuries following Mohammed's death. The map gives the dates of conquest and the names of local dynasties that were set up.

THE OMAYYADS

In **661**, Ali, the fourth caliph, was murdered and replaced by the Omayyad dynasty, who ruled Arabia from Damascus between **661** and **750**. During this period, a breakaway sect emerged, called the Shi'ites, who believed Ali to be Mohammed's true successor. They were opposed to the official interpretation of the *Koran*, which had been compiled in the reign of Othman, the previous caliph.

The Shahadah, a declaration of faith, written on a vase

THE ABBASIDS

In **750**, the Omayyads were massacred and overthrown by the Abbasid dynasty, who ruled from Baghdad. Arab civilization reached its peak under their rule, especially during the reign of Caliph Harun al Rashid (**786-809**). Baghdad was a splendid city and base for trade, learning and the arts. It was a time of great prosperity and cultural and intellectual achievement, particularly in the fields of medicine, mathematics, and astronomy. However, the Islamic world soon lost its political unity, as several parts of the empire broke away and formed their own local dynasties.

The rule of the Abbasids ended in **1258**, when Baghdad was destroyed by the Mongols.

A brass astrolabe used for navigation by Arab sailors

Islamic manuscript showing a dentist at work

Southern and Western Europe

507-711 Visigoth kingdom in Spain.

529 St. Benedict founds the first monastery in Western Europe, at Monte Cassino, Italy.

Visigoth crown belonging to King Recceswinth

535-555 Emperor Justinian reconquers the Ostrogoth kingdom in Italy.

c.537 Death of King Arthur of the Britons, at the Battle of Camlan.

Arthur, shown here as a medieval knight, is thought to have been a British chief who fought the invading Saxons.

554 Justinian reconquers part of the Spanish Visigoth kingdom.

563 St. Columba, an Irish monk, founds a monastery on Iona, and sends missionaries to England and Scotland.

568-774 Lombard kingdom in northern Italy.

Celtic cross from Ireland

596 St. Augustine is sent to Britain by Pope Gregory to convert the Saxons to Christianity.

Treasure from Sutton Hoo (c.625) - part of a memorial to one of the last pagan Anglo-Saxon kings

664 Synod of Whitby: English Christians choose Roman rather than Celtic (Irish) branch of Christianity.

c.695 Lindisfarne Gospels are produced: the first book of psalms in Anglo-Saxon.

Northern and Eastern Europe

c.500-700 Slavs begin migrating from the Pripet region, west of the River Dnieper, to the forest areas of Russia and Eastern Europe.

527-565 Reign of Emperor Justinian, of the Eastern Roman, or Byzantine, empire.

Mosaic from Ravenna of Justinian's empress, Theodora

540-561 War between Persia and the Byzantine empire.

c.600 Avars, a nomadic people from the Steppes of Central Asia, establish a kingdom in the Balkans.

603-628 Final war between Persia and the Byzantine empire ends in Persian defeat.

610-641 Reign of Byzantine Emperor Heraclius. Links with the West are neglected and the official language changes to Greek.

632 Arabs begin attacking the Byzantine empire.

Arabs, inspired by their new religion of Islam, conquered much of the Byzantine empire.

674-678 Arabs unsuccessfully besiege Constantinople.

c.680 Bulgars, a nomadic people from the Steppes of Central Asia, invade the Balkans, intermarry with Slavs and establish a Bulgar state.

Reconstruction of the Church of St. Sophia, Constantinople, in Byzantine times

Africa and the Middle East

531 Justinian sends a group of monks, led by Julian, to the Christian kingdom of Axum, Ethiopia.

Early Ethiopian painting, showing Mary and Jesus with a Nubian queen

531-579 Chrosroes I rules the Persian Sassanid empire. The empire is at its greatest extent.

543 Julian spreads Christianity to Nubia, which is divided into three Christian kingdoms - Nobatia, Makuria and Alodia - each with their own bishops. They are cut off from the rest of Christendom by the Arab conquest of Egypt (see below).

c.570-632 Life of the prophet Mohammed, founder of Islam.

611-614 The Persians take Antioch, Damascus and Jerusalem from the Byzantines and overrun Asia Minor.

618-619 Persians conquer Egypt.

622 Mohammed flees to Medina.

629 Emperor Heraclius allies with Ethiopia, and wins back lost provinces from Persia.

632 Death of Mohammed. Abu Bakr becomes caliph. Arabs overrun Syria and Iraq (**637**) and Jerusalem (**638**).

639-642 Arabs occupy Egypt.

642 Arabs conquer Persia and overthrow the Sassanids. Persia adopts the Shi'ite branch of the Muslim religion.

661-750 Omayyad dynasty rules from Damascus.

698-700 Arabs conquer Carthage and Tunis. The north African coast converts to Islam.

The Great Mosque at Kairouan, North Africa

The Far East

535 India: Gupta empire collapses. India divides into warring kingdoms.

552 Buddhism is introduced into Japan from China.

581 General Yang Chien founds the Sui dynasty. He unites China in **589**.

594 Buddhism becomes the Japanese state religion.

605-610 China: millions of people are drafted to build the Imperial Canal, linking the rivers Yangtze and Huang Ho.

606 Written examinations are introduced in China for entry into the civil service.

607 Tibet is politically unified.

618-907 T'ang dynasty in China.

T'ang dynasty pottery camel

624 Buddhism becomes the official religion in China.

627-649 Reign of T'ai tsung the Great, Emperor of China.

Emperor T'ai tsung

645 Buddhism reaches Tibet.

657 Chinese defeat Turks and extend their power in Central Asia.

668 Chinese take Pyongyang, capital of Korea.

690-713 Empress Wu siezes the throne in China.

The Americas

c.500 North America: Hopewellian mound-builders begin to decline. Mississippi mound-builders start to appear at the lower end of the Mississippi River.

Pottery bottles made by Mississippi mound-builders

c.500-900 Golden age of the Zapotec culture in Oaxaca, Mexico.

c.500-1200 Culture of the Central Gulf coast of Mexico, also known as Totonac, based around El Tajín.

c.600 Peak of Mayan civilization.

A Mayan temple at Palenque, Mexico

c.600 The Teotihuacán culture is at its peak, extending from the city to surrounding highlands. The city is about 20km (8 miles) square and laid out on a grid. Its wealth comes from agriculture, crafts and trade.

c.600-1000 The Middle Horizon Period in South America. Large towns are built. Local cultures are merged under two great empires, based around Tiahuanaco, an important religious base, and Huari, a military capital.

Gate of the Moon at Tiahuanaco

c.650-850 Teotihuacán culture slowly declines.

c.650-900 Huastecan culture in Mexico.

Early China

The earliest known farming communities in China developed along the Huang Ho River from **c.5000BC**, and along the Yangtze River from **c.4000BC**. This is known as the Yangshao culture. Farmers grew millet (grain), fruit, nuts and vegetables, and kept pigs and dogs. Farming became more developed and better organized in the Longshan Period (**c.2500BC**).

Yangshao settlement and decorated pottery

EARLY DYNASTIES

China is believed to have been ruled by the legendary Xia dynasty from **c.2205BC**. The first dynasty for which there is much evidence is the Shang, who ruled much of China from **1765-1027BC**.

Burial suit made of jade, belonging to a Han princess from the 2nd century BC

Writing developed in this period, (**c.1400BC**), and people made weapons and containers from bronze. Kings were buried in huge tombs, with food and belongings, including servants and animals. The Shang were conquered by the Zhou (**c.1027-221BC**). The Zhou period was a time of economic growth and trade, but also of instability and wars. For 250 years, from **481-221BC**, China was torn between seven warring kingdoms.

THE FIRST EMPEROR

In **221BC**, the Qin (or Ch'in) kingdom conquered the rest and united China. The ruler named himself Shi Huangdi, meaning "First Emperor of China".

Shi Huangdi improved law and government, and built roads and canals all over his empire. To protect it from northern invaders, called Hsiung-Nu, he joined and extended existing walls into the massive Great Wall of China.

When he died in **210BC**, he was buried in a vast tomb, guarded by over 7,500 terracotta soldiers, horses and chariots. The empire collapsed, but the Han dynasty took control in **202BC**.

One of the most brilliant periods in early Chinese history, both in terms of military conquest and the arts, was the T'ang dynasty (**AD618-907**), especially during the reign of the enlightened emperor T'ai tsung (**AD627-649**).

Shi Huangdi, first emperor of China

The Great Wall of China, built from 214BC

With 6,320km (4,000 miles) of wall, it is the largest man-made structure in the world.

IMPORTANT DATES

c.5000BC Farming in China.

c.2700BC Silk making begins.

c.1765-1027BC Shang dynasty.

c.1400BC Writing begins.

c.1027-221BC Zhou dynasty.

c.600BC Taoist religion and philosophy begins in China.

c.551-479BC Life of Chinese philosopher, Kung Fu-tze.

221-202BC Qin (Ch'in) dynasty.

214BC Great Wall is built.

202BC-AD222 Han dynasty.

c.105BC Chinese traders travel along the Silk Road, which stretches to the Mediterranean.

c.AD100 Paper is invented. Buddhism reaches China.

c.AD586 China is united by Yang Chien of Sui dynasty.

c.AD618-907 T'ang dynasty: China's golden age. Civil service re-established. Wood-block printing and porcelain invented.

Early America

People first arrived in America by **15,000BC**, and perhaps much earlier. They crossed a bridge of land and ice that existed between Asia and Alaska, and gradually moved south. Farming developed first in South and Central America after **5000BC**. Farmers grew corn, peppers, squashes, potatoes, tobacco and cotton, which they wove into cloth. In South America, llamas were kept for milk and meat, and carrying loads.

Corn

THE EARLY NORTH AMERICANS

The first evidence of farming in North America was in the southeast from **c.1500BC** The Adena (**c.1000-200BC**) were followed by the Hopewell (**c.300BC-AD1000**), the Hohokam (**c.100BC-AD1000**), and later a group known as the Mississippi mound-builders (**c.AD500-1200**). All these people built huge earth mounds, some pyramid shaped, others shaped like animals.

In the desert areas of the southwest, farmers known as basketmakers were thriving from **c.AD500**. From **c.AD900**, the Anasazi, who first appeared in **c.AD700**, were building villages, called pueblos, in the sides of cliffs, accessible only by ladders.

Pueblo clay pots (left) and leather bags decorated with porcupine quills (above)

EARLY CIVILIZATIONS OF CENTRAL AMERICA

One of the earliest American civilizations was that of the Olmecs (**c.1500BC-AD200**). They carved jade and pottery figures and massive stone heads and built pyramid style temples for their gods.

Mayan mask

The culture of the Maya was one of the greatest. Lasting from **c.2000BC - AD1460**, it reached its peak from **c.AD250**. The Maya built cities deep in the jungle. They were a religious people, who revered rain, earth, plant and animal gods, and studied the stars.

The jaguar, revered as a god by the Olmecs and Maya

Early cultures also include the Zapotec (**c.300BC-AD900**), as well as Totonac (**c.AD500-1200**), Huastec (**c.AD650-900**), Mixtec (**AD900-1494**), Toltec (**c.AD900-1200**) and Aztec (**c.AD1200-1521**).

An Aztec marketplace, Mexico, c.AD1350

THE CIVILIZATIONS OF THE ANDES

Most early settlement in South America was along the west coast in the area that is now Peru. Farmers learned how to cultivate the steep mountain slopes by building terraces. They were also skilled metal workers, potters and weavers. The first civilization was created by the Chavín people who were flourishing from **c.900-200BC**, and made fine objects in gold. They were followed by the Paracas (**c.200BC-AD200**), Nazca and Moche (**c.200BC-AD600**), Huari and Tiahuanaco (**c.AD600-1483**), the Chimu (**c.AD1100-1470**) and Incas (**c.AD1200-1534**).

The Byzantine empire

The Eastern Roman empire, also known as the Byzantine empire, survived for a thousand years after the fall of Rome. Based in Constantinople (formerly the city of Byzantium, now called Istanbul), it was an important political power and helped to preserve classical learning and Christianity, through the Eastern (Orthodox) Church. Its traditions were inherited by the Greeks and Slavs.

Ravenna

Black Sea

Constantinople

Rome

Córdoba

Sicily

Carthage

Mediterranean Sea

Alexandria

Empire inherited by Justinian

Justinian's reconquests

Map showing Justinian's empire

A view of the Imperial Palace in Constantinople in Justinian's day

Byzantine cross

Icons, religious pictures often painted on wood, were common in early Byzantine art. But many were destroyed between **724-843** in a movement known as iconoclasm. Icons became popular again, but very few early ones have survived.

The frontiers expanded during the Macedonian dynasty (**867-1056**), especially under Basil II (**976-1025**). The Byzantines remained a rich trading power, but constant warfare imposed a heavy strain. In **1071**, they were defeated at Manzikert by the Seljuk Turks, who took over a lot of territory in Asia Minor. This led to the Crusades (see page 44), which were disastrous for the Byzantines. During the Fourth Crusade (**1202-1204**), Constantinople was looted by crusaders, who set up a short-lived Latin empire. A Greek emperor was restored in **1261**, but the empire had become too weak to resist a new threat: that of the Ottoman Turks, who finally conquered the capital in **1453**.

Emperor Justinian (**527-565**) struggled to reunite the Roman empire by restoring the Western empire. He succeeded in retaking the Vandal kingdom in North Africa (**535**), the Ostrogoth kingdom in Italy (**553**), and part of the Visigoth kingdom in Spain (**554**).

But Justinian's longest lasting achievement was to organize the Roman legal system into the Justinian Code (**528-534**), which later became the basis for modern European law. He also commissioned many great buildings, such as St. Sophia, in Constantinople.

Justinian and his wife, Theodora, from San Vitale, Ravenna, in Italy

AFTER JUSTINIAN

Justinian's reconquests were lost after his death. In **568**, the Lombards took northern Italy, and ties with the West were largely severed. Greek replaced Latin as the official Byzantine language, and the Churches in the East and West began to move apart. Later conquests by the Persians (**611-616**) and the Arabs (**632-750**) also cost the Byzantines territory in the Middle East, North Africa, Spain and Sicily.

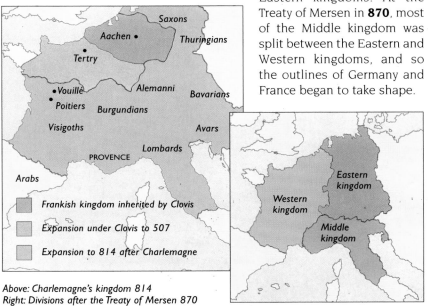

The rise of the Franks

The most successful barbarian kingdom was that of Clovis the Frank (**481-511**), a Christian ruler who founded the Merovingian dynasty. Clovis and his successors defeated other tribes: the Visigoths in **507**, the Thuringians in **531**, the Burgundians in **532-534**, and the Alemanni in **535**. In **537**, the Franks took Provence.

Carving from Charlemagne's tomb at Aachen, Germany

Gold Carolingian chalice

THE CAROLINGIANS

Following Frankish tradition, the kingdom was divided between the king's sons. But this weakened the dynasty, and power fell into the hands of important families. A powerful line of officials, known as Mayors of the Palace, emerged with Pepin I (**580-640**). Pepin II (**640-714**) defeated his rivals at the Battle of Tertry (**687**), and took control of most of the kingdom. His son, Charles Martel (**714-741**), defeated the Arabs at Poitiers in **732** and drove them out of France. Pepin III (left) deposed the Merovingian king in **731** and founded the Carolingian dynasty.

Gateway to Lorsch Abbey, in Germany, one of very few surviving Carolingian buildings

7th century copper casket

CHARLEMAGNE

The kingdom was inherited by Pepin's sons, Carloman and Charles (known as Charlemagne), who became sole ruler on his brother's death in **771**. During Charlemagne's reign (**771-814**), the Frankish empire reached its greatest extent. He conquered the Lombards (**773-774**), Bavarians (**788**), Avars (**796**) and Saxons (**804**), and set up marches (border zones) to protect the kingdom. His campaigns against the Arabs and pagan Magyars, Avars and Saxons earned him the role of defender of Christian Europe. In **800**, he was crowned "Emperor of the Romans" by the Pope, despite the protests of the Byzantines, who considered themselves to be the heirs of the Roman empire.

Charlemagne's son, Louis "the Pious", shared his inheritance with his three sons. But conflict led to the partition of the empire in **843**, into the Western, Middle and Eastern kingdoms. At the Treaty of Mersen in **870**, most of the Middle kingdom was split between the Eastern and Western kingdoms, and so the outlines of Germany and France began to take shape.

Saxons
Aachen •
Thuringians
• Tertry
• Vouillé
Poitiers
Alemanni
Bavarians
Visigoths
Burgundians
Avars
Lombards
PROVENCE
Arabs

Frankish kingdom inherited by Clovis

Expansion under Clovis to 507

Expansion to 814 after Charlemagne

Western kingdom
Eastern kingdom
Middle kingdom

Above: Charlemagne's kingdom 814
Right: Divisions after the Treaty of Mersen 870

Southern and Western Europe

c.700s Great age of art and literature in Ireland.

711 Arabs conquer Spain, except the Asturias in the northwest.

732 Battle of Poitiers: Arabs advancing into France from Spain are defeated by Charles Martel and forced to retreat.

Inside the Great Mosque, Córdoba, Spain, begun in 785

750-1031 Arab Omayyad caliphate rules southern Spain.

751 Pepin III becomes the first Carolingian king of France.

751 Lombards conquer Ravenna, the last Byzantine possession in north Italy.

756-1031 The Omayyads set up a caliphate at Córdoba, Spain.

757-796 Reign of Offa of Mercia. He builds a dyke to keep out the Welsh. Becomes ruler of all England by **779**.

768-814 Rule of Charlemagne.

793-794 Vikings plunder Lindisfarne and Jarrow in England.

800 Charlemagne is crowned Emperor of the Romans.

806 Vikings raid a monastery on Iona, a Scottish island. Monks flee to Ireland.

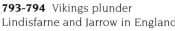

9th century Anglo-Saxon helmet

832-847 Vikings raid and settle in Ireland.

The Ardagh chalice and Tara brooch, which Vikings looted from Ireland

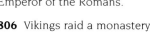

843 Kenneth MacAlpin, King of the Scots tribe, becomes King of Scotland.

858 Rhodri Mawr is recognized as Prince of all Wales.

865-874 Danish Vikings conquer Mercia, Northumbria and East Anglia.

871-899 Reign of Alfred the Great of Wessex. He resists the Danes. England is divided into Wessex and the Danelaw.

This jewel is inscribed "Alfred ordered me to be made".

Northern and Eastern Europe

716 The Bulgar state is recognized by the Byzantine emperor and lasts until **1018**.

Viking illustration of a monster

716-717 Arabs unsuccessfully besiege Constantinople.

717 Byzantine emperor Leo III allies with the Bulgars and Khazars.

726-843 Iconoclasm in the Byzantine empire: Leo III and successive emperors prohibit the use of icons in churches and many icons are destroyed.

787 Church Council of Nicaea orders the restoration of icons in churches.

c.793-794 Vikings begin raiding Europe.

812 Battle of Adrianople: Khan Krum of Bulgaria defeats the Byzantines and kills their emperor.

The battle between the Byzantines and the Bulgarians

830 Establishment of the independent Slav kingdom of Moravia. It is destroyed by Magyars in **906**.

860 Varangians unsuccessfully besiege Constantinople.

861 Vikings discover Iceland and settle there in **874**.

862 St. Cyril and St. Methodius work as Christian missionaries in Moravia. Cyril adapts the Greek alphabet for the Slavs. It becomes known as the Cyrillic alphabet.

c.862 Rurik settles in Novgorod and establishes the principality of Russia.

866 Conversion of Russia to Christianity begins.

Mosaic of Jesus Christ from St. Sophia, Constantinople

867-1056 Macedonian dynasty rules the Byzantine empire.

882 Oleg the Wise conquers Kiev and moves the Russian capital there.

889 Magyars invade Hungary and set up a state under the Arpad dynasty (**896-1301**).

c.890s-930s Norway is first organized as a single kingdom, under Harald Fairhair.

Africa and the Middle East

c.700s Arab merchants develop a flourishing trade with rich Saharan trading cities. The Arabs bring horses, copper, tools and weapons in exchange for gold, ivory, skins and slaves. This encourages the growth of strong African kingdoms and trading empires.

African king receiving Arab traders in Timbuktu

c.700-1200 Kingdom of Ghana: the first West African trading empire, rich in gold.

750-1258 The Abbasid dynasty rules from Baghdad: the golden age of Islamic culture.

Arab astronomers from the Abbasid period, taken from an Islamic illustration

786-809 Reign of the Abbasid ruler Caliph Harun al Rashid, known for the *Thousand and One Nights* stories.

788 Shi'ite kingdom is founded in Morocco.

c.800 Three small, independent Arab kingdoms are established in North Africa.

c.800-1800 Kingdom of Kanem-Bornu, a great trading empire in West Africa.

868-905 The Tulunid dynasty rules Egypt and Syria.

The Far East

710-794 First permanent Japanese capital city is established at Nara.

745-840 The Uighur empire is established in Mongolia.

c.750 Three empires in India wage war against each other: Rajputana (northwest), Rashtrakuta (south), and Bengal (northeast). Arabs begin invading the Indus region.

751 The Abbasids defeat T'ang armies at Talas River, ending China's influence in Central Asia.

794-1185 Heian Period in Japan. The emperor rules from Heian (Kyoto). Power is increasingly in the hands of the nobles.

A Heian period lute, inlaid with mother-of-pearl

Phoenix Hall, Heian, Japan

802 The Angkor kingdom is established in Cambodia under the Khmer dynasty.

842 Tibetan empire disintegrates.

c.852-1160 The Fujiwara clan controls the government in Japan.

868 The earliest printed book, the Buddhist *Diamond Sutra*, is produced in China.

Chinese paper money (right) and printing block, used for printing books

The Americas

c.700s Rise of the Mississippi River culture. The Mississippians build temples on top of flat-topped mounds.

c.700-1000 North America: Hohokam farming communities in the southwest (Arizona) reach their most prosperous stage.

The Hohokam people grew corn, beans, tobacco and cotton.

They build platform mounds and play ball games, suggesting links with the Mayan people of Mexico.

North and Central America, c.700

c.700-1000 Anasazi farmers emerge in southwestern North America.

Anasazi clifftop village, called a pueblo

c.750 Central America: the city of Teotihuacán is destroyed.

c.750 Mayan civilization begins to decline.

c.850 Mayan civilization collapses. Many cities are abandoned.

The migrations from the Steppes

The Steppes are huge plains, which stretch from Eastern Europe to Asia. A thousand years ago, they were inhabited by tribes of nomadic horsemen of Asian origin, many of whom began migrating farther west.

Migrations of peoples from the Steppes: 6th and 7th centuries (top) and 10th and 11th centuries (bottom)

Avars
Khazars
Avars (from 552)
Bulgars

Volga Bulgars (before 1257)
Magyars
Polovtsy
Patzinaks
Khazar khanate
Hungary (from 896)
Danube Bulgars
Black Sea
Turks

Steppes horsemen

The tribes of horsemen formed part of larger groups called hordes. Each horde was led by a khan, who ruled an area called a khanate.

EUROPE IN TURMOIL

The Avars moved west in **552**, drove the Slavs from their land and set up a khanate in **c.600**. This was destroyed by Byzantines in **803**.

The Patzinaks set up a state in the Balkans in the 10th century, which was wiped out in **1091** by Byzantines.

Bulgars were descended from Huns who had fled to southern Russia in the 5th century, and had been driven out by Khazars in the 6th century. One group established a state on the River Volga (until **1257**). Another settled on the Danube, intermarried with Slavs and founded a Bulgarian

Gold engraving of a Bulgar horseman

kingdom in about **680**. This was conquered by the Byzantines in **1018**.

The Khazars, who converted to Judaism, set up a khanate in the Ukraine in the 6th century, and expanded west. The state fell apart in the 11th century, after attacks from Russians and Polovtsy.

The Polovtsy were pushed from Central Asia between the 5th and the 8th centuries, and occupied Khazar land in the 10th century. Defeated by Mongols in **1237**, they merged with the Golden Horde.

The Magyars invaded Hungary in the 9th century, after the Avar kingdom had been destroyed. They raided the German frontier in **862** and fought the Bulgars. In **896**, a Hungarian kingdom was set up with the Arpad dynasty (**896-1301**). In **1001**, the Pope recognized their ruler, Stephen I (**997-1038**), as the King of Hungary.

Crown of Stephen I ("the Saint") of Hungary

THE SLAVS

The Slavs were Indo-Europeans who were originally settled in the Pripet region, west of the River Dnieper. In the 6th century, they were driven out by the Avars and spread across Eastern Europe.

By the 9th century, the Slavs were settled in their new territories and by **c.1000** had absorbed most of the original non-Slavs in the area. Slav states were founded in Moravia (**830**), Poland (**960**), Russia (**c.862**), Croatia (**815**) and Bulgaria (**716**).

Baltic Sea
Pomeranians
Russians
Abodrites
Poles
Sorbs
Pripet marshes
Bohemians
Ukrainians
Moravians
Slovenes
Croats
Bulgarian Slavs

→ Slav expansion
→ Raids of Asiatic tribes

Map showing expansion of the Slavs

The founding of Russia

From the 8th century, Swedish Vikings, also called Varangians, settled around Russia's Baltic coast to trade. They expanded along the Russian rivers, settling among the Slavs and trading between the Baltic Sea and the Islamic world. In **c.862**, Rurik, head of a tribe of Varangians called the Rus, founded a state at Novgorod. It became known as Rus, or Russia, and was ruled by Rurik's descendents until **1598**.

A Rus merchant

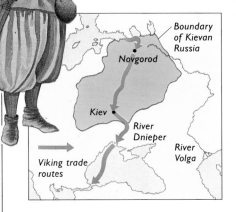

Map of Russia

Rurik's successor, Oleg the Wise (**879-912**), won the allegiance of the Slav tribes in the area and expanded south as far as Kiev, which became his capital city. Contacts with Constantinople were encouraged and, after **957**, Christianity began to spread.

Slavs converting to Christianity in a huge baptism ceremony

Vikings dragging a boat between rivers

THE CYRILLIC ALPHABET

From the 9th century, Byzantine missionaries, led by two brothers, St. Cyril and St. Methodius, were sent to convert the Slav people to Christianity. Cyril adapted the Greek alphabet for the Slav language, and it was named the Cyrillic alphabet, after him. In **990-992**, Poles and other western Slavs converted from the Eastern to the Western (Catholic) Church, while the remaining Slavs stayed with the Eastern (Orthodox) Church.

Manuscript with Cyrillic writing

KIEVAN RUSSIA

Vladimir I "the Saint" (**978-1015**) brought together what had been a loose confederation of tribes into a single state, in close contact with Constantinople. He married a Byzantine princess, and made Christianity the official religion in Russia. Under his son, Yaroslav (**1019-1054**), Kiev became a major European city and a base for culture, religion and the arts.

An icon (painting in oil on wood) of Vladimir of Kiev

Cathedral of St. Sophia, Kiev

After **1054**, Kievan Russia went into an irreversible decline. There was a new wave of invasions by the Polovtsy. Kiev was sacked in **1093**, and many people were driven north. The state dissolved into separate princedoms, which lasted until the invasions of the Mongols between **1237** and **1240** (see page 65).

Southern and Western Europe

910 Benedictine Abbey is founded at Cluny in Burgundy.

911 Rollo, a Viking chief, is made Duke of Normandy. He is given Rouen and surrounding land by the Frankish king, Charles the Simple, on condition that he swears allegiance, and becomes a Christian. The land is known as *terra Normannorum* ("the land of the northmen" in Latin).

Rollo being welcomed by the Archbishop of Rouen

912-961 Reign of Abd al-Rahman, Caliph of Córdoba in Spain: a period of prosperity and culture.

917-921 King Edward of Wessex conquers the southern half of the Danelaw.

926 Anglo-Saxon King Athelstan seizes the Danelaw.

937 Athelstan repels an invasion by Vikings, Scots and Britons at the Battle of Brunanburh.

979-1013 Reign of Anglo-Saxon King Ethelred the Unready.

986-987 Reign of Louis V, last Carolingian king of France.

987-996 Hugh Capet becomes first king of the Capetian dynasty in France (**987-1328**).

991 Danes defeat the English at the Battle of Malden. The English are forced to pay *Danegeld*, a tax to prevent more Danish attacks.

A Viking longboat

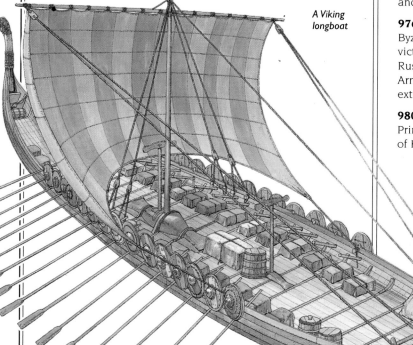

Northern and Eastern Europe

911 Death of Louis III ("the child"), the last Carolingian king of Germany. Conrad of Franconia is chosen as king.

919-936 Reign of Henry the Fowler of Saxony, first king of the Saxon dynasty in Germany.

929-967 Bohemia is united under Boleslav I after he murders his brother Wenceslas.

933 Henry I of Germany defeats the Magyars.

936-973 Reign of Otto I of Germany. He controls the German duchies and conquers Italy.

955 Otto I stops the westward advance of the Magyars at the Battle of Lechfeld, southern Germany.

960 Mieszko I (**960-992**) unites northern Poland and founds a Polish state.

961 Byzantines take Crete from the Arabs.

Otto's crown

962 Otto I is crowned Holy Roman Emperor of the German nation.

965 Harald Bluetooth, King of Denmark, becomes a Christian.

Harald Bluetooth's rune stone, the Jelling Stone, showing an image of Jesus Christ

965 Russia destroys the Khazar empire.

970-997 Geza I controls the Magyars and unites Hungary.

976-1025 Reign of Basil II, Byzantine emperor. He wins victories against the Arabs, Russians, Bulgarians, Armenians and Normans, and extends the empire.

980-1015 Vladimir, Grand Prince of Kiev, becomes sole ruler of Kievan Russia.

990-992 Poland adopts the Western (Catholic) Church.

Vladimir of Kiev

993 Olaf Skötkonung becomes the first Christian king of Sweden.

995-1000 Rule of Olaf Tryggvason of Norway. Christianity is introduced.

997-1038 Reign of Stephen I (St. Stephen) - the first Christian king of Hungary.

Africa and the Middle East

c.900 West Africa: increase in trade and prosperity in Hausaland, a region on the Lower Niger.

Samanid tomb at Bukhara, Central Asia

902-1004 The Samanid dynasty rules in Persia. With their capital at Bukhara in Samarkand, their empire covers the region between the Caspian Sea and the Hindu Kush mountains. They develop important trading contacts, both with China and the far north.

909-972 The Fatimids take over the Arab kingdoms in North Africa.

Map of Fatimid caliphate

Fez · Tahir · Kairouan · Damascus · Cairo · EGYPT

969-1171 The Fatimids take over Egypt from the Tulunid dynasty. They build Cairo, which becomes the Egyptian capital.

c.970 Cairo University is established.

997-1030 Reign of Mahmud, Sultan of Ghazni, who conquers an empire in eastern Afghanistan and northern India. Ghazni becomes a base for Islamic culture.

A minaret, a tower attached to a mosque used to call Muslims to prayer

The Far East

c.900 The Mataram dynasty is established in Java, Indonesia.

907-960 Collapse of the T'ang dynasty in China is followed by the Epoch of the Five Dynasties. China is divided by civil wars.

916 Founding of the Khitan kingdom in Mongolia.

936 Three kingdoms in Korea are united under the state of Koryo.

947-1125 Khitans overrun northern China and set up the Liao dynasty.

960-1127 The Northern Sung dynasty reunites central and southern China and rules from Kaifeng.

985-1014 Reign of Rajara I, of the Chola kingdom, southern India. He conquers Kerala, South India (**985**) and Sri Lanka (**1001**).

990 Yangtu (Beijing) becomes the capital of northern China.

Bronze statue of the Hindu god Shiva

10th century Muktesvara temple, Bhuvanesvara, northeastern India

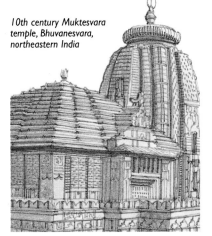

997-1030 Reign of Mahmud of Ghazni, who invades northern India 17 times between **1001-1026**, and absorbs much of it into his empire.

The Americas

c.900 The heart of Mayan culture shifts to the Yucatán peninsula.

Pyramid of Quetzalcoatl at Chichen Itza on the Yucatán peninsula, Mexico

c.900 The Anasazi begin building pueblos, clusters of buildings nestling in cliffs, reached only by ladders. They weave cotton cloth, make pots using a wheel, and work in turquoise and other stones.

c.900-1200 The Toltecs dominate much of Mexico. They destroy towns around Teotihuacán and invade Mayan territory.

Statue of a Toltec warrior

c.900-1494 Period of Mixtec culture in Mexico.

947 Mexico: birth of Quetzalcoatl, revered by the Toltecs as a god.

980 The Toltecs establish their capital at Tula.

982 Eric the Red, a Viking, begins to colonize Greenland.

The Vikings met Inuits, like this man, in Greenland.

c.990s Quetzalcoatl flees from Tula after feuds between his followers and those of another man-god. He settles in the Mayan city Chichen, which is renamed Chichen Itza. The city is rebuilt in a mixture of Mayan and Toltec styles.

The Vikings

The Vikings, also known as Northmen or Norsemen, were farmers, warriors and traders from Scandinavia. New economic pressures at home, such as an increasing population and competition for land, drove some to raiding and looting. Between the 8th and 11th centuries, Vikings terrorized much of Europe. The first raids, which began in the **790s**, came from Norway but, after the **830s**, the Danes started raiding on a larger scale.

The Vikings were not all raiders, though. They were skilled shipbuilders and navigators, and many sailed overseas to explore, trade or settle. In France, the area where they settled became known as Normandy after them. In Russia, where they were called Varangians, they founded the first Russian state, named after a Viking tribe called the Rus (see page 37).

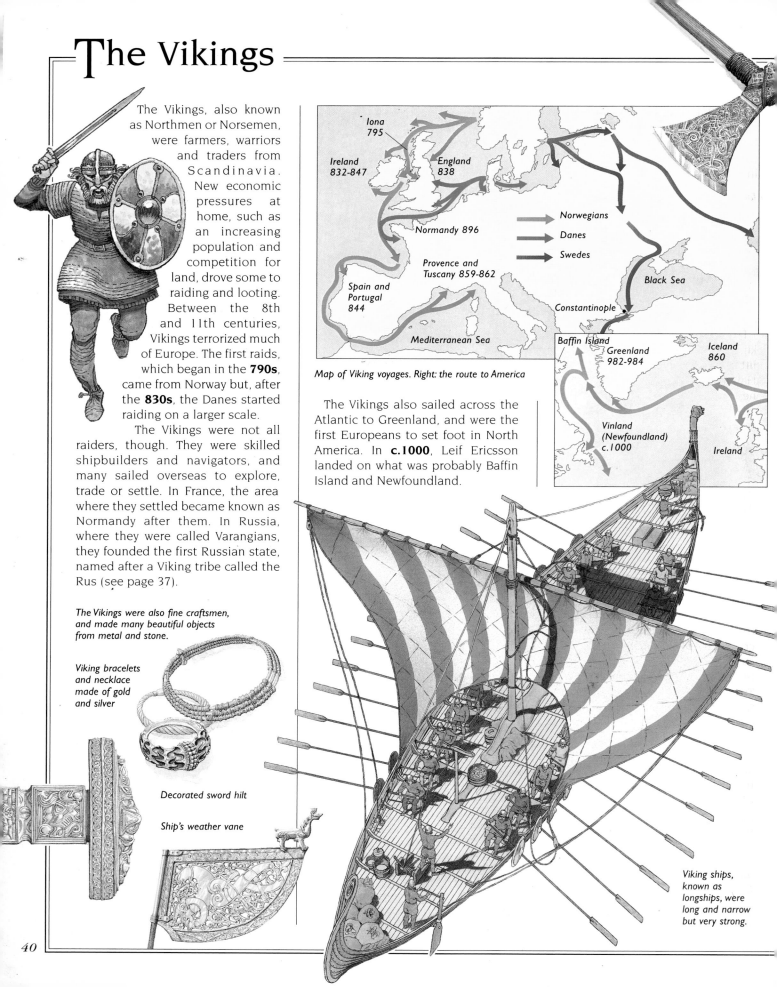

Iona 795

Ireland 832-847

England 838

Normandy 896

Provence and Tuscany 859-862

Spain and Portugal 844

Mediterranean Sea

Norwegians

Danes

Swedes

Black Sea

Constantinople

Map of Viking voyages. Right: the route to America

Baffin Island

Greenland 982-984

Iceland 860

Vinland (Newfoundland) c.1000

Ireland

The Vikings also sailed across the Atlantic to Greenland, and were the first Europeans to set foot in North America. In **c.1000**, Leif Ericsson landed on what was probably Baffin Island and Newfoundland.

The Vikings were also fine craftsmen, and made many beautiful objects from metal and stone.

Viking bracelets and necklace made of gold and silver

Decorated sword hilt

Ship's weather vane

Viking ships, known as longships, were long and narrow but very strong.

THE VIKING KINGDOMS

Denmark, Sweden and Norway first developed into separate kingdoms in Viking times.

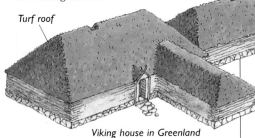

Turf roof

Viking house in Greenland

Denmark was united under one king as early as the 9th century, but little is known until the reign of Harald Bluetooth in **c.950**. In **987**, he was overthrown by his son, Sweyn Forkbeard, who conquered Norway, and invaded England in **1013**.

Viking stone, called a rune stone, decorated with pictures and writing

— *Runes, the Viking letters*

Norway was united in **c.890**, with the reign of King Harald Fairhair. His cruel son, Eric Bloodaxe (**c.930**), was overthrown, but the throne was later restored to Harald's grandson Olaf Tryggvason. Olaf was deposed by Sweyn Forkbeard of Denmark and Olof Skötkonung of Sweden.

According to legend, Olof was the son of the first powerful Swedish king, Eric the Victorious. Olof reigned from **995-1022** and became a Christian in **1008**.

Painting showing Olaf Haraldsson, a later king of Norway, being defeated by Cnut's army at the Battle of Stiklestad in 1030

THE DANELAW

Between **866** and **874**, the Danes conquered all of England, except Wessex, which was ruled by Alfred the Great (**871-899**). In **878**, Alfred defeated the Danes and set up the Danelaw, an area in which Danes could live. He and his successors, Edward (**899-924**), Ethelstan (**924-939**) and Edgar (**959-975**), gradually re-established English rule.

Jewel which may have belonged to Alfred

SCOTLAND

Iona

Lindisfarne

| | Danelaw in 878 |
| | Land held by Vikings from Norway |

NORTHUMBRIA

York

Chester

WALES MERCIA

EAST ANGLIA

London

WESSEX

But the English position again grew weaker. Ethelred the Unready (**978-1016**) was forced to pay *Danegeld*, a tax to avoid being plundered by new Danish raiders. In **1016**, England was conquered by Sweyn's son, Cnut of Denmark (**1014-1035**), who was one of the most powerful kings of the Viking age. England was then ruled by Danes until **1042**, when Ethelred's son, Edward the Confessor (**1042-1066**), became king.

Harold Hardrada, King of Norway from 1047-1066

THE NORMANS

In **895**, Danish Vikings attacked Paris, France, and settled at the mouth of the Seine. The Franks allowed them to keep the land, known as Normandy, provided they defended it against other Norsemen. In **912**, their leader, Rollo, was baptized and made Duke of Normandy. His descendent, William ("the Conqueror"), defeated Harold of Wessex at the Battle of Hastings (**1066**), conquered England and became King William I.

William I and the Bayeux tapestry, which shows scenes from the battle

THE LAST VIKINGS

By about the 12th century, the Viking age finally came to an end. The kings had united their countries and established firm control. Agriculture and trade flourished, and raiding became extremely rare. As Christianity spread through the Viking kingdoms, people adopted a more peaceful, settled way of living.

Wooden church, called a stave church, built in Norway in c.1150

Southern and Western Europe

1004 Brian Boru is proclaimed "high king" of Ireland.

1008-1028 Civil wars cause the break-up of the Muslim kingdom of Córdoba in Spain. This leads to the *reconquista*, the reconquest of the Muslim kingdoms of Spain and Portugal by the Christian kingdoms, which takes place between the 11th and 15th centuries.

El Cid, Spanish mercenary soldier and hero of the reconquista

1014 Brian Boru defeats the Vikings at the Battle of Clontarf, but is killed in battle.

1016 Normans invade South Italy, led by Robert and Roger Guiscard.

1029 Spain: Castile and Aragon become independent.

1042-1066 Reign of St. Edward the Confessor, King of England.

1054 Scotland: Macbeth, the Earl of Moray, is defeated and killed at Dunsinane by Malcolm Canmore, whose father, King Duncan, had been murdered by Macbeth.

1054 The Pope makes Robert Guiscard Duke of Apulia and Calabria and invites him to take Sicily from the Arabs.

1061-1091 Robert Guiscard's brother, Roger, conquers Sicily and is made Count of Sicily.

1066 Battle of Hastings: William of Normandy conquers England and becomes William I (**1066-1087**).

William of Normandy (left) and part of the Bayeux tapestry showing the Norman cavalry attacking English footsoldiers

1071 Normans conquer Bari, the last Byzantine possession in Italy.

1075-1122 The Investiture Controversy: a quarrel between the Pope and the Holy Roman Emperor over who has the right to invest (or appoint) bishops and abbots. Settled at the Concordat of Worms (**1122**). Part of a wider, longer-lasting power struggle between the Empire and papacy.

1085 Castile conquers Toledo. The hero of the struggle is Rodrigo Diaz de Vivar, known as El Cid.

1086 The Domesday Book is compiled in England: a survey of all the property in the land.

1094 Portugal becomes independent.

Northern and Eastern Europe

1014-1035 Cnut, King of Denmark, rules an empire which covers Denmark, England and part of Sweden. He rules Norway from **1028-1035**.

Above: Viking Christian symbols. In Cnut's reign, English missionaries converted the Danes to Christianity.

Left: map of Cnut's empire

Rostov, Russia, built in the Kievan period

1015-1028 Reign of Olaf II ("the Saint"), King of Norway. He flees to Russia in **1028**.

1019-1054 Yaroslav the Wise rules Kievan Russia.

1035 Poland becomes a fief (subject state) of the Holy Roman Empire.

1035 Norwegian kingdom is restored by Magnus the Good (**1035-1047**), who returns after the death of Cnut.

1054 A schism (or split) is established between the Eastern (Orthodox) and Western (Catholic) Churches, after the Pope insists on supremacy over the whole Church.

1059-1078 Dukas dynasty rules the Byzantine empire.

1071 Battle of Manzikert: the Byzantines are defeated by the Seljuk Turks and lose Asia Minor (Turkey).

1081-1085 Normans, led by Robert Guiscard, invade the Balkans.

Seljuk Turks, nomadic people from Central Asia

1081-1185 Comneni dynasty rules the Byzantine empire.

1086 Holy Roman Emperor recognizes Bohemia as a kingdom under Vratislav.

1093 Polovtsy sack Kiev.

1095 Byzantine emperor, Alexius Comnenus (**1081-1118**), calls on Pope Urban II for help against the Turks.

Africa and the Middle East

c.1030 The Seljuk Turks, a nomadic people from Central Asia, extend their influence in Asia Minor.

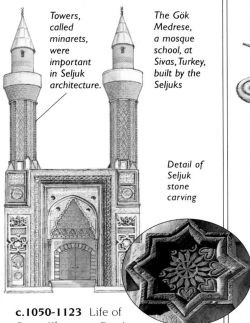

Towers, called minarets, were important in Seljuk architecture.

The Gök Medrese, a mosque school, at Sivas, Turkey, built by the Seljuks

Detail of Seljuk stone carving

c.1050-1123 Life of Omar Khayyam, Persian mathematician, astronomer and philosopher, and author of the *Rubaiyat*, a famous series of poems.

1052 The Almoravids attack Ghana, which is destroyed by **1076**.

1055 Seljuk Turks take Baghdad.

1056-1147 The Almoravids set up a kingdom in North Africa and Spain.

1076 Seljuk Turks take Jerusalem and Damascus from the Fatimids.

c.1090 The Assassins, a branch of Shi'ites who murder to destroy their opponents, are founded in Persia.

1096-1099 The First Crusade: crusaders take Jerusalem and set up states in Anatolia and Syria.

The siege of Antioch, Syria, by crusaders

The Far East

c.1000 The Chinese perfect the invention of gunpowder.

Gunpowder was used in war and in firework displays.

c.1000 Maori people settle in New Zealand, after long sea voyages across the Pacific Ocean.

1002-1050 The Angkor kingdom in Cambodia grows in importance under King Suryavarman.

1020 Japan: the *Tales of the Genji*, the first novel in any language, is written by Lady Murasaki Shikibu.

1044 A Burmese state is formed around Pagan.

1051-1062 Nine Years' Civil War in Japan: the beginning of the rise of the samurai (see below).

1083-1087 The Three Years' Civil War in Japan.

THE SAMURAI

The samurai were a highly professional Japanese warrior caste. They fought on horseback with bows and arrows, before closing in for hand-to-hand combat. Samurai were trained to win or die, and to give absolute loyalty to their feudal lord, in return for gifts of land. Running away from battle was seen as unforgivable, and the samurai were sometimes even expected to commit ritual suicide, known as *seppuku*, or *harakiri*.

Samurai warrior

The Americas

c.1000 Leif Ericsson, son of Eric the Red, travels along the North American coast, before returning to Greenland.

THE VIKINGS IN AMERICA

Viking explorers appear to have been the first Europeans to set foot in North America - almost 500 years before Christopher Columbus discovered the Caribbean. Leif Ericsson landed in three places on the East Coast - which were probably Baffin Island, Labrador and Newfoundland. The remains of Viking-style buildings and other objects were dug up in Newfoundland in **1968**.

Right: a statue of Leif Ericsson, in Iceland

Left: a Skraeling, the Viking name for Native Americans

c.1000 The Hopewellians discover how to etch designs with acid.

c.1000 The northern Iroquois people settle around eastern Great Lakes and St. Lawrence River.

c.1000 Thule Eskimo people start to spread across the North American Arctic region.

c.1000-1483 Late Intermediate Period in South America. Decline of the Huari-Tiahuanaco culture. Local styles and cultures re-emerge.

Early Peruvian pot

The Crusades

In **1071**, the Seljuk Turks defeated the Byzantines at Manzikert, and in **1076** took over Jerusalem from the Fatimids. As recent converts to Islam, the Turks were more militant than the previous rulers, and began persecuting Christian pilgrims. This sparked off the Crusades, a series of military expeditions fought by European Christians to win back Palestine, known as the Holy Land.

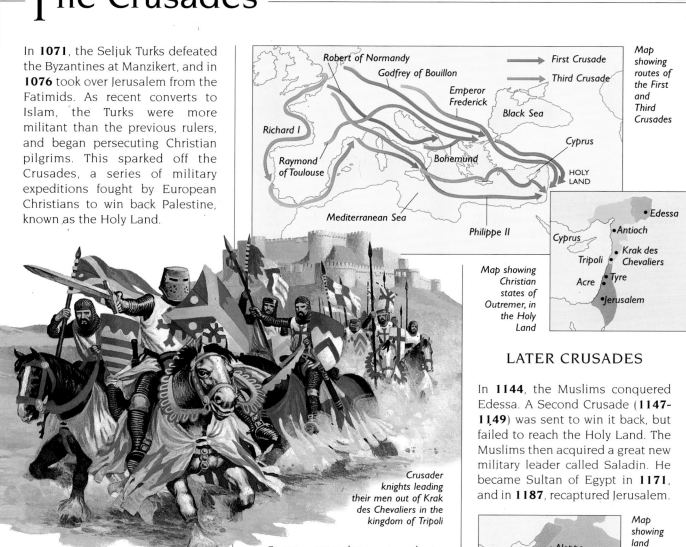

Map showing routes of the First and Third Crusades

First Crusade
Third Crusade

Robert of Normandy
Godfrey of Bouillon
Emperor Frederick
Black Sea
Richard I
Raymond of Toulouse
Bohemund
Cyprus
HOLY LAND
Mediterranean Sea
Philippe II

Map showing Christian states of Outremer, in the Holy Land

Edessa
Antioch
Cyprus
Krak des Chevaliers
Tripoli
Acre
Tyre
Jerusalem

Crusader knights leading their men out of Krak des Chevaliers in the kingdom of Tripoli

In **1095**, the Byzantine emperor, Alexius Comnenus, appealed to Pope Urban II for help to fight the Turks. The Pope preached the idea of a crusade, or "holy war". This attracted many followers, as it combined religious zeal with the chance to become rich and acquire new land.

The First Crusade (**1096-1099**) was made up of armies of French, Flemish and Normans. The crusaders captured Nicaea in **1097**, Antioch in **1098**, and Jerusalem in **1099**, killing many Muslims. They divided the land into the states of Jerusalem, Antioch, Edessa and Tripoli, known collectively as Outremer.

Some crusaders stayed to protect their new lands, while many others returned to Europe, taking with them silks, spices and other luxuries, as well as new ideas from Islamic culture, such as bathing. Meanwhile the Muslims grew in strength and started to band together to drive out all the Christian "unbelievers".

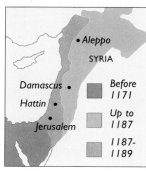

A crusader fighting a Saracen (Muslim). The crusaders wore crosses on their shields and clothing.

LATER CRUSADES

In **1144**, the Muslims conquered Edessa. A Second Crusade (**1147-1149**) was sent to win it back, but failed to reach the Holy Land. The Muslims then acquired a great new military leader called Saladin. He became Sultan of Egypt in **1171**, and in **1187**, recaptured Jerusalem.

Map showing land claimed back by Saladin between the Second and Third Crusades

Aleppo
SYRIA
Damascus
Hattin
Jerusalem

Before 1171
Up to 1187
1187-1189

The Third Crusade (**1189-1192**), led by Emperor Frederick I, Richard I ("the Lionheart") of England and Philippe II of France, failed to win back Jerusalem, although they won the right for Christians to enter. The disastrous Fourth Crusade (**1202-1204**) ended with an attack on Constantinople by crusaders, who set up a Latin empire (**1204-1261**). There were later attempts, but the age of crusades was over.

The rise of the Ottomans

The Ottomans were Turkish Muslims from Turkestan in Central Asia, driven west by the Mongols. By **c.1250**, they had settled in northwest Turkey, working for the Seljuk Turks.

In **1288**, their *emir* (or chief) Osman I proclaimed himself "Sultan of all the Turks", and founded a small state which became the nucleus of an empire.

Osman I

SULEIMAN THE MAGNIFICENT

The empire expanded in the 16th century, especially during the reign of Suleiman II "the Magnificent" (**1520-1566**). Under him, the Turks took control of Egypt and parts of North Africa, and occupied most of the modern territories of Lebanon, Israel, Iraq, Syria and the Yemen, as well as parts of the Caucasus mountains. They also held land in the Balkan region of Eastern Europe.

Roxelana, Suleiman's Russian wife (above left)
Painting from the Ottoman period (above)

Suleiman's reign was a golden age for the Ottomans. Beautiful mosques and other public buildings were built in Istanbul, especially by the architect Sinan. But the empire began to decline under Suleiman's son, Selim II (**1566-1574**).

Above: a tile from a mosque in Istanbul, decorated with verses from the holy book, the Koran

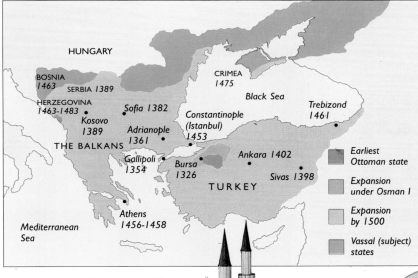

HUNGARY

BOSNIA
1463
SERBIA 1389
CRIMEA
1475
HERZEGOVINA
1463-1483
Sofia 1382
Black Sea
Kosovo
1389
Adrianople
1361
Constantinople
(Istanbul)
1453
Trebizond
1461
THE BALKANS
Gallipoli
1354
Bursa
1326
Ankara 1402
Sivas 1398
TURKEY
Athens
1456-1458
Mediterranean
Sea

Earliest
Ottoman state

Expansion
under Osman I

Expansion
by 1500

Vassal (subject)
states

Map showing the early expansion of the Ottoman empire, with dates of conquest

Osman built up a huge army, which included the janissaries, Christian children taken as slaves and raised as Muslims.

In **1453**, Mehmet II (**1451-1481**) conquered Constantinople and finally overthrew the Byzantine empire. The city was renamed Istanbul and became the Ottoman capital. By the end of the 15th century, the Ottomans had established themselves as leaders of the Islamic world.

The Byzantine church of St. Sophia in Constantinople was converted into a mosque by the Ottomans.

The four minarets (towers) were added by the Ottomans after 1453.

Southern and Western Europe

1105 Roger II is Count of Sicily. He acquires Calabria (**1122**), Apulia (**1127**) and is made King of Sicily (**1130-1154**).

1128 Mathilda, heir to Henry I of England, marries Geoffrey of Anjou, nicknamed "Plantagenet".

1135 Stephen of Boulogne seizes the English throne, on the death of his uncle, Henry I.

1137-1144 St. Denis, Paris, the first great Gothic cathedral, is built by Abbot Suger.

Stained glass window of Abbot Suger at St. Denis

1139 Alfonso I is crowned first King of Portugal.

1139-1148 Civil war in England between Stephen and Mathilda. Mathilda is defeated.

Mathilda, though Queen of England, was never crowned.

c.1150 Paris University is founded.

1152 Mathilda's son, Henry of Anjou, renews the struggle for the English throne.

The tomb of Eleanor of Aquitaine (1102-1169), wife of Henry II

1153 Stephen recognizes Henry of Anjou as his heir.

1154-1189 Henry of Anjou becomes Henry II and rules England and France.

1157 Malcolm IV of Scotland cedes Northumberland, Cumbria and Westmoreland to Henry II.

1159 Henry II introduces scutage, allowing knights to pay money instead of fighting in his wars.

1167-1168 Oxford University founded.

1170 Thomas à Becket, Archbishop of Canterbury, is killed by Henry II's knights. Becket is made a saint in **1173**.

15th century illustration showing Becket's murder

1171 Henry II invades Ireland and proclaims himself Lord of Ireland.

1186 Constance, daughter of Roger II of Sicily, marries Emperor Henry VI.

Mosaic of Roger II of Sicily

1189-1199 Reign of Richard I of England. He recognizes the independence of Scotland.

Northern and Eastern Europe

1105 West Germans begin colonizing East Germany.

1122 Byzantines wipe out the Patzinaks.

1122 Concordat at Worms, Germany, ends the power struggle between the Pope and the Holy Roman Emperor.

1137-1268 The Hohenstaufen dynasty rules the Holy Roman Empire.

c.1147 Moscow is founded by Kievan Prince Yuri Dolgoruky.

1147-1149 Second Crusade ends in complete failure, never reaching the Holy Land.

A crusader's shield had a cross on it, the sign of his promise to go to Jerusalem.

1152-1190 Reign of Frederick I Barbarossa, Holy Roman Emperor. He fights six campaigns in Italy, putting down rebellions by the Normans in southern Italy, and helping the Pope fight rebellions by the Romans in Rome.

c.1170s Serbia becomes independent from the Byzantines.

Map showing territory of Byzantines and Seljuk Turks in the 12th century

1171 Emperor Manuel Comnenus arrests all Venetians on Byzantine territory, but loses the resulting war with Venice.

1176 Byzantines are decisively defeated by the Seljuk Turks at Myriokephalon and lose more territory in Asia Minor.

1185-1205 Angeli dynasty rules Byzantine empire.

1186 Bulgarians rebel and establish independence from Byzantium.

c.1190 Teutonic Knights, a military order of monks, are founded in Germany to defend the Christian states in the Holy Land.

Africa and the Middle East

c.1100 The kingdom of Ife in Nigeria grows in importance.

A bronze head of a ruler from Ife

1135-1269 The Almohads rule a kingdom in North Africa.

1147-1149 Second Crusade.

1171 The Fatimids are thrown out of Egypt by Saladin, who founds the Ayyubid dynasty. He becomes ruler of Syria (**1174**) and Aleppo (**1183**).

Saladin

1187 Saladin defeats the Christians at the Battle of Hattin and takes Jerusalem.

1189-1192 The Third Crusade: Philippe II of France and Richard I "the Lionheart" of England fail to retake Jerusalem.

1190 Accession of Lalibela, Christian King of Ethiopia. He has 10 chapels and churches cut from rock in the Lasta mountains.

1191 Crusaders take Acre.

1192 Peace of Ramlah. Saladin keeps Jerusalem, but recognizes the Christian kingdom of Acre.

The castle of Krak des Chevaliers in Syria, rebuilt by crusaders in the 12th century, on the site of an earlier Islamic castle

The Far East

1126-1234 The Chin dynasty overruns northern China.

1127-1279 The Southern Sung dynasty is established at Nanking, southern China.

c.1150 Suryavarman II of Cambodia (**1112-1152**) completes the temple of Angkor Wat (see below).

A procession at Angkor Wat

1156-1185 Civil wars in Japan: struggles between the Taira, Fujiwara and Minamoto clans.

1159 The Taira clan controls Japan.

1170 The height of the Srivijaya kingdom in Java under the Indian Shailendra dynasty.

c.1180 The Angkor empire is at its greatest extent.

1185 Japan: Yoshitsume Minamoto defeats the Taira clan. The Kamakura Period (**1185-1333**), named after the home district of the Minamoto.

1192 Yoritomo Minamoto is given power under the title *shogun* (hereditary military dictator). His family rules Japan until **1219**.

The Americas

c.1100 Cahokia, at the junction of the Missouri and Mississippi rivers, is the largest town in North America.

c.1100s The Chimu peoples build large towns, including their capital Chanchan, on the north Peruvian coast. Ancestors of the Incas start to gather around Cuzco, Peru.

c.1100s Statues are erected on Easter Island in the Pacific Ocean.

Early Central American peoples

MEXICO

Huastec

Tula ·

Totonac

Aztec

Zapotec   Mixtec

Chichen Itza

Yucatán peninsula

Maya

Huari empire

Tiahuanaco empire

· San Agustín

· Chanchan

Moche ·

Chavín ·

Huari ·

Nazca ·   · Cuzco — Lake Titicaca

PERU   ·Tiahuanaco

Map of early South American settlements

Carving from San Agustín, in the northern Andes region of South America

c.1170 Chichimec people overrun the Toltec city of Tula. The Toltec civilization is destroyed.

1179 Mayan city of Chichen Itza is burned and destroyed.

1190 Second era of Mayan civilization begins.

Life in the Middle Ages

The period in Europe from just before **1000** to about **1450** is known as the Middle Ages. During this time, most people lived by farming, under a system called feudalism, based on the ownership of land.

A medieval peasant farmer sowing seed

A bishop of the Catholic Church

Religion played a crucial part in people's daily lives. In Western Europe, the Pope, as head of the Catholic Church, was an important political, as well as religious, leader. Europe was divided into small kingdoms, ruled by kings, princes and dukes. But real power was often in the hands of local landowners. Wars were frequent, as the feudal lords fought to defend their land, or win more.

HOW FEUDALISM DEVELOPED

The break-up of the Roman empire, then that of Charlemagne, and the threat posed by the Viking raids, created disruption in Western Europe. People looked to powerful leaders to help defend them. In the 8th and 9th centuries, a system of rights and duties developed, known as feudalism, between lords and their vassals (those they protected). In return for a fief (a piece of land), the vassal had to perform military duties, and pay certain rents and dues. Peasants worked on the vassal's land in return for protection.

The King

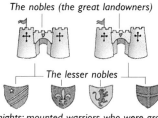
The nobles (the great landowners)

The lesser nobles

The knights: mounted warriors who were granted a fief to support themselves and their households

Free peasants, or freemen, owned land or rented it from the lord.

Villeins and serfs had their own plot of land, but also had to work on the lord's land, and pay other dues.

THE BIRTH OF PARLIAMENT

For much of the Middle Ages, feudal lords were often more powerful than the kings they were supposed to serve. In **1215**, the English nobles succeeded in forcing King John to sign a document, called *Magna Carta* ("Great Charter"), limiting his power and establishing their right to a Council to discuss problems.

Later, Council meetings grew to include knights, churchmen and townspeople too. This formed the basis for the English Parliament. Similar institutions developed elsewhere, such as the Estates-General in France, the Cortes in Spain, and the Diet in Germany. Supported by these assemblies, kings were able to raise taxes and pay for their own armies. This meant they were no longer dependent on the feudal lords for protection. By the 16th century, the feudal system had virtually disappeared.

Manuscript showing Edward I at a meeting of Parliament

The most powerful feudal lords lived in magnificent castles, like this one.

Chapel

Great Hall

Servants' quarters

Sentries on lookout duty

Private quarters of the lord and family

Within the castle walls vegetables were grown and animals were kept.

Towers strengthened the castle wall and made good lookout posts.

THE GROWTH OF TOWNS AND TRADE

Merchants and craftsmen did not fit into the feudal system. They tended to settle together in towns, and lived by selling their goods or skills for money. In the 11th century, they began organizing themselves into guilds.

Guild badge of the fishermen of Zurich

Guilds regulated prices and wages, set standards of work, and looked after their members. They were a little like trade unions. By the 12th century, each trade had its own guild.

In the 12th and 13th centuries, most of Europe enjoyed growing prosperity. The population increased and new land was brought into cultivation. Some landlords began allowing villeins to pay rent, instead of working for them, which meant they were no longer tied to the land.

Gold coins from Florence

Prosperous towns and cities grew in the main trading areas. The Baltic and North Sea trade was dominated by the Hanseatic League, a group of cities, including Hamburg and Lübeck, which set up trading associations, called *hanse*, for mutual protection. The luxury trade in silks and spices from the East was under the control of the northern Italian cities. In **1381**, Venice defeated her rival, Genoa, and became the foremost naval and trading power.

The Hanseatic city of Lübeck, northern Germany

In many places, kings and nobles sold charters to the guilds, allowing them to rule the city. By **1500**, some of the great cities in Italy, such as Florence and Venice, had become independent states with their own governments. A complex economy soon developed throughout Europe.

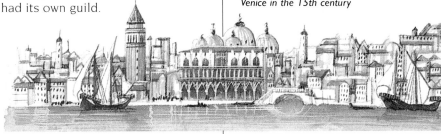

Venice in the 15th century

The first banking system was introduced in the 13th century by the Lombards, merchants from northern Italy. They soon set up a network of banks all over Europe. Other bankers followed, the most famous being the Medici family of Florence. They began as cloth traders, rose to public office in the 14th century, and in **1434** became rulers of the city.

The growing number of freemen, the importance of cities, the use of money and of paid soldiers, known as mercenaries, all helped to contribute to the eventual decline of feudalism.

FAMINE, PLAGUE AND UPRISINGS

In the early 14th century, bad weather brought poor harvests and famine (**1315-1317**). Then, from **1347** to **1353**, a plague known as the Black Death swept through Europe from the East, killing as many as one in three people. Wages rose at first, but fell again, causing hardship. There were struggles between some of the poorer craftsmen and richer guilds, and uprisings against taxes and poor working conditions.

DATES OF UPRISINGS

1302 Craftsmen in Ghent and Bruges seize power from wealthy pro-French merchant guilds. They defeat the French at Courtrai, but are beaten at Cassel.

1355 Etienne Marcel, a cloth merchant, leads an uprising in Paris against taxes.

1358 The Jacquerie: uprisings of French peasants against harsh conditions. They try to ally with the Parisian rebels, but are crushed by nobles and merchants.

1378 Unsuccessful uprising of the *ciompi* (clothworkers) in Florence.

1381 Peasants Revolt: an uprising of English peasants led by Jack Straw and Wat Tyler. They disperse when the King agrees to some of their demands.

1382 Paris uprising against taxes.

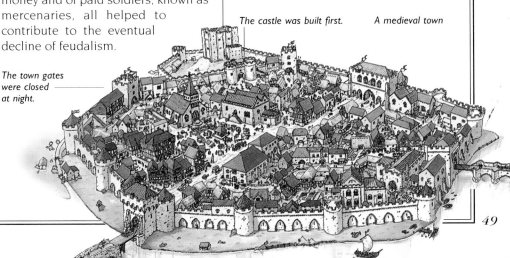

The castle was built first. *A medieval town*

The town gates were closed at night.

Southern and Western Europe

c.1200s Rise of Gothic architecture in Europe, characterized by the lancet arch, ribbed vault and flying buttress.

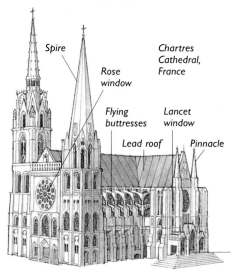

Spire
Rose window
Flying buttresses
Lead roof
Chartres Cathedral, France
Lancet window
Pinnacle
Porch

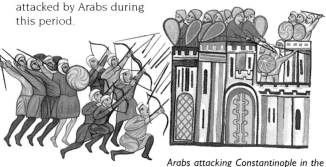

Gothic lancet window from Chartres Cathedral

c.1200s Flourishing of the first universities, established in Bologna (**1119**), Paris (**1150**) and Oxford (**1170**).

1202 Arabic numerals are introduced in Europe.

1209-1229 Albigensian Crusade, led by Simon de Montfort the elder against the Albigensians (see page 53).

1212 Battle of Las Navas de Tolosa: Christian kings of Castile, Aragon and Navarre defeat the Muslims. Starts the break-up of the Muslim kingdom in Spain.

1214-1294 Life of Roger Bacon, English monk, scholar and scientist. He carried out research into optics and was one of the first to suggest the use of lenses as spectacles.

1215 English King John signs *Magna Carta* (see page 48).

1225-1274 Life of Thomas Aquinas, Italian theologian and philosopher.

c.1258-1265 Uprising of English barons against Henry III, led by Simon de Montfort the younger. Defeated by Prince Edward at Evesham.

Henry III of England (1207-72) being crowned at Gloucester Cathedral

Northern and Eastern Europe

1204 Crusaders sack Constantinople, depose the Byzantine emperor and set up a Latin empire, ruled by Western Roman emperors until **1258**. The city is also attacked by Arabs during this period.

Arabs attacking Constantinople in the 13th century, based on an early drawing

1218 The ruling family in Switzerland dies out. Small independent states, called cantons, are formed.

1220-1250 Reign of Emperor Frederick II (see page 56).

A Teutonic Knight

1222 Andreas II of Hungary issues the Golden Bull, giving power to the nobles and certain rights to the national assembly.

1226-1283 The Teutonic Knights are sent by Frederick II to convert Prussians to Christianity.

1227 Denmark is defeated at Bornhöved by north German princes, who increase trade with the Baltic.

1231 German secular princes are given the same rights over territory as ecclesiastical princes.

1237-1242 Mongols invade Russia, Hungary and Poland and set up the Khanate of the Golden Horde.

1249 Birger Jarl of Sweden conquers Finland and gives trading privileges to the Hanseatic League (**1250-1266**), an association of German and Scandinavian trading cities, led by Lübeck.

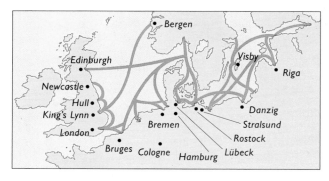

Bergen
Edinburgh
Visby
Riga
Newcastle
Hull
King's Lynn
Bremen
Danzig
London
Stralsund
Rostock
Bruges
Cologne
Hamburg
Lübeck

Map showing sea trade routes of the Hanseatic League

1250 Collapse of imperial power in Germany and Italy, followed by the Great Interregnum (**1254-1273**).

1253-1278 Rule of Ottokar II of Bohemia.

1258-1282 Michael Paleologus restores Byzantine rule.

Africa and the Middle East

1200s Trans-Saharan trade continues. Ghana is in decline.

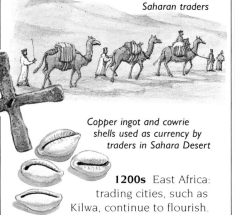

Saharan traders

Copper ingot and cowrie shells used as currency by traders in Sahara Desert

1200s East Africa: trading cities, such as Kilwa, continue to flourish.

c.1200 Church of St. George is built at Lalibela, Ethiopia.

1218 Ayyubid empire breaks up, but the Ayyubids still rule in Egypt.

1228 War between Saladin's heirs.

1228-1229 Fifth Crusade: Frederick II is crowned King of Jerusalem.

c.1235 Sun Diata Keita establishes kingdom of Mali (lasts until **c.1500**).

1240 Destruction of Kumbi, former capital of Ghana.

1244 Egyptians retake Jerusalem.

1248-1254 Sixth Crusade, by Louis IX of France against Egypt.

Crusader galleon cut away to show cargo inside

1250 North Africa: Berber states flourish for over 200 years. Europeans call North Africa the Barbary Coast.

1250 Mamelukes seize power and found their own military state in Egypt.

1258 Baghdad is destroyed by Mongols.

Cabin for the king

Asia

1206-1526 Rule of the Islamic Sultanate of Delhi, known as the Slave Dynasty.

1206 Genghis Khan unites Mongols and begins conquest of Asia.

1211 Mongols invade China.

1218-1224 Mongols attack the empire of Khwarizm.

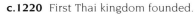

Mongol soldiers were trained to fight on horseback.

c.1220 First Thai kingdom founded.

1221 Mongols attack Delhi.

1227 Death of Genghis Khan. His son, Ogadei, is elected Great Khan (**1229-1241**).

1234 Mongols overthrow the Chin dynasty in China.

1239 Mongols sack Ani, the capital of Armenia.

1251-1265 Hulagu, grandson of Genghis Khan, conquers Persia and sets up Il-Khan empire.

Crusader flag

The Americas

c.1200 North America: the Mississippians dominate a wide area. They develop a remarkable culture, influenced by Mexico, building large cities on flat-topped mounds.

Mound-dwellers village

Objects found in tombs of mound-dwellers

c.1200 North America: Pueblo builders are at their peak in the southwest.

c.1200 The Aztecs begin to found small states in Mexico.

c.1200 The Mayan capital, Chichen Itza, is abandoned and a new capital built at Mayapán, defended by 8 km (5 miles) of wall.

c.1200-1300 Chimu kingdom continues in Peru.

Chimu gold mummy burial mask

c.1200-1300 Beginning of the early Inca period in Peru.

The Church in the Middle Ages

The Catholic Church played a central role in daily life in Europe during the Middle Ages. The continent itself was sometimes described as Christendom, because it was united by religion.

THE FIRST MONASTERIES

During the 3rd century, some Christians in Egypt moved into the desert to live alone as hermits. They were first brought together into communities by Basil of Caesarea (**330-379**).

Monk Amalric of Bena lecturing at the University of Paris

St. Catherine's monastery at Mount Sinai, Egypt, founded c.337

Monasticism in Western Europe was started by Benedict of Nursia (**480-543**). In **c.529**, he founded an order of monks, called Benedictines, who lived in a monastery at Monte Cassino in Italy. They worked and prayed together, following a set of regulations known as the Rule.

Monks at their daily work, from an illuminated manuscript

By the 8th century, there were monasteries and convents (for women called nuns) all over Europe. Until the spread of universities in the 13th century, monasteries were the main focus for education and culture. They also provided care for the poor and sick, and hospitality to people on journeys.

NEW MONASTIC ORDERS

The monasteries became great landowners, but as they grew richer, discipline often became relaxed. There were frequent attempts at reform, and new orders of monks and nuns were established. The first of these were the Cluniacs, who were founded at Cluny in France in **910** and spread rapidly from **c.950** to **1100**. The Cistercians, founded at Cîteaux in France in **1098**, were influential in the 12th century under St. Bernard of Clairvaux (**d.1153**). They wanted a simpler way of life, away from towns.

The 12th century was the great age of the monasteries, but by the end of the century their popularity was in decline. New religious orders were founded, such as the Franciscans (**1210**) and the Dominicans (**1215**), but these were based in towns. They were called mendicant friars and went around preaching and lived on alms (donations).

Milan Cathedral, Italy, c.1385-1485, an example of late Gothic architecture

RELIGIOUS ARCHITECTURE

The larger monasteries commissioned important works of art and inspired the Romanesque style, which flourished from the 9th to 12th centuries. Romanesque buildings are identified by rounded arches, groined vaults and massive stone walls.

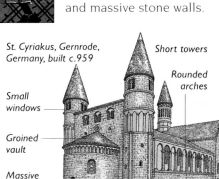

St. Cyriakus, Gernrode, Germany, built c.959

Short towers

Rounded arches

Small windows

Groined vault

Massive stone walls

In the 12th century, Romanesque began to be replaced by a new style, later described as Gothic. It was characterized by churches that were lighter, taller, and more delicate-looking, with pointed arches and bright stained-glass windows.

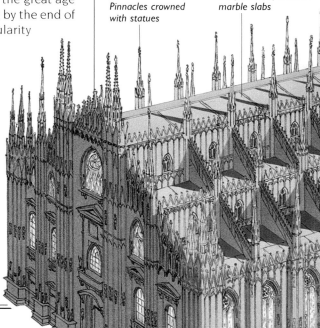

Pinnacles crowned with statues

Roof made of massive marble slabs

MEDIEVAL POPES

In the 13th century, the popes, the leaders of the Church, began claiming they were superior to temporal (non-religious) rulers. This provoked clashes, especially with the Holy Roman Emperor, over taxation, imperial elections, and church appointments. Conflict came to a head with the rivalry between Emperor Frederick II and Innocent III (see page 56).

Pope Innocent III

Pope Boniface VIII issued two documents, known as bulls: *clericos laicos* (**1296**) and *unam sanctam* (**1302**). These bulls banned churchmen from paying taxes to temporal rulers and proclaimed the sovereignty (authority) of the Church.

Spire

Tower

Tall stained-glass windows and pointed arches

THE GREAT SCHISM

Both England and France opposed these bulls. In **1303**, Philippe IV of France imprisoned Pope Boniface and had a French pope, Clement V (**1305-1316**), elected instead.

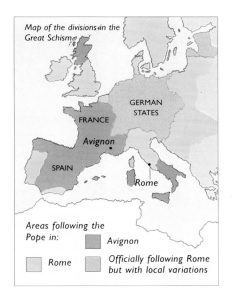

Map of the divisions in the Great Schism

GERMAN STATES

FRANCE

Avignon

SPAIN

Rome

Areas following the Pope in:

Avignon

Rome

Officially following Rome but with local variations

Between **1309-1377**, the papal court was moved to Avignon, France, and a series of Frenchmen was elected pope, under the influence of the French kings. Pressure built up for reform, and for a return to Rome. In **1378**, Urban VI was elected pope and took up residence in Rome. At the same time, a rival French pope, Clement VII, was elected in Avignon. For 40 years (**1378-1418**), Catholic Europe was divided. This period is known as the Great Schism.

At the Council of Pisa in **1409**, both popes were deposed and a new one elected, but the first two refused to stand down. At the Council of Constance (**1414-1418**), all three were deposed. A new pope, Martin V, was elected and ruled from Rome.

HERETICS

As the Church grew wealthier, it also grew more corrupt, and this inspired a number of movements for reform. Complaints about abuses by priests sometimes developed into attacks on the authority of the Church itself, and even on official teaching. The popes condemned these attacks as heresy. In **1184**, an organization called the Inquisition was founded, to seek out and suppress heresy.

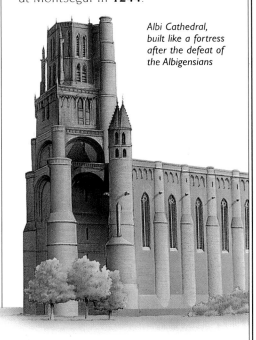

Dominican monks, who were put in charge of the Inquisition

Heretics (people found guilty of heresy) were savagely punished and condemned to death by burning. Despite this, some heretical sects became popular. One group, the Cathars, attracted a big following in southern France. They were known there as Albigensians, after Albi, where they began. The Albigensians were attacked and virtually wiped out after the fall of their stronghold at Montségur in **1244**.

Albi Cathedral, built like a fortress after the defeat of the Albigensians

Southern and Western Europe

1282 The death in battle of Prince Llewelyn of Wales marks the end of Welsh independence from England.

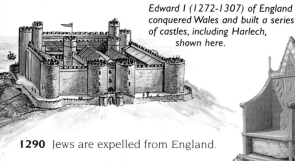

Edward I (1272-1307) of England conquered Wales and built a series of castles, including Harlech, shown here.

1290 Jews are expelled from England.

1290 Margaret, child Queen of Scotland, dies. Edward I is asked to judge the claims of 13 rivals for the Scottish throne, but later claims it himself.

1295 Mateo Visconti seizes control in Milan. His dynasty rules until **1447**.

1295 Edward I of England calls the Model Parliament, which forms the basis for the House of Commons.

Edward I's coronation chair

1297 French occupy Flanders (now in Belgium).

1297 Scots, led by William Wallace, defeat the English at Stirling Bridge.

1301 Wales becomes the principality of the heir to the English throne.

1302 Flemish craftsmen defeat the French army at the Battle of Courtrai.

1306 Jews are expelled from France.

Knight Templar on horseback

1307-1314 The Knights Templars, a military religious order, are investigated for heresy.

1309-1378 The Avignon Papacy: the Pope's court moves to Avignon, France.

1314 Robert Bruce, King of Scotland (**1306-1329**) defeats the English at the Battle of Bannockburn.

Portrait and seal of Robert Bruce

1317 The Salic Law in France bans women from inheriting the throne.

Northern and Eastern Europe

1261 Greenland is conquered by Norway.

1262-1264 Iceland comes under Norwegian rule.

Inuit carving

1263 Norway is defeated by the Scots and cedes the Hebrides to Scotland.

Inuit fishermen from Greenland

1266 Norway cedes Isle of Man to Scotland.

1273-1291 Rudolf of Hapsburg becomes Holy Roman Emperor, despite the efforts of his enemy, Ottokar II.

1278 Ottokar II of Bohemia is killed at Marchfeld. Bohemia and Moravia become estates of the Holy Roman Empire.

1282 Rudolf of Hapsburg makes his son, Albert, Duke of Austria.

1291 Three Swiss cantons (Unterwalden, Schwyz and Uri) sign the Pact of Rutli forming the Swiss Confederation.

Map showing Swiss cantons in the 13th and 14th centuries

ZURICH
Sempach
LUCERNE ZUG Morgarten
BERN SCHWYZ
UNTERWALDEN
URI
GLARUS

Cantons by 1315
Cantons by 1389

1293 Sweden conquers Karelia (Finland).

1298-1308 Rule of Albert I Hapsburg as Holy Roman Emperor.

1301 End of the Arpad dynasty in Hungary.

1306 King Wenceslas III of Hungary and Bohemia is murdered. The Premsyl dynasty dies out.

Hungarian coat-of-arms

1308-1313 Henry VII of Luxembourg becomes Holy Roman Emperor.

1310 John of Luxembourg inherits Bohemia.

1315 Battle of Morgarten: Swiss peasants repulse an attack by the army of Leopold I of Austria.

Africa and the Middle East

1260-1277 Reign of Sultan Baibars of Egypt.

13th century water clock, built for an Arab sultan. Every hour the bird whistled.

1261 Battle of Ain Jalut, Palestine: the Mongol advance is halted by the Egyptians, led by Baibars.

1262-1263 Baibars takes the Ayyubid lands in Syria.

1265-1271 Baibars takes most of Outremer.

1268 Baibars captures Antioch.

1270 Seventh Crusade, led by Louis IX of France, who dies in Tunis.

Louis IX

1281-1326 Reign of Osman I, *emir* (chief) of a small Turkish princedom. In **1290** he declares himself Sultan of the Turks and becomes the founder of the Ottoman empire.

1291 Mamelukes take Acre, the last stronghold of Outremer.

c.1300 Emergence of the empire of Benin in Nigeria.

Asia

1264 Kublai Khan founds the Yuan dynasty in China.

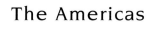

Kublai Khan, Mongol ruler of China

1271-1295 Marco Polo of Venice travels across Asia to China. From **1275-1292**, he works for Mongol ruler Kublai Khan.

1274 Unsuccessful Mongol invasion of Japan.

1279-1368 The Sung dynasty in China is overthrown by Kublai Khan. The Yuan (Mongol) dynasty rules all China.

1281 Second attempted invasion of Japan by Mongols. The Japanese attack the Mongol fleet and capture several ships. Finally, the rest of the fleet is scattered by *kamikaze* ("divine winds").

Japanese woodcut showing a Mongol ship under attack

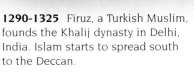

1290-1325 Firuz, a Turkish Muslim, founds the Khalij dynasty in Delhi, India. Islam starts to spread south to the Deccan.

1293 The first Christian missionaries reach China.

c.1300 Ghazan, Mongol ruler of Persia, declares Islam the state religion.

1307 The first Catholic archbishop is established in Beijing, China.

The Americas

c.1300 Constant warfare among the Maya people in Yucatán contributes to the decline of their civilization.

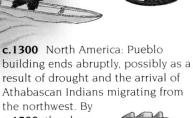

INUIT

ATHABASCANS

MISSISSIPPI MOUND BUILDERS

PUEBLO BUILDERS

Chichen Itza

Yucatán peninsula

Tenochtitlán

AZTECS

MAYA

American peoples 1200-1500

Quito

CHIMU

INCA

Cuzco

Patterned pots made by pueblo builders

c.1300 North America: Pueblo building ends abruptly, possibly as a result of drought and the arrival of Athabascan Indians migrating from the northwest. By **c.1500**, they have completely taken over the southwest.

Totem poles, like this one, were built by tribes on the northwest coast.

The Holy Roman Empire

From the coronation of Charlemagne (see page 33) in **800** to the mid 13th century, the Holy Roman Empire, based on the German states and princedoms, was the most powerful political force in Europe. At the height of its power in the 13th century, the emperors ruled over territories from the Baltic Sea to Sicily.

Charlemagne

The emperors were the temporal (non-religious) heads of Christian Europe. They had great influence over the Church, choosing their own bishops and sometimes even controlling the elections of popes.

Otto I, the first to be crowned Holy Roman Emperor

Otto's crown

THE EMPIRE DECLINES

Unlike the other kings in western Europe, however, the Holy Roman emperors never succeeded in breaking the power of the local lords. As the feudal system broke down, imperial authority declined rather than increased. By the 16th century, many states within the Empire had become efficient independent units, over which the Emperor had little control. Despite this, the title continued to exist until **1806**, when Napoleon finally abolished it (see page 133).

FREDERICK II & THE FALL OF THE HOHENSTAUFEN

Frederick II of Hohenstaufen (**1194-1250**), King of Sicily and Germany, became Holy Roman Emperor in **1220**. Resident in Sicily at the heart of a brilliant court, he reorganized the Sicilian government in **1231** (with his *Constitutions of Melfi*), making Sicily one of the most advanced states in Europe. Frederick was a well-educated man, with a thirst for knowledge. His lively personality won him the nickname *Stupor Mundi* ("Wonder of the World"). But his conduct and attitudes offended many people.

The empire at the time of Frederick II Above: a falcon perching on the thick leather glove used to protect the falconer's hand

Falconry was a popular sport at Frederick II's court.

Frederick's ambitions in Italy brought him into conflict with the papacy. Pope Gregory IX officially deposed him, even though he had played a major part in the Fifth Crusade (**1228-1229**), winning back Jerusalem by treaty from the Turks. In North Italy, rivalry developed between two factions: the Ghibellines (Frederick's allies) and the Guelphs (the Pope's supporters). Frederick sucessfully fought off a rebellion by Guelphs in **1237**.

The feuds continued after his death and led to the fall of the Hohenstaufen dynasty. The result was political chaos in Germany and Italy, where independent city-states grew up in place of imperial authority. The Pope gave Sicily to Charles of Anjou, who defeated Frederick's son Manfred and grandson Conradin at the battles of Benevento (**1266**) and Tagliacozzo (**1268**). The Sicilians hated their new French rulers and massacred them at the Sicilian Vespers in **1282**.

Holy Roman Emperor Frederick II

Sicily then passed to Frederick's granddaughter, Constance, who was the wife of Peter III of Aragon in Spain.

The Wars of the Roses

The Wars of the Roses is the name given to the struggle between the descendents of Edward III for the English crown. The name comes from the emblems of the two rival families involved: the white rose of York and the red rose of Lancaster.

The white rose of York and the red rose of Lancaster

Bitter rivalries developed during the long minority rule of Henry VI (**1422-1461**) of Lancaster. When he was old enough to rule, he proved incompetent and subject to bouts of madness. Added to his problems was the humiliation caused by defeat in the Hundred Years' War.

Coat of arms of Henry VI

In **1454**, Parliament made Richard, Duke of York, Protector, giving him the authority to rule on behalf of the king. But, in **1455**, he was excluded from the Royal Council and fighting broke out.

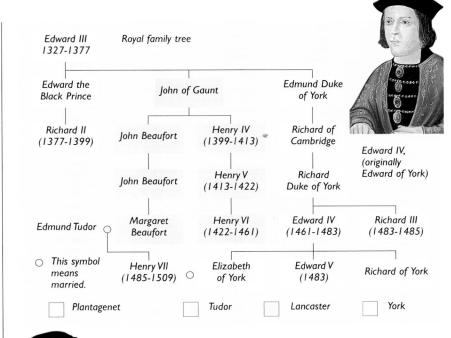

Royal family tree

Edward IV, (originally Edward of York)

This symbol ○ means married.

Plantagenet · Tudor · Lancaster · York

The wars ended with the victory of Henry Tudor, who became Henry VII, first king of the Tudor dynasty (**1485-1603**).

Henry VII

Boys' skeletons found in The Tower of London may have been those of Edward V and his brother Richard Duke of York. They had been imprisoned there by their uncle, who became Richard III.

The Tower of London

The White Tower, where bones of two children were found

KEY DATES

1455 Yorkists win at St. Albans.

1460 Northampton: Yorkists win. Henry VI is taken prisoner. Lancastrians win at Wakefield. Richard of York is executed.

1461 Edward of York defeats Henry VI at Mortimer's Cross, and is crowned Edward IV.

1469 Earl of Warwick defeats Edward IV at Edgecote, forcing him to flee to Flanders. Henry VI regains the throne.

1471 Henry VI is murdered. Edward IV kills Warwick at Barnet and regains the throne.

1483 Edward IV dies, succeeded by his young son, Edward V. Edward and his brother are kept in the Tower of London by their uncle, Richard of Gloucester, later Richard III. The boys disappear, and are presumed murdered.

1485 Henry Tudor, the Lancastrian heir, defeats Richard III at Bosworth. He marries the Yorkist heiress, Elizabeth, and becomes Henry VII.

Southern and Western Europe

1323 The Declaration of Arbroath sets the wishes of Scotland's people above those of the Scottish kings.

1328 Start of the Valois dynasty in France.

1337-1453 The Hundred Years' War breaks out between England and France after Edward III of England claims the French throne.

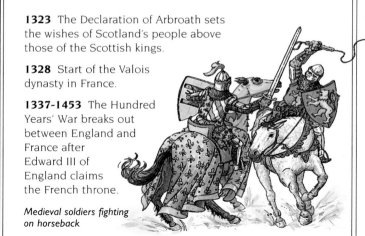

Medieval soldiers fighting on horseback

THE BLACK DEATH

The Black Death, a bubonic plague carried by fleas on black rats, reached Genoa, Italy from the East, via the Crimea, in **1347**. It swept through Europe until **1353**, killing as many as 20 million people, or one person in three. Many towns saw their populations halved and some villages were completely deserted.

This illustration from a medieval manuscript shows people trying to stop the spread of infection by burning the clothes of the plague victims.

1346 The English defeat the French at Crécy.

c.1350 The first firearms, muzzle-loading cannon, are used in Europe.

The picture shows a 16th century muzzle-loading cannon.

The fuse was lit, the gunpowder exploded, and the cannon ball shot out.

Gunpowder was pushed to the bottom of the barrel through the open end (muzzle) followed by the cannon ball.

1355 Revolt against taxes led by cloth merchant Etienne Marcel in Paris.

1358 The Jacquerie: an uprising of peasants in France.

1371 House of Stewart rules in Scotland.

1373 Treaty of Anglo-Portuguese friendship.

1378-1415 Europe is divided by the Great Schism in the Catholic Church (see page 53).

Northern and Eastern Europe

1320 The unity of Poland is restored when Vladislav Lokiekek becomes king.

1328-1340 Moscow expands under Duke Ivan I.

1333-1370 Casimir III the Great strengthens Poland.

1342-1382 Reign of Louis the Great of Hungary. He conquers Croatia, Serbia, Bosnia, Wallachia, Bulgaria, Transylvania and Moldavia.

Territory held by the Teutonic Knights

1343 Teutonic Knights acquire Estonia from Denmark.

1346 Golden age of kingdom of Bohemia and city of Prague begins with the reign of Charles IV of the Luxembourg dynasty.

1354 The Turks acquire Gallipoli, their first European possession.

1355 Charles IV becomes Holy Roman Emperor.

15th century Prague

Charles IV's crown

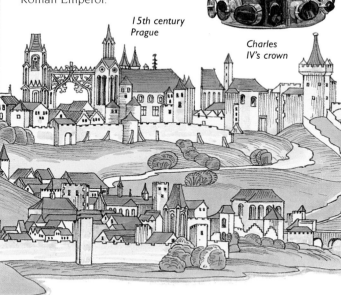

1361 Denmark is defeated by the Hanseatic League.

1370 The Lithuanians are defeated at Rudan by the Teutonic Knights.

1370 Hungary and Poland are unified under the Hungarian king, Louis of Anjou.

1370 Peace of Stralsund between Denmark and the Hanseatic League. The League's power is at its height.

1373 Byzantine emperor becomes an Ottoman vassal.

Africa and the Middle East

1324 Mansa Musa, King of Mali, goes on pilgrimage to Mecca. He visits Cairo and impresses everyone with his wealth.

Mansa Musa, from a 14th century map

1325 Ibn Battuta, a Moroccan Muslim, travels to Mecca, Arabia, via Egypt, Jerusalem and Damascus.

c.1350 Founding of the kingdom of Songhai in West Africa.

1352 Ibn Battuta travels in West Africa and visits Mali and writes an account of all he sees. He reaches Timbuktu in **1353**. From the writings of other Arab scholars, and archeology, other African states from this period are known: Kanem-Bornu, Kongo and Benin.

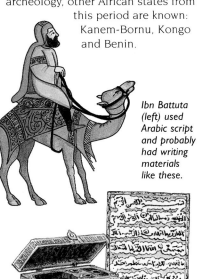

Ibn Battuta (left) used Arabic script and probably had writing materials like these.

1375 Mamelukes conquer Sis, Armenia: the end of Armenian independence.

Asia

c.1325 The development of Nō plays in Japan: classic Japanese drama, using music and dancing.

Nō masks of a young girl and a devil

1325-1351 Reign of Mohammed Ibn Tughluk, Sultan of Delhi. He expands his territories and briefly conquers the Deccan (South India).

1333 China suffers drought, famine, floods, and plague. Five million die.

1333 End of Kamakura shogunate in Japan. Emperor Go-daigo rules without a shogun (**1333-1336**).

1336 The Il-Khan empire is replaced by a Turcoman dynasty.

1340 India: the Hindu empire of Vijayanagar becomes a base for resistance to Islam. It is dominant in southern India by **c.1370**.

1349 The earliest Chinese settlement in Singapore.

c.1350 Cultural peak of the Majapahit empire in Java.

1368 The Yuan dynasty in China is overthrown and replaced by the native Chinese Ming dynasty.

1369 Thais invade Cambodia.

1369-1405 Tamerlane rules the Mongols from his capital at Samarkand. He conquers Herat (**1381**), destroys Delhi (**1398-1399**) and annexes the Punjab.

The Americas

c.1325 Rise of the Aztecs in Mexico. A great warrior civilization, they build up a large, well-organized empire. Their culture is highly sophisticated in many areas, especially science, art, architecture and agriculture, and they have strict laws and complex religious beliefs and ceremonies. The city of Tenochtitlán is built by a group led by Chief Tenoch, on islands in Lake Texcoco. It becomes the residence of the major tribe.

The quetzal bird, sacred to the Aztecs

c.1335 Tenochtitlán is increased in size by the building of floating gardens in the lake.

CENTRAL AMERICA · Texcoco · Tenochtitlán · Gulf of Mexico · PACIFIC OCEAN · Aztec

Aztec territory at its peak c.1519

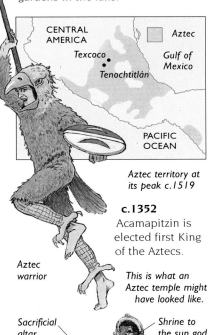

Aztec warrior

c.1352 Acamapitzin is elected first King of the Aztecs.

This is what an Aztec temple might have looked like.

Sacrificial altar

Shrine to the sun god

The unification of France

At the beginning of the 13th century, much of France was made up of semi-independent provinces in the hands of powerful nobles, including the King of England. The direct control of the King of France was limited to less than half the country.

Edward III of England and his coat of arms, which included the fleur-de-lis, symbol of the French kings

By the end of the 15th century, however, most of France was united under the French kings.

In **1204**, Philippe II of France conquered the English land in northern France: Normandy, Maine, Anjou and Touraine. At the Battle of Bouvines in **1214**, he retook all the remaining English lands, except Guyenne and Gascony. Despite early losses in the Hundred Years' War (see opposite), the French won back all their land from England, except Calais and the Channel Islands.

The kings acquired Chartres, Blois, and Sancerre (**1234**), Macon (**1239**), Poitou and Toulouse (**1271**), Bar (**1301**), Montpellier and Dauphiné (**1349**) from French nobles. Dauphiné became the province of the heir to the throne, known from then on as the *dauphin*. Louis XI seized Burgundy and Artois in **1477** and Lorraine in **1480**. In **1491**, Charles VIII married Anne of Brittany, adding Brittany to the French kingdom.

Edward I of England paying homage to Philippe I of France for his land in Gascony

THE DUCHY OF BURGUNDY

In **1363**, Jean II of France made his younger son, Philippe, Duke of Burgundy. By buying and inheriting more land, the dukes of Burgundy increased their territory in France, Germany and the Netherlands. They were among the richest princes in Europe, and influenced politics and culture for over a century. They were known especially for their splendid courts and patronage of the arts.

Holland 1433
Gelderland 1473
Zeeland 1328
Brabant 1430
Artois 1384
Flanders 1384
Limburg 1430
Luxembourg 1451
Picardy 1435
Hainault 1328
Paris
Lorraine 1475
Nancy
FRANCE
Alsace 1469
Dijon
Burgundy
Franche-Comté 1384
Charolais 1390

French lands after 1482 | Hapsburg lands after 1482

Map of the Burgundian kingdom, with dates when territories were acquired

The Burgundians provoked civil war in France (**1410-1411**) and took England's side in the 100 Years' War. In **1477**, when Charles the Bold was killed at Nancy, Louis XI of France seized Picardy and Burgundy. At the Peace of Senlis (**1493**), the rest of Burgundy passed to Maximilian Hapsburg. This gave the Hapsburgs a base from which, under Charles V (see page 76), they rose to dominate Europe.

Philippe the Good, Duke of Burgundy

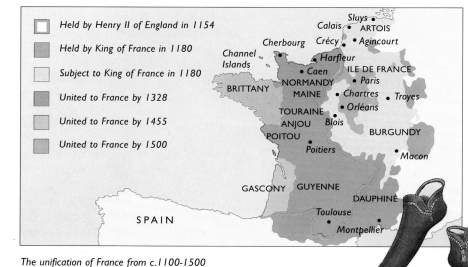

Held by Henry II of England in 1154
Held by King of France in 1180
Subject to King of France in 1180
United to France by 1328
United to France by 1455
United to France by 1500

Sluys
Calais
ARTOIS
Cherbourg
Crécy
Agincourt
Channel Islands
Harfleur
Caen
ILE DE FRANCE
BRITTANY
NORMANDY
Paris
MAINE
Chartres
Troyes
TOURAINE
Orléans
ANJOU
Blois
POITOU
BURGUNDY
Poitiers
Macon
GASCONY
GUYENNE
DAUPHINÉ
Toulouse
Montpellier
SPAIN

The unification of France from c.1100-1500

THE HUNDRED YEARS' WAR

The Hundred Years' War is the name given to the struggle between England and France which lasted from **1337** to **1453**. Ever since **1066**, there had been quarrels and wars between the two countries, over land held in France by the English kings.

Longbows, which could shoot much farther than crossbows, helped the English win many battles.

But, added to this, a dispute broke out over the crown itself. In **1328**, Charles IV of France died without a male heir and was succeeded by his cousin Philippe VI. Later, in **1337**, Charles's nephew Edward III of England decided to claim the French throne for himself.

In **1338**, Edward formed an alliance with Flanders and, in **1339**, invaded France. The English made early gains, winning victories at Sluys (**1340**), Crécy (**1346**), Calais (**1347**) and Poitiers (**1356**), where they took the French king captive. By the Treaty of Brétigny (**1360**), the English won large areas of France.

In **1367**, civil war broke out in Castile, Spain, and England and France backed opposite sides. By **1369**, the war had spread to

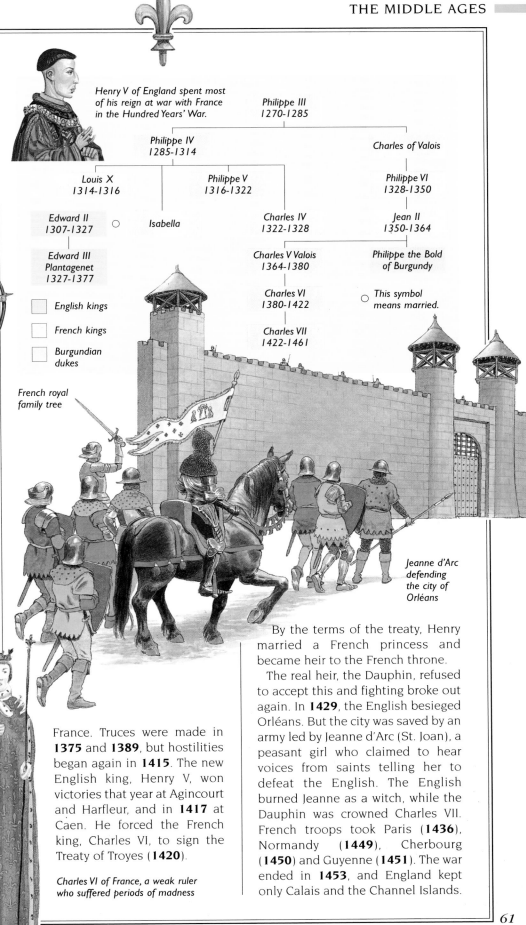

Henry V of England spent most of his reign at war with France in the Hundred Years' War.

French royal family tree

English kings

French kings

Burgundian dukes

Philippe III 1270-1285

Philippe IV 1285-1314

Charles of Valois

Louis X 1314-1316

Philippe V 1316-1322

Philippe VI 1328-1350

Edward II 1307-1327 ○ Isabella

Charles IV 1322-1328

Jean II 1350-1364

Edward III Plantagenet 1327-1377

Charles V Valois 1364-1380

Philippe the Bold of Burgundy

Charles VI 1380-1422

○ This symbol means married.

Charles VII 1422-1461

Jeanne d'Arc defending the city of Orléans

Charles VI of France, a weak ruler who suffered periods of madness

France. Truces were made in **1375** and **1389**, but hostilities began again in **1415**. The new English king, Henry V, won victories that year at Agincourt and Harfleur, and in **1417** at Caen. He forced the French king, Charles VI, to sign the Treaty of Troyes (**1420**).

By the terms of the treaty, Henry married a French princess and became heir to the French throne.

The real heir, the Dauphin, refused to accept this and fighting broke out again. In **1429**, the English besieged Orléans. But the city was saved by an army led by Jeanne d'Arc (St. Joan), a peasant girl who claimed to hear voices from saints telling her to defeat the English. The English burned Jeanne as a witch, while the Dauphin was crowned Charles VII. French troops took Paris (**1436**), Normandy (**1449**), Cherbourg (**1450**) and Guyenne (**1451**). The war ended in **1453**, and England kept only Calais and the Channel Islands.

Southern and Western Europe

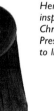

c.1380 John Wycliffe, an English scholar, begins preaching that the Bible alone is the authority for Christian belief. His teachings are condemned and his followers, the Lollards, are persecuted.

1381 The Peasants' Revolt in England (see page 49).

1381 Genoa is defeated by Venice after a hundred years of war.

A Spanish mercenary captain. Mercenaries, men who were hired to fight for foreign armies, began to be used in the 14th century.

1387 Geoffrey Chaucer (**c.1345-1400**), the first great poet to write in English, writes *The Canterbury Tales*.

1394-1466 Life of Henry the Navigator, Prince of Portugal, who inspired many expeditions and voyages of discovery.

Henry the Navigator was inspired by stories of a Christian priest-king, known as Prester John, who was believed to live somewhere in Africa.

Prester John

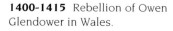

1400-1415 Rebellion of Owen Glendower in Wales.

1407 Casi di San Georgio, the first European public bank, is established in Genoa, Italy.

1410-1411 Civil war in France. Power struggle between Armagnacs and Burgundians.

1415 Henry V of England defeats the French at the Battle of Agincourt.

1416 Prince Henry of Portugal founds a school of navigation.

1431 Jeanne d'Arc is burned.

1434 Cosimo de Medici takes control of Florence, Italy. The Medici dynasty rules Florence until **1737**.

Dome of Florence Cathedral, built by Brunelleschi, c.1420-1436

Northern and Eastern Europe

1380 Muscovites defeat Mongols at Kulikova.

1386 Union of Poland and Lithuania.

1389 Battle of Kosovo: Turks gain control of the Balkans.

1397 The Union of Kalmar unites Scandinavia under Margaret, Queen of Denmark and Norway (**1387-1412**).

1410 Poles defeat the Teutonic Knights at Tannenberg.

1415 John Huss, a Bohemian religious reformer, is condemned by the Council of Constance and burned as a heretic.

Eastern Europe in the 14th century

Mount Tabor Castle, a Hussite stronghold

1415 Frederick VI of Hohenzollern is made Frederick I, Elector of Brandenburg.

1416 Venetians defeat the Turks off Gallipoli.

1419-1436 Hussite wars between Bohemia and Moravia and the HRE are triggered by the death of John Huss.

1422 First siege of Constantinople by the Ottoman Turks. Sultan Murat I invades Greece and the Peloponnese.

1430 Murat I of Turkey conquers Thessalonika, Greece.

1437 Albert II Hapsburg of Austria becomes King of Hungary and Bohemia, and is elected King of Germany in **1438-1439**. The Hapsburgs are king-emperors until **1918**.

1439 Russian and Greek Orthodox Churches are formally separated.

Africa and the Middle East

1397 Portuguese explorers reach the Canary Islands.

c.1400s Chinese traders join the Arab and Indian merchants trading in East Africa.

East Africans traded gold, ivory, coconuts and grain.

1401 Tamerlane conquers Damascus and Baghdad.

1415 Portuguese conquer Ceuta, North Africa.

1419 Portuguese reach Madeira.

c.1420 Chinese are believed to have rounded Cape of Good Hope (South Africa).

15th century Chinese map showing the Cape of Good Hope at the top

c.1430 Massive stone buildings are erected at Great Zimbabwe.

1431 Portuguese reach the Azores.

1434 Portuguese courtier Gil Eannes sails around Cape of Bojador, near Canary Islands, after several failed Portuguese attempts.

Portuguese ship

Asia

1387 Ming conquest of China.

1392-1636 The great age of the Choson dynasty in Korea.

1394 Temple of the Golden Pavilion is built, near Kyoto, Japan.

Temple of the Golden Pavilion

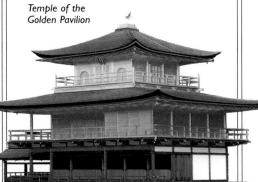

1405-1433 Chinese courtier, Cheng Ho, with a fleet of 317 ships and 27,000 men, makes seven great voyages. He visits Indochina, Indonesia, Siam (Thailand), the Maldives, Borneo, the Persian Gulf, Arabia and East Africa.

Chinese boat called a junk

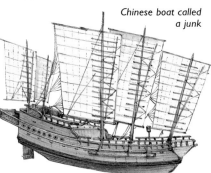

1421 Beijing becomes the capital of China.

1424 King of Siam dies. His two eldest sons fight each other for the throne on elephants and both die.

The princes fighting on elephants

1428 The Chinese are expelled from Vietnam.

The Americas

Early **1400s** Peru: Viracocha Inca (8th emperor) takes the title Sapa Inca, meaning "Supreme Inca".

c.1427 Mexico: a causeway is built from the Aztec island city of Tenochtitlán to the mainland. Emperor Itzcoatl adopts an aggressive policy toward local tribes. He forces them to pay tribute and establishes a three-city league with Texcoco and Tlacopán, to gain political control of the region.

c.1436-1464 Rule of Emperor Montezuma I of the Aztecs.

Aztec soldiers from a 16th century illustration

Aztec sacrificial knife

THE INCA EMPIRE

The Late Inca (or Empire) Period in Peru began with the reign of Pachacuti Inca (**1438-1471**), who started conquering an empire from his capital Cuzco. He was regarded as half-god, half-human. The Incas had a well-developed social system. Everyone had to work in accordance with their rank and ability. In return, orphans, the sick and elderly were looked after. The Incas were also expert stonemasons and farmers, and built good roads across very difficult, rough land.

The Incas kept records with knotted strings called quipu.

The Mongol empire

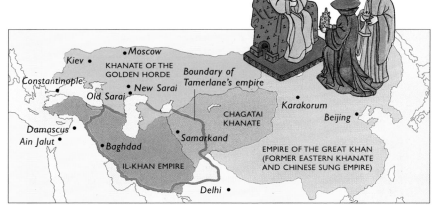

The Mongols were nomadic tribes from the part of the Steppes which is now Mongolia. In **1206**, they were united by Temujin (**c.1162-1227**), who overpowered the other Mongol tribes and took the name Genghis Khan, meaning "supreme ruler". He and his sons and grandsons made the Mongols into a formidable fighting force, which threatened the civilizations of Europe and Asia. They built up a vast empire from northern China to the Black Sea, which would have taken two years to ride across.

Map of the Mongol empire and Kublai Khan meeting the Polo brothers, who were Italian explorers

Genghis Khan, the first great Mongol ruler

From **1211**, Genghis Khan attacked the Chin empire in northern China, and in **1221** invaded India. When he died in **1227**, his son Ogadei became Great Khan and the empire was divided between him and his three brothers. Between **1237-1241**, they invaded Russia, Hungary and Poland. In **c.1251**, they established the Khanate of the Golden Horde in South Russia. The Mongols invaded Persia (**1251-1265**) and set up the Il-Khan empire which survived until **1336**. They sacked Baghdad in **1258**, but their advance was halted in **1260** by the victory of the Egyptian Mamelukes at Ain Jalut.

THE EMPIRE DIVIDES

Kublai Khan

Unity came to an end in **1259**, when Kublai Khan took over as Great Khan, ruling the Eastern Khanate. He conquered the Sung empire of China and set up the Yuan dynasty (**1280-1368**). Kublai Khan was a very powerful and efficient ruler, but his empire broke up after his death.

Mongol power was revived under Timur the Lame, or Tamerlane, who built up an empire from Samarkand, from **1369-1405**. But his empire did not survive him, and Mongols came increasingly under attack. The territories of the Golden Horde were absorbed by Russia, and in **1696**, Mongolia itself came under Chinese rule.

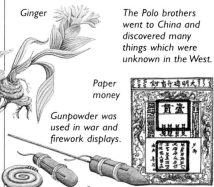

Ginger

The Polo brothers went to China and discovered many things which were unknown in the West.

Paper money

Gunpowder was used in war and firework displays.

A tent, called a yurt, which the Mongols carried from place to place

Mongol armies leaving a city they have destroyed

Chief's tent being carried by ox-drawn cart

Russia and the rise of Moscow

Between **1237-1240**, Russia was overrun by Mongols, also known as Tartars. In **1240**, they captured Kiev, destroying the cultural heart of medieval Russia. In **c.1251**, the Mongols withdrew to South Russia and established the Khanate of the Golden Horde, while exacting tribute from the rest of the country. From this time, Russia was cut off from all contact with western Europe.

Russian treasure c.1170-1240, hidden from the Mongols

In northern Russia, Alexander of Novgorod fought off the Swedes at the Battle of the River Neva (**1240**) and the Teutonic Knights at Lake Peipus in **1242**. Nicknamed "Nevsky", he became a national hero and a saint of the Orthodox Church, although he too was forced to pay tribute to the Mongols.

Nevsky's father's helmet

Nevsky's youngest son, Daniel, became Prince of Moscow (**1280-1303**). Under his dynasty, Moscow slowly expanded in size and importance to become the state of Muscovy.

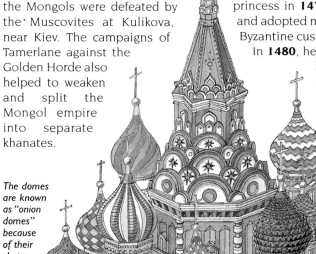

Prince Dimitri of Moscow and his army at the Battle of Kulikova

In **1328**, Moscow became the residence of the Metropolitan, the head of the Orthodox Church in Russia. Meanwhile, Mongol power was declining. In **1380**, the Mongols were defeated by the Muscovites at Kulikova, near Kiev. The campaigns of Tamerlane against the Golden Horde also helped to weaken and split the Mongol empire into separate khanates.

THE FIRST CZARS

The position of Moscow was strengthened further by Ivan III "the Great" (**1462-1505**). He extended control over new territory and in **1478** conquered Novgorod, the old Russian capital.

Ivan III, "the Great", 1462-1505. He adopted the double-headed eagle as the symbol of Russia.

Ivan married a Byzantine princess in **1472** and adopted many Byzantine customs.

In **1480**, he declared himself Czar (sole ruler) of all the Rus and finally ended Mongol control by refusing to pay tribute to them. Russia continued to grow under his son, Vassily, and grandson, Ivan IV "the Terrible".

The domes are known as "onion domes" because of their shape.

The exterior of the cathedral is covered in bright tiling.

The building of St. Basil's Cathedral in Moscow was started by Ivan IV, known as "the Terrible", in 1552.

SWEDEN

River Neva

RUSSIA

Novgorod

Lake Peipus

Moscow

◼ Moscow at end of 13th Century

◼ Expansion of Moscow to 1462

◻ Expansion of Moscow to 1505

Map showing the expansion of Moscow

Southern and Western Europe

1442 Alfonso of Aragon conquers Naples.

1447 French Orléans family claims Milan by inheritance.

1450 Francesco Sforza becomes Duke of Milan.

1455-1485 The Wars of the Roses (see page 57).

1462-1492 Rule of Lorenzo de Medici ("the Magnificent") in Florence.

1469 Ferdinand of Aragon marries Isabella of Castile.

Spanish coin showing Ferdinand and Isabella

1477 Charles the Bold, Duke of Burgundy, is killed. His daughter Marie marries Maximilian Hapsburg of Austria.

1477-1493 France and Austria fight over Burgundian lands. Austria keeps Burgundy and the Netherlands.

1479 Ferdinand of Aragon succeeds his father as King of Aragon and unites the kingdom with Castile.

1483 Charles VIII of France claims Naples as part of his Anjou inheritance.

1485 The Battle of Bosworth: Henry Tudor becomes first king of the Tudor dynasty in England.

1487 Rebellion in England by Lambert Simnel who claims to be the nephew of Edward IV.

1492 Ferdinand and Isabella conquer Granada, the last Muslim kingdom in Spain. Jews are expelled and many go to Eastern Europe.

The Alhambra, Granada, palace of the Spanish Muslim Nasrid dynasty

Many Jews in Europe were forced to wear special clothes to distinguish them from Christians.

1494-1495 France invades Italy and is driven back after early successes. The start of a struggle for power between France and the Hapsburgs.

1497 Rebellion in England by Perkin Warbeck who claims to be the son of Edward IV.

1498 Louis XII of France invades Italy and takes Milan.

Northern and Eastern Europe

1445 Johann Gutenberg (**1397-1468**), a German, develops printing presses and publishes the *Gutenberg Bible*, the first printed book in Europe.

Reconstruction of Gutenberg's press

Engraving of Gutenberg and a page from his Bible

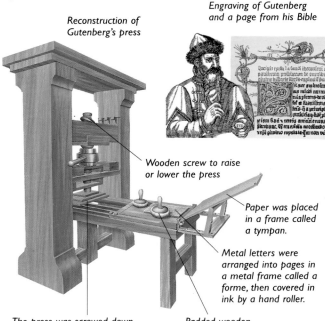

Wooden screw to raise or lower the press

Paper was placed in a frame called a tympan.

Metal letters were arranged into pages in a metal frame called a forme, then covered in ink by a hand roller.

The press was screwed down so that the inked letters printed clearly onto paper.

Padded wooden hammers were used to make the letters level.

1453 Ottomans capture Constantinople. The end of the Byzantine empire.

Byzantine chalice

Byzantine culture was preserved in Greece, in monasteries like this one in Meteora.

1456-1467 Ottomans take over Balkan states.

1462-1505 Rule of Ivan III ("The Great") of Moscow.

1468-1469 Denmark pawns Orkney and Shetland to Scotland.

1471-1480 Turkish raids in Styria.

1480 Ivan III liberates Moscow from Mongol rule and declares himself first Czar of Russia.

1488 South German cities, knights and princes establish the Swabian League, to preserve peace.

1499 Swiss independence is recognized at the Peace of Basle.

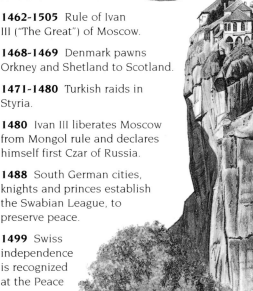

Africa and the Middle East

1445 Portuguese reach the mouth of the River Congo.

1451-1481 Reign of Ottoman Turkish Sultan Mehmet II, known as "the Conqueror".

Mehmet II

1461 The Portuguese reach Sierra Leone, West Africa.

1463-1479 Ottoman Turks are at war with Venice.

1464-1492 Reign of Sunni Ali, ruler of Songhai in West Africa, who conquers Timbuktu and expands his empire at the expense of Mali.

The trading city of Timbuktu

1471 Portuguese conquer Tangier.

1482 Portuguese establish a fort at El Mina on the Gold Coast (Ghana).

1487 Portuguese navigator, Bartholomeu Diaz, rounds the Cape of Good Hope, South Africa.

This map of 1489 shows Europeans had some knowledge of the West African coast.

1490 King Nzinga Nkuwu of the Kongo becomes a Christian.

1493 The Songhai empire reaches its peak.

Asia

1447 The empire of Tamerlane breaks up. Indian, Persian and Afghan provinces win independence.

1451-1489 Rule of Bahlol Lodi, the first Pathan king of Delhi.

1467-1477 First Onin War in Japan.

1469-1539 Life of Guru Nanak, who founds the Sikh religion.

Guru Nanak

1471 Vietnamese expand south.

1477-1568 Provincial wars in Japan (see page 80).

1494 Babar, a descendent of Genghis Khan and Tamerlane, becomes Prince of Ferghana, central Asia.

Babar, Prince of Ferghana

1497-1499 Vasco da Gama, a Portuguese navigator in search of trade, makes the first sea voyage by a European to India and back.

Da Gama's ship being attacked

Da Gama met with hostility on the East African coast, where trade was controlled by Arabs.

Jewels, spices and silk from the East

The Americas

1460 Mayapán is destroyed. The Mayan civilization comes to an end.

c.1470 Incas conquer the Chimu kingdom in Peru.

1471-1493 Reign of Emperor Topa Inca, who extends the empire south.

1493-1525 Reign of Huayna Capac, the greatest Inca conqueror. He founds a second capital at Quito.

1492-1493 Christopher Columbus reaches Bahamas and West Indies.

Portuguese influence

SOUTH AMERICA

Quito

Expansion of the Inca empire in Peru

Cuzco

Lake Titicaca

Spanish influence

Under Parachuti, to 1463

Parachuti and Topa Inca, to 1471

Topa Inca, to 1493

1494 Treaty of Tordesillas: Pope Alexander VI fixes a line (see map) to divide spheres of influence in the New World (America) between the Spanish and the Portuguese.

1497 John Cabot, an Italian explorer employed by Henry VII of England, reaches Newfoundland.

1498 Christopher Columbus reaches Trinidad and the coast of Venezuela.

1499-1502 Amerigo Vespucci, a Florentine navigator, explores the South American coast.

The Renaissance

Renaissance means "rebirth". It is the name given to the renewed interest in the art and learning of classical Greece and Rome, that stimulated the changes which mark the end of medieval and the beginning of modern times. A gradual process, it began in Italy, but eventually influenced all of Europe, reaching its height in the 15th and 16th centuries. Technical improvements, such as the invention of printing, helped the new ideas to spread.

Medieval illustration showing the Church at the top, ruling all other classes in society

HUMANISM

The Renaissance was not just a revival of the past; but a time of exploration and new ideas. But classical ideas provided an inspiration, particularly in the emphasis on what human beings could achieve for themselves. This new attitude became known as humanism. Learning was no longer solely in the hands of the Catholic Church. Many new schools and universities were set up, and scientific and medical experiments were carried out.

The artist Leonardo da Vinci dissected bodies to learn more about how they worked.

A soldier operated a gear mechanism which pulled back the arrow.

The arrow was released after pulling a lever.

The crossbow was set on wheels.

THE ARTS

Painters and sculptors tried to portray people, and landscapes, in a more natural, realistic style. To achieve this, they looked at classical statues and studied human anatomy. Artists also began to make use of perspective, to make paintings look less flat.

In addition to traditional religious themes, subjects now included contemporary and classical events, and portraits. Artists became more independent, and more famous, than medieval craftsman had been.

Primavera ("Spring") by Alessandro Botticelli

Renaissance architects, such as Alberti (**1404-1472**), Brunelleschi (**1377-1446**) and Palladio (**1508-1580**), used classical forms in their designs, including rounded arches, central domes and barrel vaults.

Many Renaissance rulers believed in the ideal of the "universal man", with wide-ranging talents. Lorenzo de Medici, ruler of Florence, was a soldier, politician, banker and poet. Men like this were the patrons of great artists, and lived in luxurious palaces designed by contemporary architects.

Reconstruction of a flying machine, based on designs in da Vinci's sketchbooks

Sketches by Leonardo showing various anatomical features

A reconstruction of a giant crossbow sketched in Leonardo da Vinci's notebook

System of cranks and pulleys

The wings were to be powered by the feet working a crank and pulley system, so they flapped up and down.

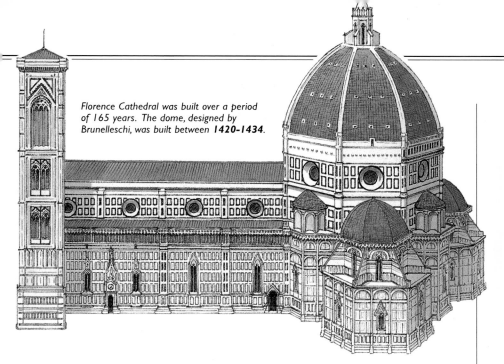

Florence Cathedral was built over a period of 165 years. The dome, designed by Brunelleschi, was built between 1420-1434.

FINANCE & DIPLOMACY

The capitalist skills that financed the Renaissance first developed in Italy, and the political links between the city-states formed the origins of diplomacy. The first banking system was introduced in the 13th century by the Lombards, a group of North Italian merchants. Over the next 200 years or so, the Italian cities won a reputation as the bankers of Europe.

Gold coins from Florence

RENAISSANCE ITALY

At the time of the Renaissance, Italy was divided into a number of city-states, nominally under the control of the Holy Roman Empire. In fact, the emperors never succeeded in imposing their authority over the Italian states. The popes, who ruled over part of Central Italy, contested their claim to political power.

In the first half of the 15th century, Italy was free from the threat of foreign invasion, and five powers emerged: Venice, Florence, Milan, Naples and the Papal States.

ITALIAN RENAISSANCE PEOPLE

Boccaccio, Giovanni (**1313-1375**), poet and writer of the *Decameron*, a collection of short stories.

Botticelli, Alessandro (**1444-1510**), Florentine painter, noted for his graceful linework.

Brunelleschi, Filippo (**1377-1446**), Florentine architect, whose work includes the dome of Florence Cathedral.

Dante Alighieri (**1265-1321**), poet and writer, famous for *La Divina Commedia* (the Divine Comedy).

Cellini, Benvenuto (**1500-1571**), Florentine sculptor, goldsmith and writer of a famous autobiography.

Donatello (**c.1386-1466**), Florentine sculptor.

Giotto di Bondone (**c.1266-1337**), Florentine painter, who was the first to break with the Byzantine style and develop a more naturalistic style.

Leonardo da Vinci (**1452-1519**), painter, inventor, musician, architect and sculptor.

Machiavelli, Niccolò (**1469-1527**), Florentine politician and philosopher, author of *The Prince*.

Masaccio (Tomasso Guidi) (**1401-1428**), Florentine painter, the first to use perspective in painting.

Michelangelo Buonarroti (**1475-1564**), Florentine painter, sculptor. and architect, one of the greatest Renaissance artists. Painter of the Sistine Chapel, in Rome.

Palladio, Andrea (**1508-1580**), Italian architect who revived and developed classical architecture.

Petrarch (Francesco Petrarca) (**1304-1374**), Italian poet.

Raphael (Raffaello Sanzi) (**1483-1520**), painter and architect, one of the greatest artists of the High (or Late) Renaissance.

Each wing would have been 11m (36ft) long by 3.2m (10.5ft) wide.

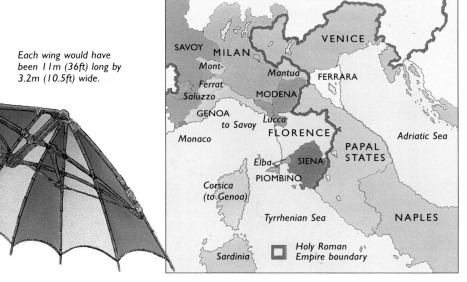

SAVOY
MILAN
Mont-Ferrat
Saluzzo
Mantua
VENICE
FERRARA
MODENA
GENOA
to Savoy
Lucca
Monaco
FLORENCE
Elba
SIENA
PIOMBINO
Corsica
(to Genoa)
PAPAL
STATES
Adriatic Sea

Tyrrhenian Sea
NAPLES

Sardinia
◻ Holy Roman Empire boundary

Beechwood struts

Map of Renaissance Italy

Southern and Western Europe

1501 Louis XII of France conquers Naples, Italy.

1509-1547 Reign of Henry VIII.

1510 Holy League formed to drive France from Italy.

Catherine of Aragon	*Anne Boleyn*	*Jane Seymour*

Henry VIII of England and his six wives

1512 The French invade Milan, but are defeated and expelled from Italy.

1512 Ferdinand II of Castile annexes Navarre.

Anne of Cleves	*Catherine Howard*	*Catherine Parr*

1513 Battle of Flodden between England and Scotland. James IV of Scotland is killed.

1513 Niccolò Machiavelli (**1469-1527**), a Florentine statesman, writes *The Prince*, advocating ruthlessness and cunning in order to achieve political success.

1515-1547 Reign of François I of France.

The Château of Chambord, built by François I of France

1515 François I of France defeats the Swiss at the Battle of Marignano and conquers Milan, Italy.

1516 Charles Hapsburg becomes Charles I of Spain.

1516 Coffee is first imported into Europe.

Coffee beans **1520** The Field of the Cloth of Gold: peace talks between Henry VIII and François I.

1520 Europe first imports chocolate.

1521 Silk manufacture begins in France.

1521-1544 Four wars between Charles V and the French in Italy.

Northern and Eastern Europe

1513 Scandinavia: the Union of Kalmar ends.

1516 The Netherlands comes under the control of Spain, with the accession of Charles I.

1517 Martin Luther, a monk and professor of theology, nails his 95 theses (complaints) to a church door in Wittenburg, Germany (see page 84).

Martin Luther

1519 Ulrich Zwingli begins preaching church reform in Zurich, Switzerland.

1519 Charles I, King of Spain, is elected Holy Roman Emperor, Charles V (see page 76).

1521 The Diet of Worms: Luther is called to account for himself and is condemned as a heretic.

1521 Charles V gives the Austrian Hapsburg lands to his brother, Ferdinand.

1521 Belgrade, Serbia, falls to the Ottoman Turks.

1522-1523 The imperial knights rebel against their overlord, the Archbishop of Trier, in protest against their declining economic and social position.

1523 Reformation begins in Switzerland with the writings of Ulrich Zwingli, a priest at Zurich Cathedral.

1523 Sweden gains independence from Denmark. Vasa dynasty begins with the reign of Gustav I (**1523-1560**).

1523 Imperial knights are defeated by an alliance of princes at Landstuhl.

1524-25 Peasants rise up against their landlords in South and Central Germany.

A mercenary soldier, known as a landsknecht, employed by the Emperor

The cathedral at Worms, South Germany, where the 1521 Diet was held

Africa and the Middle East

1500 Mohammed Turre (**1494-1528**) of Songhai expands his territory in West Africa.

1502 Safavid dynasty is established in Persia (now Iran) by Ismail I.

1504 Nubians destroy the Christian kingdom of Meroë (now Sudan).

1504-1546 Reign of the Christian king, Afonso of the Kongo.

1505 Songhai people invade Mali.

1505-1507 Portuguese establish forts on the East African coast.

1508 Portuguese set up a factory in Mozambique.

1509 Spain takes Oran, North Africa.

1513 Portuguese establish posts at Sena and Tete on the Zambezi River.

1514 Turks fight the Persians.

1516-1518 Selim conquers North Iraq, Syria and Palestine.

1517 Turks conquer Egypt.

1518 First full cargo of slaves sails from Guinea to the New World.

1520-1566 Reign of Suleiman the Magnificent: the great age of the Ottoman Turks.

1521-1522 Turks take Cyrenaica, Belgrade and Rhodes.

Suleiman the Magnificent riding into battle

Asia

c.1500 Guru Nanak (**1469-1539**) founds the Sikh religion in the Punjab, a region of Pakistan and India.

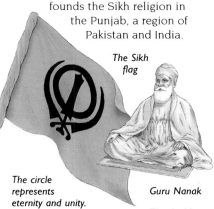

The Sikh flag

The circle represents eternity and unity.

Guru Nanak

The double-edged sword stands for the power of truth.

The crossed daggers remind Sikhs to be prepared to defend their faith.

1504 Babar becomes Master of Kabul, Afghanistan.

1510 Portuguese annex Goa, on the west coast of India.

1511 Portuguese take Malacca, Malaya.

1514 Portuguese reach China. By **1516**, they are trading from Canton.

A Chinese ship known as a junk

1519-1522 The first circumnavigation of the World is led by Ferdinand Magellan, a Portuguese navigator, sponsored by Charles V of Spain. He was heading for the Molucca islands in the East Indies, which were rich in spices, by sailing west around the tip of South America.

1521 Magellan reaches the Molucca islands, but is killed in the Philippines.

1523 European traders are expelled from Chinese ports.

The Americas

1500 Aztec empire reaches its greatest extent under Ahuizotl.

1501 Anglo-Portuguese expedition to Newfoundland.

1504 Amerigo Vespucci, a Florentine navigator, publishes an account of his voyages to South America. The new discoveries are known as the New World.

c.1507 The New World becomes known as America.

1510 The first African slaves are brought to America.

1513 Ponce de León, a Spanish explorer, discovers Florida.

1513 Nuñez de Balboa, a Spanish explorer, crosses the Isthmus of Panama and discovers the Pacific Ocean.

Leatherback turtle, frigate bird and octopus found in the Pacific Ocean

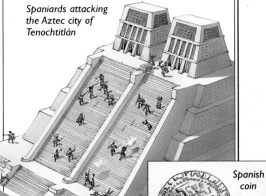

1519-1521 Hernando Cortés, a Spanish explorer, conquers Mexico: the end of the Aztec empire.

1520 Ferdinand Magellan, a Portuguese navigator, finds the Magellan Straits.

1521-1549 Spaniards colonize Venezuela.

Spaniards attacking the Aztec city of Tenochtitlán

Spanish coin

Aztec god Quetzalcoatl

The Age of Discovery

In the 15th and 16th centuries, European seafarers began to explore the world. Until then, Europeans had had only a vague knowledge of other continents. The areas they knew were limited to the north and west coasts of Africa and the overland routes to the East.

Sailors navigated by the Sun and stars using equipment such as this astrolabe.

In the early 15th century, Prince Henry of Portugal (**1394-1460**) set up a school of navigation and encouraged Portuguese sailors to search for a sea route to India.

Christopher Columbus and his ship, the Santa Maria

Their plan was to gain direct access to the valuable spice trade of the East Indies. In **1488**, Bartholomeu Diaz reached the Cape of Good Hope, the tip of South Africa. In **1497**, Vasco da Gama sailed into the Indian Ocean, arriving in India in **1498**.

In **1492**, Christopher Columbus, a Genoese navigator employed by Spain, tried sailing west instead. By doing so, he accidentally discovered the Bahamas and the West Indies. Further expeditions succeeded in reaching the South American mainland. The new territories were known as the New World, though at first people believed they had reached Asia, not realizing that a new continent had been discovered.

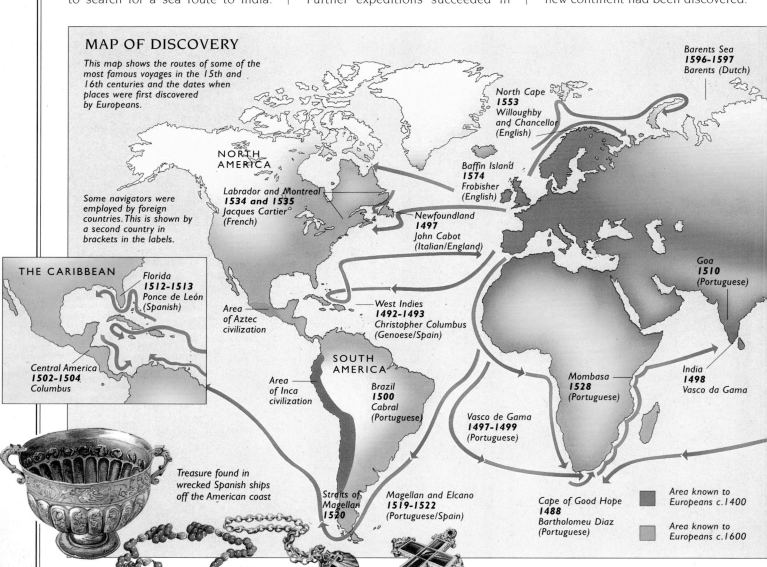

MAP OF DISCOVERY

This map shows the routes of some of the most famous voyages in the 15th and 16th centuries and the dates when places were first discovered by Europeans.

Some navigators were employed by foreign countries. This is shown by a second country in brackets in the labels.

Barents Sea
1596-1597
Barents (Dutch)

North Cape
1553
Willoughby and Chancellor (English)

Baffin Island
1574
Frobisher (English)

NORTH AMERICA

Labrador and Montreal
1534 and 1535
Jacques Cartier (French)

Newfoundland
1497
John Cabot (Italian/England)

Goa
1510
(Portuguese)

THE CARIBBEAN

Florida
1512-1513
Ponce de León (Spanish)

Area of Aztec civilization

West Indies
1492-1493
Christopher Columbus (Genoese/Spain)

Central America
1502-1504
Columbus

SOUTH AMERICA

Area of Inca civilization

Brazil
1500
Cabral (Portuguese)

Mombasa
1528
(Portuguese)

India
1498
Vasco da Gama

Vasco de Gama
1497-1499
(Portuguese)

Treasure found in wrecked Spanish ships off the American coast

Straits of Magellan
1520

Magellan and Elcano
1519-1522
(Portuguese/Spain)

Cape of Good Hope
1488
Bartholomeu Diaz (Portuguese)

Area known to Europeans c.1400

Area known to Europeans c.1600

THE CONQUEST OF MEXICO AND PERU

By the Treaty of Tordesillas of **1494**, Portugal and Spain agreed to divide up the New World between them. The French and English did not accept this, and adventurers, such as John Hawkins and Francis Drake, attacked Spanish shipping in the Caribbean. Others, such as John Davis and Henry Hudson, looked for an alternative route East by sailing northwest. Although they failed to find a northwest passage, this led to the discovery of North America.

Aztec warrior

The early explorers of the New World returned to Europe with legends of the great wealth to be found. Spanish fortune-hunters, known as *conquistadores*, followed in search of land and gold. Cortés, who conquered Peru between **1519** and **1521**, and Pizarro, who conquered Mexico between **1532** and **1534**, were the most famous. They came up against two great warrior civilizations - the Aztecs of Mexico and the Incas of Peru.

Hernando Cortés

The Incas and Aztecs had large, well-organized empires, with beautiful cities, strict laws and complex religious beliefs. The Aztecs had their own writing and number system, and built huge pyramid-shaped temples to their gods. The Incas were skilled metalworkers and potters, and built excellent roads. But the Spaniards had the advantage of horses and cannons, and soon destroyed these native civilizations.

Silver was found in Peru (**1545**) and in Mexico (**1548**) and shipped back to Europe, boosting Spanish wealth and prestige. The native Americans were forced to work in the mines, but they were physically unsuited to the work and many died, often from European diseases.

This is an Aztec carving showing stars and planets.

China
1514
(Portuguese)

The Philippines
1521
*Magellan and Elcano
(Portuguese/Spain)*

Guanacos (shown here) and llamas are found in Peru. The Incas bred them for wool.

The Incas terraced steep mountainsides, where crops such as corn, potatoes, squash, peppers and tomatoes were grown.

Southern and Western Europe

1525 Battle of Pavia: Spain defeats France and Francis I is taken prisoner.

1525 England and France make peace with Charles V.

1527 The troops of Charles V sack Rome and capture Pope Clement VII.

1527-1530 The Medici family is expelled from Florence.

Silver coin showing Emperor Charles V

1529 Peace of Cambrai: the French renounce their claim to Italy and Charles V renounces his claim to the lost Burgundian lands.

1530 The Knights Hospitallers establish a base in Malta.

1531 The Inquisition is established in Portugal.

1532 John Calvin begins work in Paris (see page 84).

1534 Ignatius Loyola founds the Jesuits.

1536 The English and Welsh governments are unified.

1541 John Knox starts the Reformation in Scotland.

1542 Mary Stuart (**1542-1587**) becomes Queen of Scotland, aged one week.

1543 Andreas Vesalius, a pharmacist from Brussels, is the first scholar to make a detailed study of the human body.

An illustration from Andreas Vesalius's study of the human body showing details of muscles

1543 Alliance of Henry VIII of England and Charles V of Spain against France and Scotland.

1544 Peace of Crespi ends wars between France and Charles V in Italy.

1545 Council of Trent: the Counter-Reformation begins.

Mary, Queen of Scots

1547 England invades Scotland and defeats the Scots at the Battle of Pinkie. Mary, Queen of Scots, is sent to France to marry the Dauphin (the heir to the throne).

1547-1559 Reign of Henri II of France.

1547-1553 Reign of Edward VI of England.

Diane de Poitiers, the mistress of Henri II of France

Northern and Eastern Europe

1525 Albert of Hohenzollern, ruler of Prussia, becomes a Lutheran and secularizes the state.

1526 Battle of Mohacs: Louis II of Hungary is defeated and killed by the Turks. Charles V's brother, Ferdinand, and John Zapolya are both elected kings of Hungary.

1529 The Turks besiege Vienna, Austria.

1529 Second Diet of Speyer, Gemany.

1529 War between Swiss Catholics and Protestants.

1530 Charles V is crowned Holy Roman Emperor by the Pope: the last imperial coronation by a pope.

1531 Protestant League of Schmalkalden is formed.

1531 Copernicus (**1473-1543**), a Polish astronomer, circulates his revolutionary theory, demonstrating that the planets move around the Sun, not around the Earth as the Church had taught.

An engraving showing the Copernican view of the Universe with the planets orbiting the Sun

1532 Peace of Nuremburg: Protestants in the Holy Roman Empire are allowed to follow their religion.

1532-1533 War between Turkey and Austria over Hungary.

1533-1584 Reign of Ivan IV ("the Terrible") in Russia.

1534-1535 Münster in northern Germany is taken over by Anabaptists, who deny the need for any government.

1536 John Calvin, the founder of Calvinism, goes to Geneva and publishes *Institutes*, containing his ideas for reform.

1541 Calvin starts organizing the Church in Geneva.

1541-1688 Hungary becomes a Turkish province.

1547 Charles V defeats League of Schmalkalden at Muhlberg.

1547 Ivan IV takes the title "Czar of all the Russias".

An engraving of Ivan the Terrible

Africa and the Middle East

1535 Charles V takes Tunis, North Africa.

1538 Ottoman Turks capture Aden.

1543 Ethiopian Christians, helped by Portugal, repel the Muslim advance into Ethiopia.

Ethiopian crosses

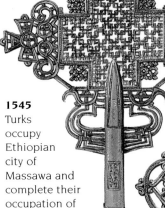

1545 Turks occupy Ethiopian city of Massawa and complete their occupation of Ethiopia.

1546 The destruction of the Mali empire by the Songhai.

1549-1582 Reign of Askia David, King of Songhai.

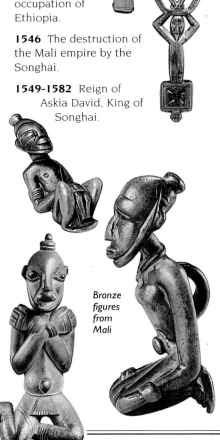

Bronze figures from Mali

Asia

1525 Babar, a descendent of the Mongol Tamerlane, enters India from Afghanistan and conquers the Punjab.

Babar, the first Mogul emperor

1526 Babar wins a victory over the Sultan of Delhi at Panipat. The Moguls are established in India.

1527 Babar defeats Hindus at Kanwaha..

1529 Babar wins a victory at Gogra.

1533 North Vietnam splits into Tongking and Annam.

1539 Burmese kingdom of Toungoo conquers Mons kingdom of Pegu.

1540 Babar's son, Humayun, is driven out of India by the Afghan, Sher Shah.

1542 Francis Xavier, a Portuguese Jesuit missionary, arrives in Goa, on the west coast of India.

Kabul •   Lahore •   TIBET
PERSIA   Delhi •   • Panipat
  Bengal
INDIA   Bay of Bengal
Mogul empire 1526   Goa •

Map showing the early Mogul empire

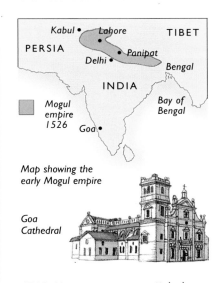

Goa Cathedral

1545 Humayun captures Kabul.

1549-1551 Francis Xavier and his missionaries spread Christianity in Japan and participate in trade.

The Americas

1526 John Cabot sails to the River Plate, Argentina.

1528 Germans attempt to colonize Venezuela.

1530 Portuguese begin to colonize Brazil.

1531 Rio de Janeiro is founded.

1532-1534 Francisco Pizarro conquers Peru: the collapse of the Inca empire.

1534 A French expedition, led by Jacques Cartier, reaches Labrador, Canada.

1535 Buenos Aires and Lima are founded.

1535 Jacques Cartier discovers the St. Lawrence River, and sails to the site of Montreal.

Jacques Cartier (above) and North American moose

1535-1538 Gonzalo Jiminez de Quesada, a Spanish *conquistador*, conquers Columbia.

1536 Jesuits found Asunción, Paraguay.

1536 Inca rebellion in Peru, led by Manco Inca. He rules from Villcabamba until **1545**.

1540-1544 Pedro de Valdivia, a Spanish *conquistador*, explores Chile.

1541 Indian revolt in Mexico.

1542 Charles V's New Laws abolish native slavery in Spanish colonies and limit the colonists' control.

1545 Silver mines are discovered in Peru and Mexico (**1548**).

Llamas made of Peruvian silver

The empire of Charles V

In the first half of the 16th century, Europe was dominated by the vast empire of Charles V (**1500-1558**), the heir of the Austrian Hapsburg family. He became King of Spain in **1516** and Holy Roman Emperor in **1519**, making him the most powerful monarch in Europe. He defeated his great rival,

Charles V on a horse and shown on a silver coin called a thaler

Francis I of France, after five wars with the French in Italy, and stopped the advance of the Ottoman Turks. Under him, Spain acquired wealth and prestige, as a result of the discovery of the New World (see pages 72-73).

However, there were constant problems in Germany, both social and economic (such as uprisings by imperial knights in **1522-1523** and peasants in **1525**), in addition to the religious turmoil caused by the Reformation (see page 84). Peace finally came at the Peace of Augsburg in **1555**.

In **1521**, Charles handed over government of Hapsburg lands in Austria to his brother, Ferdinand. In **1526**, Ferdinand also claimed Hungary and Bohemia, through his

Flag of Charles V

wife Anne on the death of her brother, King Lewis of Hungary. Charles abdicated in **1556**, leaving the imperial title to Ferdinand and the Spanish possessions to his son, Philip II.

The Escorial Palace, outside Madrid, built by Philip II

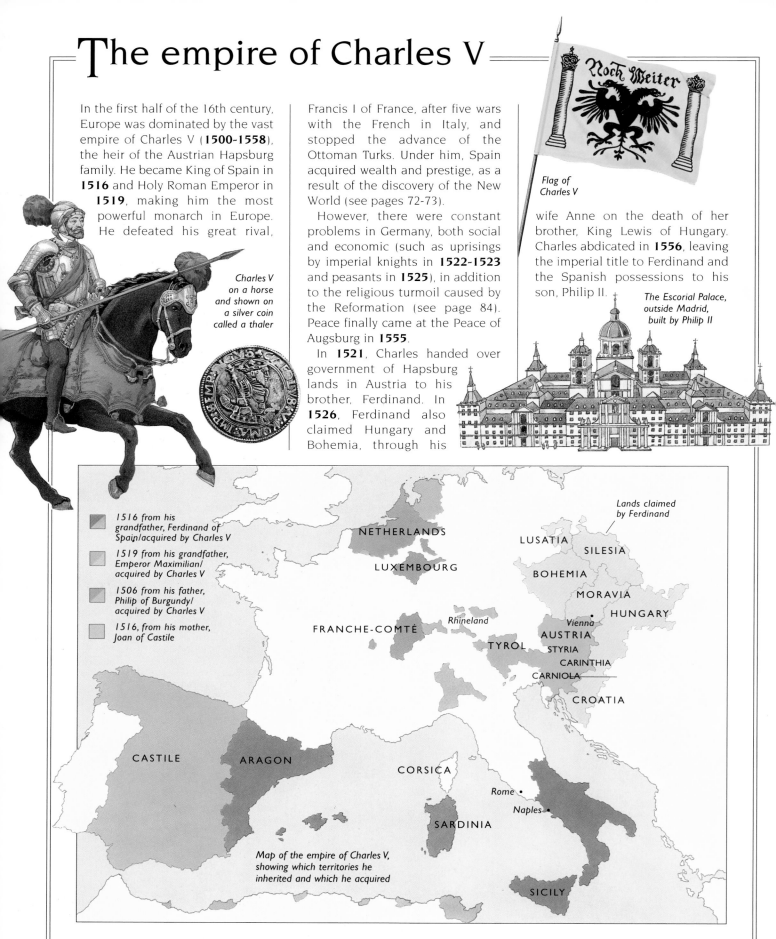

1516 from his grandfather, Ferdinand of Spain/acquired by Charles V

1519 from his grandfather, Emperor Maximilian/acquired by Charles V

1506 from his father, Philip of Burgundy/acquired by Charles V

1516, from his mother, Joan of Castile

Lands claimed by Ferdinand

NETHERLANDS

LUXEMBOURG

LUSATIA

SILESIA

BOHEMIA

MORAVIA

HUNGARY

FRANCHE-COMTÉ

Rhineland

Vienna

AUSTRIA

TYROL

STYRIA

CARINTHIA

CARNIOLA

CROATIA

CASTILE

ARAGON

CORSICA

Rome

Naples

SARDINIA

SICILY

Map of the empire of Charles V, showing which territories he inherited and which he acquired

The Dutch Revolt

In the early 16th century, Calvinism made many converts in the Netherlands. In **1555**, the territory was inherited by Philip II of Spain, an unpopular foreigner who ruled through a series of governors. Philip tried to impose Catholicism, but many people opposed it, including Counts Egmont and Hoorn, and William, Prince of Orange (**1533-1584**).

In **1566**, Calvinists began to worship openly and there were attacks on Catholic churches. The the Spanish governor, the Duke of Alva, introduced widespread persecution and in **1568** had Hoorn and Egmont executed.

Dutch soldier

Many of the rebels, described as Sea Beggars, escaped to sea and attacked Spanish ships. This began a long struggle for independence, known as the Dutch Revolt (**1568-1648**). The Dutch were supported by the English and French, who sent help in **1585**.

Confrontation between Dutch rebels and Spanish troops at the port of Briel

IMPORTANT DATES

1572 Sea Beggars capture Briel (Brill) and Vlissingen (Flushing).

1576 Spanish soldiers sack Antwerp. This leads to the Pacification of Ghent: all 17 provinces unite against Spain.

1578 Peace of Arras: the ten southern (Catholic) provinces unite with Spain.

1579 Union of Utrecht: the seven northern (Calvinist) provinces unite against Spain.

William of Orange

1581 Northern provinces claim independence as the United Provinces. William of Orange is elected hereditary stadtholder (governor).

1584 William of Orange is assassinated. He is succeeded by Maurice of Nassau (until **1625**).

1648 Peace of the Hague: Spain recognizes the United Provinces.

Southern and Western Europe

1552-1556 War between Henri II of France and Charles V of Spain.

Nicotiana alata, the tobacco plant

1553 Tobacco is first introduced into Europe (from America to Spain).

1553-1558 Reign of Mary I of England, who marries Philip II of Spain. England returns to Catholicism and 300 Protestants are burned.

1555 Emperor Charles V abdicates. His son becomes Philip II of Spain, and inherits Hapsburg land in Italy, the Netherlands and America.

Mary I

1558 England loses Calais to France.

1558-1603 Reign of Elizabeth I of England. She reinstates the Anglican Church.

1559 Mary, Queen of Scots, is widowed and returns to Scotland from France.

1559 Jean Nicot first imports tobacco into France from America. The word nicotine is named after him.

1559 Treaty of Cateau-Cambresis makes peace between France and Spain.

1560-1574 Reign of Charles IX of France.

1562 Start of the French Wars of Religion (see page 87).

1563 English Poor Law: Justices of the Peace are entitled to raise a poor rate to look after the poor in each parish.

1564-1616 Life of William Shakespeare, English playwright and poet.

1567-1625 Reign of James VI of Scotland.

1572 St. Bartholomew's Day Massacre: 20,000 Huguenots (French Protestants) are murdered by troops acting on behalf of the regent, Queen Catherine de Medici.

The Globe Theatre, London, where Shakespeare's plays were performed.

The building had no roof. If it rained, plays were called off. Here the walls have been cut away to show wealthy guests and musicians sitting in wooden galleries.

Northern and Eastern Europe

1553-1555 Richard Chancellor, an English navigator, goes on expeditions to Russia.

1555 Peace of Augsburg: Emperor Charles V allows the Protestant princes freedom of worship.

1555 The English Muscovy Company is given a charter to explore and trade with Russia.

Muscovy Company coat of arms

1556 Ferdinand, the brother of Charles V, becomes Holy Roman Emperor.

1557-1582 Russia, Poland, Sweden and Denmark fight over territories in the Baltic.

1563-1570 War between Sweden and Denmark, which ends with the Peace of Stettin. Livonia is partitioned between Poland and Denmark.

1564-1576 Reign of Maximilian II, Holy Roman Emperor.

1566 Rebellions in the Netherlands against Spanish rule.

1571 Battle of Lepanto (off the west coast of Greece). Turks are defeated by Spanish and Venetians. The end of Turkish sea power in Europe.

Turkish ships

Spanish and Venetian ships

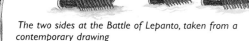

The two sides at the Battle of Lepanto, taken from a contemporary drawing

1571 Tartars from the Crimea destroy Moscow.

1572 Poland introduces a system of electing kings.

1572 The beginning of the Dutch Revolt (see page 77).

1573 Henri of Valois (later Henri III of France) becomes first elected King of Poland.

Africa and the Middle East

c.1550s England starts trading with West Africa.

1551 Turks take Tripoli. War between Turkey and Hungary.

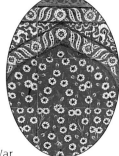

Ceramic tiles from the Blue Mosque, Istanbul, Turkey, built by Suleiman the Magnificent

1554-1555 War between the Turks and the Persian Safavids.

1562 England joins the slave trade, shipping slaves from West Africa to the Caribbean. John Hawkins, a navigator, allies with two kings in Sierra Leone and attacks local tribes, taking captives as slaves.

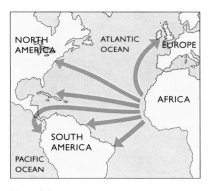

Map of slave routes

1566 The Ottoman empire is now at its greatest extent (see page 45).

1566-1574 Reign of Sultan Selim II of Turkey.

1573 Don John of Austria captures Tunis and Turkey goes to war with Austria.

1574 -1595 Reign of Sultan Murad III of Turkey.

1574 Portuguese colonize Angola.

1574-1575 The Ottoman Turks retake Tunis from Spain and conquer the rest of Tunisia.

Asia

1550 The Mongol leader, Altan-Khan, invades northern China. Japanese pirates raid China.

1555 Humayun regains his Indian empire from Sher Shah.

1555 The King of Toungoo captures the northern Burmese kingdom of Ava. This results in a unified Burmese state, which grows at the expense of the Thai kingdom.

1556-1605 Reign of Akbar the Great, greatest of the Mogul rulers. A new phase of conquest begins.

Akbar (on the second elephant) pursuing his enemies

1556 Astrakhan annexed by Russia.

1557 Portuguese establish a settlement at Macao. Trade with China is restricted to Macao.

1560 Oda Nobunaga becomes leading *daimyo* (landowner) in Japan.

1564 Spaniards occupy the Philippines and build Manila.

1565 Akbar extends the Mogul empire to the Deccan.

1567 Oda Nobunaga becomes *shogun* (military dictator) of Japan.

1570 Nagasaki, Japan, is opened to foreign traders. Traders come via Macao, China bringing silk.

1573-1577 Akbar conquers Gujerat and Bengal and unifies northern India.

The Americas

1554 The founding of São Paulo in Brazil.

SOUTH AMERICA

São Paulo •

Golden conure (left) and macaws from the Amazon rainforest in Brazil

c.1560 Silver from Mexico and Peru is established as chief export from Americas to Spain.

Gold and silver from South America were made into ingots in Mexico. These ones were salvaged from a shipwreck.

1560 Titi Cusi Inca rules at Villcabamba, Peru.

1562-1565 French colony in Florida is destroyed by the Spaniards.

1562 John Hawkins makes his first slave trade voyage to Hispaniola (Haiti). Second and third voyages follow: **1564-1565** and **1567-1568**.

1572 Francis Drake, an English navigator, attacks Spanish American ports.

1572 Topa Amaru, the last Inca ruler, is captured and executed.

Inca priest

Cacao pod, used by Incas for food and medicine

Inca farmers grew crops on terraces dug into the mountainside.

China - the Ming and Ch'ing dynasties

The Ming dynasty was established in **1368** by a Buddhist monk named Chu Yuan-chang, also known as Hung Wu. He drove out the Mongols and set up a capital at Nanking.

The Ming ruled China until **1644**: it was a period of prosperity, peace and stability. Farming improved and the population began to grow. Industry, trade and the arts developed, with the making of fine crafts in porcelain, jade, silk and lacquer.

THE FORBIDDEN CITY

The early rulers strengthened their army and extended the Great Wall of China, to defend themselves against outside attacks. They invaded Mongolia and Vietnam, and sent diplomatic missions across the world. One of the greatest of the Ming emperors was Yung-Lo, who ruled from **1403-1424**. He built up the empire and personally led five

Ming porcelain and a lacquered wood food box

Emperor Yung-Lo

military campaigns against the Mongols.

Yung-Lo moved the Ming capital from Nanking to Beijing, and was active in promoting the arts, including literature, sculpture and painting .on bamboo. He built a magnificent walled palace in Beijing, surrounded by a moat. The palace was called "the Forbidden City".

One of the bronze lions, which guard the Forbidden City

GREAT EXPLORATION

The Ming were also great explorers. Admiral Cheng Ho was put in charge of a major project of exploration, involving a fleet of 317 ships.

Woodcut of flat-bottomed boat called a junk

Between **1405** and **1433**, he made seven long sea voyages, visiting Indochina, Arabia and East Africa. Soon, however, the Chinese decided to stop all contacts abroad. They were self-sufficient and regarded foreigners as uncivilized barbarians.

THE DYNASTY DECLINES

By the 16th century, the Ming were under attack from Mongols and Japanese pirates, and had to install huge armies along the Great Wall. A period of weak, corrupt government provoked a series of rebellions. In **1644**, bandits occupied Beijing and the dynasty was overthrown.

The Forbiddden City during the Ming period

THE RISE OF THE CH'ING DYNASTY

Between **1600** and **1615**, a Manchu nation emerged in Manchuria, northern China. In **1627**, the Manchus expanded into other parts of China, and Korea, and Inner Mongolia from **1629** to **1635**.

When the Ming dynasty was overthrown in **1644**, the Chinese people invited the Manchus in to help them deal with the bandits. As a result, the Manchus set up a new dynasty, called the Ch'ing, which ruled from their capital at Beijing until **1911**.

Despite Ming resistance in the south, by **1652** most of the country was under Ch'ing control. From **1674** to **1681**, there were unsuccessful rebellions, known as the Rebellion of the Three Feudatories, by the governors of the southern and western provinces. But this was followed by a long period of peace.

The population grew from about 100 million in **1680** to about 176 million a century later.

Under Emperor K'ang Hsi (**1662-1722**), the Ch'ing built up a great empire, which included Tibet and Eastern Turkestan. It was at its largest in the late 18th century, after wars with Burma (**1767-1769**) and Tibet (**1791-1792**).

Manchu armies on the attack

FOREIGN TRADE

In the 17th and 18th centuries, China had a flourishing export trade through the port of Canton, exporting porcelain, tea, silk and crafts to Europe.

Silk, jade, tea and porcelain were all exported.

Chinese style became increasingly fashionable in Europe, although the Chinese maintained their lack of interest in western goods, and asked to be paid only in silver.

Under the Ch'ing Emperor Ch'ien Lung (**1736-1796**), there was growing hostility to missionaries from Europe, and to the imports of opium from India which began in the late 18th century. This provoked tensions and led to the outbreak of the Opium Wars (see page 134).

A 17th century model used to teach acupuncture. Chinese culture remained independent of Western influences.

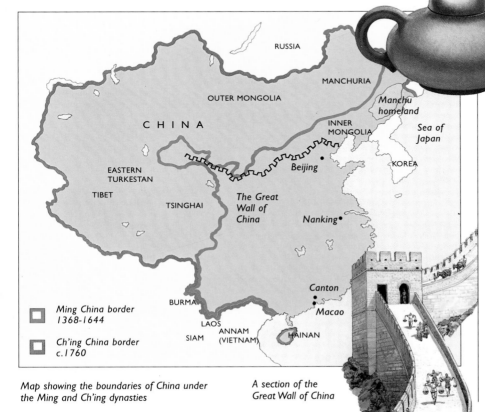

RUSSIA

MANCHURIA

OUTER MONGOLIA

Manchu homeland

CHINA

INNER MONGOLIA

Sea of Japan

EASTERN TURKESTAN

KOREA

TIBET

Beijing

TSINGHAI

The Great Wall of China

Nanking

BURMA

Canton

LAOS

Macao

SIAM

ANNAM (VIETNAM)

HAINAN

☐ Ming China border 1368-1644

☐ Ch'ing China border c.1760

Map showing the boundaries of China under the Ming and Ch'ing dynasties

A section of the Great Wall of China

Southern and Western Europe

1580-1640 Union of Spain and Portugal.

1581 First known ballet, *Le Ballet Comique de la Reine*, is performed at the marriage of the Queen of France's sister.

Music for early ballet was played on a viol (shown here). Dancing shoes were worn, as there were no special ballet shoes.

1582 The Gregorian Calendar, devised by Pope Gregory XIII, is introduced in Catholic countries only.

1587 Mary, Queen of Scots, is executed by Elizabeth I for plotting against her. Elizabeth accepts Mary's son, the Protestant James VI of Scotland, as her heir.

1588 The Spanish Armada, a fleet of ships sent by Philip II to conquer England, is defeated.

Gold coins and chain found in the wreckage of the Spanish ship Girona, sunk off the Irish coast

1589 Henri of Navarre becomes Henri IV of France. The start of the Bourbon dynasty.

Spanish galleons were huge, cumbersome and slow, more suited to defending than attacking.

1592 Presbyterianism (a form of Calvinism) is adopted in Scotland, influenced by the teachings of John Knox.

1596 Galileo Galilei (**1564-1642**), an Italian astronomer, mathematician and physicist, invents the thermometer.

1596 The English attack Cadiz, on the southwest coast of Spain, and hinder the preparation of a second Armada.

1597 Irish rebellion against the English, led by Hugh O'Neill, Earl of Tyrone.

1598 Henri IV of France issues the Edict of Nantes, allowing religious toleration to Huguenots (French Protestants). This ends the French Wars of Religion.

Northern and Eastern Europe

1576 Pacification of Ghent: the 17 provinces of the Netherlands unite to drive out the Spaniards.

1576 Russia begins expanding across the Ural mountains.

1578 Peace of Arras: 10 southern provinces of the Netherlands unite with Spain.

1579 Union of Utrecht: the seven northern provinces of the Netherlands unite against Spain.

1581 Russians begin the conquest of Siberia.

Russian aristocrats, known as boyars

1581 The seven northern provinces of the Netherlands proclaim independence as the United Provinces and elect William of Orange as their ruler.

1582 Peace between Russia and Poland. Russia is cut off from the Baltic Sea.

1584 William of Orange, ruler of the United Provinces, is assassinated.

1585 Gerardus Mercator (**1512-1594**), a Flemish geographer and map-maker, introduces a more accurate way of drawing maps than had previously been used.

1587-1688 The Catholic Vasa dynasty rules Poland.

1596 France, England and the United Provinces unite against Spain.

1598 Death of Czar Theodor, last of the Rurik dynasty: the start of a period known as "the time of troubles" in Russia.

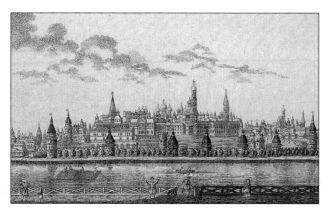

Early print of the city of Moscow

Africa and the Middle East

1578 King Sebastian of Portugal invades Morocco, but is defeated at the Battle of al-Ksar al-Kabir. Ahmed al Mansur of Fez establishes the Sharifian dynasty and Morocco expands in power.

1580-1617 Reign of Idris Alooma, greatest of the kings of the Kanem-Bornu.

1581 Moroccans begin penetrating the Sahara Desert.

Dromedary camel found in the Sahara

1581 Peace between Turkey and Spain.

1585 The Ottoman empire begins to decline.

1586-1622 Reign of Shah Abbas the Great in Persia.

1590 Moroccans reach the River Niger and take Timbuktu.

1590 Shah Abbas of Persia makes peace with Turkey.

Shah Abbas's helmet

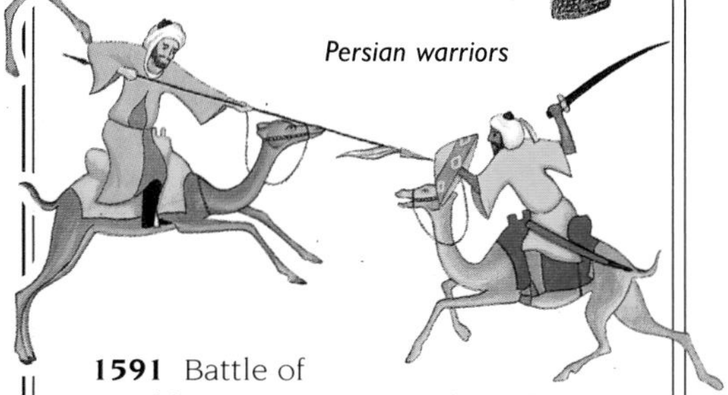

Persian warriors

1591 Battle of Tondibi: Moroccans invade and defeat Songhai and cause the collapse of the kingdom.

1592 The Portuguese take Mombasa, on the East African coast.

1598 The Dutch take Mauritius.

1598 Shah Abbas makes Isfahan the capital of Persia.

Asia

1579 A Portuguese trading station is established in Bengal, India.

1581 Akbar subdues Afghanistan, formally annexing it in **1585**.

1581 The Russians take Siberia.

1582-1598 Toyotomi Hideyoshi succeeds as leader in Japan.

1584 Phra Narai creates an independent kingdom of Siam.

1587 Akbar takes Kashmir, northern India.

1591 First English voyage to the East Indies.

Hindu statue from Java, Indonesia, East Indies

1592 Annamese take Hanoi and unite North Vietnam.

1592 Akbar conquers Sind, India.

1593 Japanese leave Korea under pressure from the Chinese.

1594 English begin trading in India.

1594 Akbar takes Kandahar.

1595 The Dutch start to establish colonies in the East Indies.

1597 Japanese invade Korea, but the Chinese help the Koreans to expel them.

1598 Death of Toyotomi Hideyoshi, ruler of Japan. He is succeeded by a child, and five regents compete for power.

A Japanese building called a pagoda

1599 Akbar begins to conquer the Deccan.

Pagodas are often built next to Buddhist temples.

The Americas

1576-1577 Martin Frobisher, an English navigator, explores North Atlantic and discovers Baffin Island.

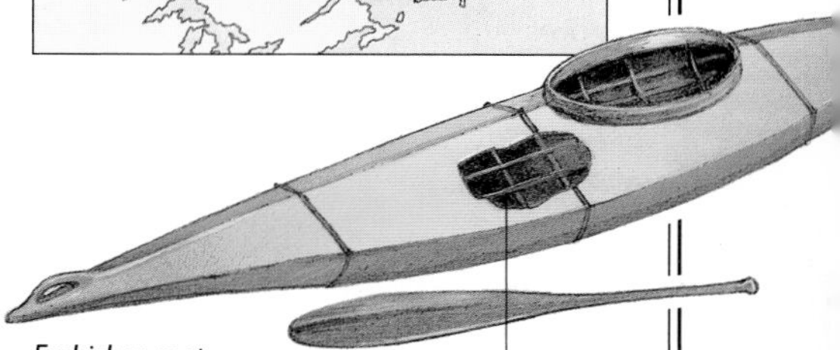

[Map showing GREENLAND, Baffin Island, Frobisher Bay, Hudson Bay, Labrador, CANADA, ATLANTIC OCEAN]

Frobisher met local people, the Inuits, paddling in one-manned canoes called kayaks.

Wooden frame with sealskin covering

1577 Humphrey Gilbert, an English navigator, is granted a patent to found colonies in North America.

1579 Francis Drake claims New Albion (California) during his voyage round the world (**1577-1580**).

Francis Drake

1583 Humphrey Gilbert establishes the first English colony in Newfoundland.

1584 Walter Raleigh, (English) discovers and annexes Virginia. He founds a colony in **1585**, but it is abandoned by settlers in **1586**. A second colony is set up in **1587-1591**.

1585-1587 John Davis (English) searches for a northwest passage to Asia and explores the Davis Strait.

The Reformation

The Reformation began as an attempt to reform the Catholic Church, but it provoked a religious upheaval that led to the creation of Protestant Churches and a split in Christian Europe. The Reformation also became associated with radical social and political protest and helped to inspire movements such as the Dutch Revolt (see page 77).

Martin Luther

It began with Martin Luther (**1483-1546**), a monk and professor at Wittenburg in Germany. In **1517**, he nailed 95 theses, or proposals for reform, to the door of the church. They were printed and attracted wide public interest.

The original doors of Wittenburg Church were damaged by fire and replaced by these ones on which the theses are inscribed.

For many years people had been criticizing the Church for a number of abuses. These included absenteeism (a priest's absence from his parish), nepotism (giving benefices, or church positions, to relations), and simony (selling things such as benefices, saints' relics and pardons for sins). Ordinary priests were criticized for their lack of education, and Church leaders for their wealth and involvement with politics.

In **1521**, Luther was called to account for himself at the Diet of Worms, a council held by the Holy Roman Emperor. There he stressed the need to base religious beliefs on the Bible, rather than the teachings of the Church.

For this, Luther was condemned as a heretic. He went into hiding in Wartburg Castle, where he began developing his ideas for the organization of a Lutheran Church.

In **1525**, Lutheranism became the official religion in Saxony. It quickly spread to other German states and provoked a number of quarrels and wars. At the Peace of Augsburg (**1555**), the Emperor gave each ruler within the Empire the right to choose his state's religion.

Metal letters were arranged into pages in a metal frame and covered in ink. Padded wooden hammers were used to make the letters level.

Paper was placed in this frame.

Gutenberg's printing press. The invention of printing c.1445 was very important in allowing the new ideas to spread.

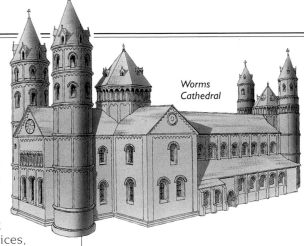

Worms Cathedral

ZWINGLI

In **1523**, Ulrich Zwingli (**1484-1531**), a priest at the cathedral in Zurich, inspired by Luther's teachings, wrote 67 theses providing for even greater changes in belief, services and church organization. They were accepted by the city council and his influence soon spread in South Germany as well as Switzerland.

A camp follower in the German religious wars

CALVIN

Another great leader of the Reformation was Jean Cauvin, known as John Calvin (**1509-1564**), a Frenchman based in Geneva. In **1536**, he published Institutes, containing his ideas for reform. Calvinism was a stricter religion than Lutheranism, but better organized, and it quickly made many converts.

In **1541**, Calvin began organizing the Genevan Church. The Church was to govern itself, electing pastors (to preach in church), doctors (to decide matters of faith, or doctrine), elders (to enforce discipline) and deacons (to care for the poor) - with a committee, called a synod, to arrange elections.

John Calvin (1509-1564)

THE REFORMATION IN ENGLAND & SCOTLAND

The Reformation in England was prompted by political rather than religious motives. Henry VIII (**1509-1547**) was desperate for a son to secure his dynasty, but all his children by his wife, Catherine of Aragon, had died, except a daughter, Mary. Henry wanted to divorce Catherine and marry Anne Boleyn. But the Pope, under the influence of Catherine's nephew, Charles V, was very unlikely to consent to a divorce. So Henry chose to break with the Catholic Church in Rome. However, although he refused to submit to the Pope's authority, he still did not accept Protestant doctrines.

Henry VIII's coat of arms

The Anglican (English Protestant) Church was established during the reign of Henry's young son, Edward VI (**1547-1553**). Changes were made by his regent, the Duke of Somerset, bringing the English Church closer to the ideas of other European Protestants.

Edward's sister, Mary (**1553-1558**), restored Catholicism as the state religion, but this was revoked by Elizabeth I (**1558-1603**), and the Anglican Church was reinstated.

In Scotland, many people, led by John Knox, were influenced by the ideas of Calvin. They became known as Presbyterians. Civil war broke out in **1559**. After the abdication of the Catholic Mary Stuart in **1567**, Presbyterianism emerged as the established religion in Scotland.

IMPORTANT DATES IN THE ENGLISH REFORMATION

1531 The English clergy recognizes Henry VIII as Supreme Head of the English Church.

1533 Henry's marriage is declared void. He marries Anne Boleyn and is excommunicated.

1534 Act of Supremacy is passed in Parliament, cutting off all ties with the Pope in Rome.

1534-1539 The Dissolution of the Monasteries: monasteries are closed and sold on the pretext of the discovery of fraud, immorality and other abuses.

1536-1537 Pilgrimage of Grace: a Catholic uprising against the Reformation in the north of England.

1539 Six Articles are issued, setting out points of Catholic doctrine still to be followed.

1547-1553 Reign of Edward VI.

1549 The Act of Uniformity and a new Prayer Book are issued to establish the new faith.

1552 A Second Act of Uniformity and Prayer Book bring the Anglican Church closer to Swiss Protestants.

1553-1558 Reign of Henry VIII's daughter, Mary Tudor. The Catholic Church is reinstated.

1558-1603 Reign of Henry VIII's daughter, Elizabeth I, who reinstates the Anglican Church.

1559 New Act of Supremacy and Prayer Book, closer to the moderate **1549** version. These are unacceptable to radical Protestants who want to move closer to Calvinism.

1563 39 Articles set out the beliefs of the Anglican Church.

1570 Elizabeth I is excommunicated by the Pope. Catholics are now under suspicion as possible traitors.

1593 Act against sectaries (members of Protestant sects who find the Anglican Church too moderate; also called non-conformists or Puritans).

Henry VIII, whose break with the Pope led to the formation of the Anglican Church

Elizabeth I, who established a Church that represented a compromise between Protestant and Catholic beliefs

The Counter-Reformation

The successes of the Reformation forced the Catholic Church to reform itself and counterattack. This movement is known as the Counter-Reformation. By the early 17th century, it had succeeded in reversing Protestant gains in Poland, France, Bavaria, Austria and the Southern Netherlands.

Colleges were set up to train priests to win back Protestant converts, and to educate Catholics from non-Catholic countries. New religious orders were founded, the most influential of which were the Jesuits (**1534**), who were employed as teachers and missionaries, as far afield as India and Japan.

Ignatius Loyola, founder of the Jesuit order

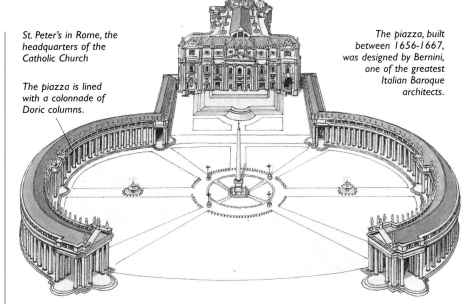

St. Peter's in Rome, the headquarters of the Catholic Church

The piazza is lined with a colonnade of Doric columns.

The piazza, built between 1656-1667, was designed by Bernini, one of the greatest Italian Baroque architects.

A Council of the Catholic Church met at Trent, on the Italian-German border in **1545-1547**, **1551-1552** and **1562-1563**, which launched an energetic campaign. The Inquisition was reinstated, and Protestants were convicted of heresy and burned. The Baroque movement in the arts also helped to win people back to Catholicism, with flamboyant religious painting, music and architecture.

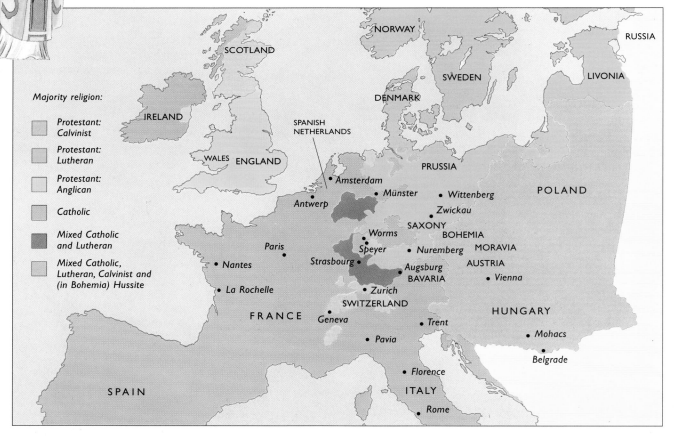

Majority religion:

- Protestant: Calvinist
- Protestant: Lutheran
- Protestant: Anglican
- Catholic
- Mixed Catholic and Lutheran
- Mixed Catholic, Lutheran, Calvinist and (in Bohemia) Hussite

Map of Europe in 1560, showing the different Christian groups

The French wars of religion

In the mid-16th century, rival Catholic and Protestant factions emerged at the French Court, after many nobles became Calvinists (known in France as Huguenots). This situation was made worse by a succession of weak kings after the death of Henri II in **1559**. Struggles between the two sides provoked a series of bloody civil wars between **1562-1598**.

The Catholics were led by the Guise family, supported by King Charles IX, who was still a child, and his mother, Catherine de Medici, who was the regent. The Huguenots were led by the Coligny brothers, the Bourbon Prince of Condé and King Henri of Navarre.

Catherine de Medici, who ordered the massacre of Huguenots on Saint Bartholomew's Eve

The wars were brought to an end with the accession of Henri of Navarre, the Protestant heir, in **1589**. As Henri IV of France, he became the first king of the Bourbon dynasty. Henri succeeded in uniting the country, first by making a politically wise conversion to Catholicism in **1593**, and then by allowing the Huguenots religious toleration, with the **1598** Edict of Nantes.

Bourbon coat of arms

IMPORTANT DATES

1562 Massacre of Huguenots at Vassy by the Duke de Guise and his retainers leads to civil war.

1563 Murder of the Duke de Guise by Protestants.

Murder of the Duke de Guise

1567-1570 Second civil war ends with the Peace of Saint Germain.

1572 St. Bartholomew's Eve massacre of thousands of Huguenots in Paris leads to another civil war.

1584 The Guise family joins Philip II of Spain in the League of Joinville against the Huguenots.

1586 War of the Three Henries: Henri III, Henri of Navarre and Henri de Guise.

1589 Henri III is murdered. The crown is claimed by Henri of Navarre, as Henri IV, first king of the Bourbon dynasty.

1590 Henri IV defeats Catholics at the Battle of Ivry.

1593 Henri IV converts to Catholicism.

1594 Henri IV enters Paris and begins his reign.

1598 Edict of Nantes grants religious toleration to Huguenots.

Henri IV and, above, his sword, a wedding present from the city of Paris

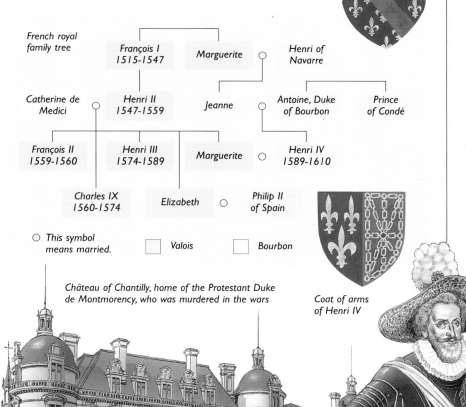

French royal family tree

| François I 1515-1547 | — | Marguerite | ○ | Henri of Navarre |

| Catherine de Medici | ○ | Henri II 1547-1559 | Jeanne | ○ | Antoine, Duke of Bourbon | Prince of Condé |

| François II 1559-1560 | Henri III 1574-1589 | Marguerite | ○ | Henri IV 1589-1610 |

| Charles IX 1560-1574 | Elizabeth | ○ | Philip II of Spain |

○ *This symbol means married.*

☐ Valois   ☐ Bourbon

Château of Chantilly, home of the Protestant Duke de Montmorency, who was murdered in the wars

Coat of arms of Henri IV

Southern and Western Europe

1603 Death of Queen Elizabeth I of England marks the end of the Tudor dynasty.

Funeral procession for Elizabeth I

1603-1625 James VI of Scotland becomes James I of England and Scotland. The start of the Stuart dynasty.

James I of England

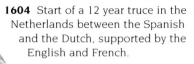

1604 Start of a 12 year truce in the Netherlands between the Spanish and the Dutch, supported by the English and French.

1605 The Gunpowder Plot: a failed attempt by a group of English Catholics, including Guy Fawkes, to blow up the Houses of Parliament. They are caught and executed.

1608 The first practical telescope is invented by Hans Lippershey, a Dutch lens maker.

1609 Expulsion of the Moors (North African Arabs) from Portugal.

1610 Galileo Galilei, an Italian scientist, publishes *The Starry Messenger*, about his discoveries with the use of a telescope.

1610 Assassination of Henri IV of France. Start of reign of Louis XIII (**1610-1643**).

1614 John Napier, a Scottish mathematician, invents his logarithm tables.

Two of Galileo's telescopes, mounted on a stand

1614-1616 Civil war in France.

1616 William Harvey, an English doctor, introduces the idea of the circulation of the blood around the body.

Northern and Eastern Europe

1603 Grigoriy Otrepieff, a monk, claims to be Dimitri, youngest son of the late Ivan IV, and heir to the Russian throne. (Dimitri had in fact been murdered in **1591**.) Grigoriy invades Russia and is crowned Czar, but soon becomes unpopular.

Czarevich Dimitri (top) and Grigoriy Otrepieff, the False Dimitri (bottom)

1606 The false Dimitri is defeated and murdered in a revolt led by Boris Gudunov.

1607 The reign of Charles IX of Sweden.

1608 Formation of a Protestant Union in Germany.

1609 Maximilian of Bavaria forms a Catholic league.

1609 Johannes Kepler (**1571-1630**) a German astronomer, announces his laws of planetary motion. Kepler had developed Copernicus's idea that planets revolve around the Sun, but suggested that they did so in ellipses rather than circles.

Diagram showing Kepler's idea of planetary motion, based on Copernicus's ideas.

1611-1613 War between Sweden and Denmark.

1611-1632 Reign of Gustavus Adolphus II of Sweden, a great soldier and statesman. Sweden acquires land on the Baltic and becomes a major power.

1613 The founding of the Romanov dynasty (**1613-1917**) in Russia by Czar Michael.

Crown jewels made for Czar Michael Romanov

1613 Turks conquer Hungary.

1617 Treaty of Stolbovo: Russia gives up Ingria and Karelia to Sweden.

1618-1648 Thirty Years' War is fought between Protestant provinces and Catholic imperial forces in the Holy Roman Empire. The war breaks out after two Catholic governors are thrown out of the window of Prague castle by Bohemians wanting independence.

1619-1637 Reign of Emperor Ferdinand II of the HRE.

Africa, India and the Middle East

1600 Oyo kingdom in West Africa is at its height.

An Oyo carving

1602-1627 Wars between the Persian Safavids and the Ottoman Turks.

1604 Persians recover Tabriz from the Ottomans.

1605 Death of the Mogul emperor, Akbar the Great. He is succeeded by Jahangir (**1605-1627**).

Jahangir, Mogul emperor

1609 Dutch take Ceylon from Portugal.

1610 English East India Company sets up a factory at Madras.

1611 English East India Company establishes its first trading post in India, at Surat.

1612 Persians take Baghdad from the Turks.

The Blue Mosque, Isfahan, Persia

1616 Dutch and French establish trading posts in Senegal and the Gold Coast, West Africa.

1616 British East India Company trades with Persia.

The Far East and Australasia

1596-1619 Dutch trading bases in Java and Sumatra.

1600 Civil War in Burma: Burmese empire breaks up.

1600 English East India Company is founded.

Dutch tile

1600 Ieyasu Tokugawa defeats his rivals at the Battle of Sekigahara and establishes supremacy in Japan.

Ieyasu Tokugawa

1602 Dutch East India Company is founded. The first Dutch traders arrive in Cambodia and Siam.

1603 Ieyasu Tokugawa assumes the title of *shogun* (military ruler) and founds the Tokugawa dynasty.

1604 Russians expand across Siberia and found Tomsk.

1605 Hidetada Tokugawa becomes ruler in Japan.

1606 Willem Jantszoon, a Dutch navigator, becomes the first European to reach Australia.

1613-1646 Reign of Sultan Agung of Mataram, who tries to rule Java.

1614-1636 Europeans begin to explore Australia.

1616 Manchu Tartars invade China.

1618-1629 Dutch expel Portuguese from East Indies. They found a base at Batavia (Jakarta), Sumatra in **1619**.

Puppets from Java, East Indies

The Americas

1602 Spaniards explore the coast of California.

1603 Start of French colonization in North America: Newfoundland, Nova Scotia and New France.

1605 Spaniards found Santa Fé, New Mexico.

1605 James 1 of England is proclaimed King of Barbados.

1607 First permanent English settlement in North America, at Jamestown, Virginia.

1608 French found Quebec.

Native North Americans swapped furs for guns, knives and blankets.

A tomahawk, a traditional Native American weapon

1608 Paraguay founded by Jesuits.

1609 English settlers on Bermuda.

1609 Dutch found Manhattan.

1610-1611 Henry Hudson (English) explores Hudson Bay, in search of the Northwest passage to the East.

1610 Etienne Brulé (French) discovers Lake Huron.

1612 Tobacco cultivation is begun in Virginia.

1613 Samuel de Champlain (French) explores Ottawa River.

1613 English destroy French settlement at Port Royal, Jamaica.

1616 Willem Schouten, a Dutch navigator, rounds Cape Horn.

1619 First slaves imported into Virginia from West Africa.

1619 First colonial assembly is held at Jamestown, Virginia.

African kingdoms

Much of Africa south of the Sahara Desert remained unknown and unexplored by Europeans until the 19th century. Since the people there did not develop literacy, much of their history has vanished. However, during the Middle Ages in Europe, there existed fabulously rich empires in Africa, particularly in West Africa, around such cities as Gao, Timbuktu, and Jenne. These empires prospered from trade with Arab merchants in gold, ivory, animal skins and slaves.

THE GREAT TRADING EMPIRES

One of the earliest trading empires was Ghana (**c.700-1200**), which was absorbed into the kingdom of Mali (**c.1235-1500**), and later that of Songhai (**c.1350-1600**). Another was Kanem-Bornu (**c.800-1800**).

In southern Africa, Zimbabwe was established by the Rozwi kings of Mwenemutapa and thrived from **c.1270-1450**.

The fortress at Great Zimbabwe, where the rulers lived

THE EAST AFRICAN TRADING CITIES

Along the East African coast, Arab merchants had been trading with ports such as Kilwa, Mombasa, Zanzibar and Malindi since before the 8th century. From the 10th century, the Arabs began to settle there too. Trade in gold, ivory and other goods came from as far away as India and China, as well as all over the Islamic world.

An Arab boat called a dhow

The outside walls were 5m (16ft) thick.

In 1414, East Africans gave the Chinese emperor a giraffe as a gift.

Objects used as trading currency

In the 15th century, Chinese merchants joined Indian and Arab traders on the East coast. At about the same time, the Portuguese began exploring the coast of West Africa and discovered a sea route to India. In the 16th century, they set up forts along the East African coast. The prosperity of the area declined, as they took over the trade for themselves.

THE MUSLIM KINGDOMS OF THE NORTH

From the 7th century, the Arabs made conquests all over North Africa and converted the people to Islam (see page 27). This meant that North Africa became part of the Mediterranean world, rather than that of continental Africa.

By the mid-13th century, the Muslim Berber people had set up several states along the North African coast, which lasted for more than 200 years. Europeans named it the Barbary Coast, after them.

In the 16th century, the Ottoman Turks took control of Egypt, Tripoli, Tunisia and, indirectly, Algeria. Morocco remained independent from **1578**, under the Muslim Sharifian dynasty, which expanded south, taking over Songhai.

ETHIOPIA

Ethiopia was a remarkable kingdom, which remained Christian, stable and unchanged for centuries. In the 19th century, it was almost the only African country to stay uncolonized by Europeans.

Church of St. George, Ethiopia, one of a series of 11 cross-shaped churches carved out of rock by King Lalibela in the 13th century

IMPORTANT DATES

c.100-700 Kingdom of Axum.

c.333 Ethiopia converts to Christianity.

c.700-1200 Kingdom of Ghana.

c.800-1800 Kingdom of Kanem-Bornu.

c.1235-1500 Kingdom of Mali, established by Sun Diata Keita.

c.1240 Kumbi, former capital of Ghana, is destroyed.

c.1270-1450 Zimbabwe kingdom, ruled from Great Zimbabwe.

1324 Mansa Musa of Mali visits Cairo, displaying great wealth.

c.1350-1600 Songhai kingdom.

1352 Ibn Battuta, a Berber explorer, describes Mali.

c.1380-1662 Kongo kingdom.

1578 The Muslim Sharifian dynasty is established in Morocco.

c.1700 Kingdoms of Benin, Oyo and Ashanti are flourishing.

c.1800 Kingdoms of Buganda and Lunda are at their height.

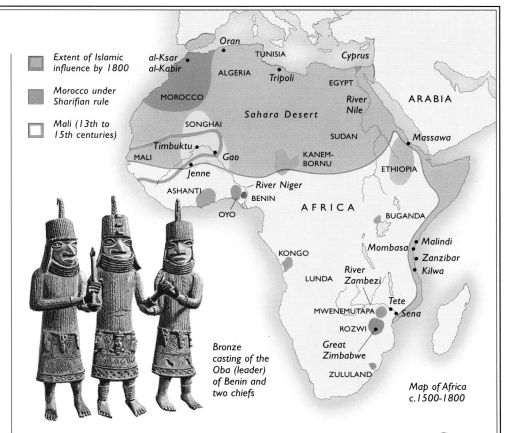

Extent of Islamic influence by 1800

Morocco under Sharifian rule

Mali (13th to 15th centuries)

Bronze casting of the Oba (leader) of Benin and two chiefs

Map of Africa c.1500-1800

WEST AFRICAN KINGDOMS

By **1500**, some African kingdoms, such as Kanem-Bornu, Kongo and Songhai in West Africa, were growing into larger political units, with expanding territory and population. But the growth of the slave trade in the 16th century spread disorder and eventually led to a fall in population. By the end of the century, many of these kingdoms were in decline.

For many centuries, West African tribes speaking Bantu languages had been expanding south and east, setting up new kingdoms at the expense of weaker local tribes. By the 17th century, they had reached their present territory of South Africa, and began taking over from the native Khoisan. In **c.1700**, other Bantu tribes founded the kingdoms of Buganda in East Africa, and Lunda in Central Africa.

By **1700**, the kingdoms of Ashanti in Ghana, and Benin and Oyo in Nigeria, were flourishing. The Ashanti were known for their work in gold, and the people of Benin for their highly skilled works of art in bronze.

Bronze head of a Benin queen

Mosque at Jenne, Songhai

Arab slave traders crossing the Sahara Desert

Southern and Western Europe

1620 Uprising of Huguenots (Protestants) in France.

1621-1625 Philip IV of Spain (**1621-1665**) resumes war against the Dutch.

1624-1629 France and England at war.

1624-1642 Cardinal Richelieu is first minister to Louis XIII of France.

1625-1649 Reign of Charles I of England.

1628 Cardinal Richelieu captures the Huguenot stronghold of La Rochelle, ending the Huguenot threat to French unity.

Cardinal Richelieu

Siege tower at La Rochelle

Charles I

1629-1640 England: King Charles I dissolves Parliament after disagreements with the House of Commons over customs and excise duties and Catholicism. He does not call it again until **1640**. Charles builds up his navy to rival that of the Dutch, levying an old tax called Ship Money to cover the cost.

1632 Galileo Galilei (**1564-1642**), an Italian astronomer and mathematician, publishes his *Dialogues*, which revolutionizes scientific thinking.

Galileo's sketches of his observations of the moon, showing mountains and "seas"

1635 France declares war on Spain and joins the Thirty Years' War (see page 94).

Northern and Eastern Europe

1620 Battle of the White Mountain outside Prague: victory for the imperial forces in the Thirty Years' War.

1621 Gustavus Adolphus gains Livonia from Poland.

1622 England sends first ambassador to Turkey.

1623 Protestant worship is forbidden in Bohemia.

1625 Denmark enters the Thirty Years' War.

1628 Swedish royal flagship, the *Vasa*, sinks in Stockholm shortly after being launched.

The Vasa

1629 Peace of Lübeck between Denmark and the Holy Roman Empire.

1630 Sweden enters the Thirty Years' War.

1631 Battle of Breitenfeld: imperial defeat.

17th century gauntlets (gloves), used in battle

1632 Battle of Lützen: Swedish victory, but Gustavus Adolphus is killed.

1632-1654 Reign of Queen Christina of Sweden, guided by the great statesman, Axel Oxenstierna.

1634 Battle of Nördlingen: Sweden loses South Germany.

Sweden, 1560
Expansion to 1645
Expansion to 1658
Boundary 1658

RUSSIA

KINGDOM OF NORWAY AND DENMARK

SWEDISH KINGDOM

KARELIA

Narva
INGRIA

Stockholm
ESTONIA

HALLAND
GOTLAND
LIVONIA

Kalmar

Copenhagen
Baltic Sea

Roskilde
Lund

POLISH KINGDOM

Lübeck

The growth of the Swedish empire in the 16th and 17th centuries

Africa, India and the Middle East

1627-1658 Rule of Mogul emperor, Shah Jahan, who adds further territories to the empire.

Shah Jahan

1628 Portuguese destroy the Mwenemutapa kingdom in southern Africa.

1629 Death of Shah Abbas the Great of Persia.

1631-1642 Dutch West India Company ousts the Portuguese from the Gold Coast (Ghana).

1632-1653 Shah Jahan builds the white marble Taj Mahal, at Agra, as a tomb for his wife, Mumtaz Mahal.

A Mogul sword

The Taj Mahal, Agra, India

1636 The sultans of the Deccan, India, become vassals (subject princes) of the Mogul empire.

1637 The Dutch take El Mina, West Africa, from the Portuguese.

1637 The French establish trading posts in Senegal, West Africa.

1639 Ottoman Turks make peace with the Persians after capturing Iraq from them.

The Far East and Australasia

1621 The Manchus (see page 81) set up a capital at Loyang, China.

1622-1624 Christian missionaries in Japan are executed.

1623 The Amboyna Massacre: Dutch destroy the English base in the East Indies, at Amboyna.

1623-1651 Rule of the powerful shogun, Iemitsu Tokugawa, in Japan.

1626-1662 Dutch trade with China from Formosa (Taiwan).

1627 Manchus overrun Korea, which becomes a vassal (subject state) in **1637**.

1627 Rebellions against the Ming dynasty in China.

Ming bowl

Statue of a Ming official

1632 Russians continue to expand in Siberia: Irkutsk is founded.

Engraving of Russian fur traders in Siberia

1636 The Manchus proclaim the start of a new Chinese dynasty, the Ch'ing, at Mukden, Manchuria.

1637 English establish a trading post in Canton, China.

1639 Japan enforces isolationist policies. Japanese are forbidden to travel abroad and foreigners are banned from entering Japan.

The Americas

1620 *The Mayflower* sails from Plymouth, England, to Massachusetts, carrying the Pilgrims (English Puritans).

Wild American turkey, eaten at Thanksgiving

Pilgrims at a Thanksgiving meal

1625 French establish a port at Cayenne, Guiana.

1626 Dutch found New Amsterdam (now New York).

1627 French Cardinal Richelieu sets up a company to colonize all land between Florida and the Arctic.

1629 English capture Quebec from France (restored to France **1632**).

1630-1642 16,000 settlers join the Massachusetts Bay Colony.

1634 Maryland is founded for Catholic colonists.

1634 Dutch establish a base at Curaçao, West Indies.

1634 Jean Nicolet (French) explores Lake Michigan and St. Lawrence and Mississippi rivers.

1636 Founding of Dutch Guiana (British Guiana in **1814**).

Native Americans from the East coast

The Thirty Years' War

The Thirty Years' War (**1618-1648**) began as a revolt by the Bohemian provinces of the Holy Roman Empire, but it soon merged with several other conflicts. Fought mainly in Germany, the war devastated the land, killing thousands.

Bohemian nobles throwing two imperial governors out of the window, an event that helped spark off the war

Catholic

Reclaimed by Catholics

Protestant: Lutheran

Protestant: Calvinist

Mixed Protestant

Mixed Catholic/Protestant

Gustavus Adolphus

Map of Germany during the Thirty Years' War

War broke out after the Bohemians rejected the claim of Austrian Archduke Ferdinand to the throne of Bohemia, and chose instead the Protestant Elector Frederick of the Palatinate. The Emperor attacked, supported by Spain and the Catholic German states. Bohemia was supported by Denmark and Protestant German states. Neither side won clear victories, although the imperial army, under General Wallenstein, won several destructive battles.

Although the two sides were originally divided on religious lines, political factors later grew more important. In **1630**, the Swedes entered the war, led by their brilliant commander, Gustavus Adolphus. His aim was to expand his own power in the Baltic. France was already at war with Spain and joined the Protestant side in **1635**.

The Peace in **1648** ended the threat of Hapsburg domination, ensuring the survival of German Protestant states. While Spain's status declined, that of France, Prussia and Sweden increased.

KEY DATES

1620 Battle of the White Mountain: imperial victory.

1625 Denmark enters the war.

1629 Peace of Lübeck.

1630 Sweden enters the war.

Musket

Arquebus

Sword

Weapons were improved during the war, especially by Sweden

Cannon

1631 Battle of Breitenfeld: the imperial forces are defeated.

1632 Battle of Lützen: Swedish victory, but Gustavus Adolphus is killed in battle.

1634 Battle of Nördlingen.

1635 France enters the war on the Protestant side.

1648 Peace of Westphalia.

The city of Magdeburg on fire in 1631

The rise of the Dutch

Engraving of Amsterdam in the 16th century by D.G. Hucquier

The 17th century was a golden age for the Dutch Republic (also known as the United Provinces). Having gained independence from Spain at the end of the 16th century, the Dutch grew into the most successful trading nation in Europe. They founded a major colonial empire in Asia, South Africa and the New World, and Amsterdam grew to be one of the largest and most prosperous cities of its day. Dutch engineers became experts at land drainage and reclamation, and their farms were the most productive in Europe.

Under the patronage of wealthy merchants, the Dutch also made important contributions to art, science and technology.

By the second half of the 17th century, their greatest rivals were the English, who were also expanding rapidly as a trading and colonial power. Between **1652** and **1674**, there were three Anglo-Dutch trade wars. But, by the **1680s**, growing French ambition brought the English and Dutch together again. The Dutch ruler, William of Orange, married the English Princess Mary. In **1688,** he became King of England, after the fall and abdication of her father, James II.

Dutch china, influenced by porcelain imported from the Far East

FAMOUS 17TH CENTURY DUTCH PEOPLE

Hugo Grotius (**1583-1645**), lawyer and statesman, regarded as founder of modern international law.

Frans Hals (**1580-1666**), painter best known for portraits.

Christiaan Huygens (**1629-1695**), physicist. Defined wave theory of light, and built the first accurate pendulum clock.

Huygen's pendulum clock mechanism

Willem Jantszoon (born **c.1570**), explorer. The first European to reach Australia.

Anton van Leeuwenhoek (**1632-1723**), microscope maker. First person to describe blood corpuscles accurately.

Hans Lippershey (**c.1570-1619**), optician. One of the first people to make a practical telescope.

Rembrandt van Rijn (**1606-1669**), painter noted for his treatment of light and shade.

Baruch Spinoza (**1632-1677**), writer and philosopher. Author of *Ethics*.

Jan Steen (**1626-1679**), painter of scenes of daily life.

Abel Tasman (**1603-1659**), explorer. Sights Tasmania and discovers the west coast of New Zealand.

Jan van der Meer van Delft (**1632-1675**), known as Vermeer, painter of daily life, famous for his interiors and delicate use of light and shade.

Leeuwenhoek's microscope

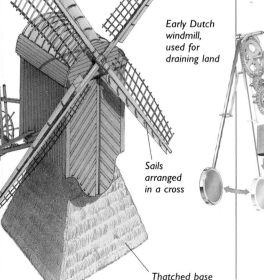

Early Dutch windmill, used for draining land

Sails arranged in a cross

Thatched base

Southern and Western Europe

1640 Charles I of England summons Parliament as he needs to raise money to fight the Scots.

1640 Portugal becomes independent under the house of Braganza (until **1910**).

1642 Blaise Pascal, a French mathematician, designs a mechanical adding machine.

Numbers appeared in windows.

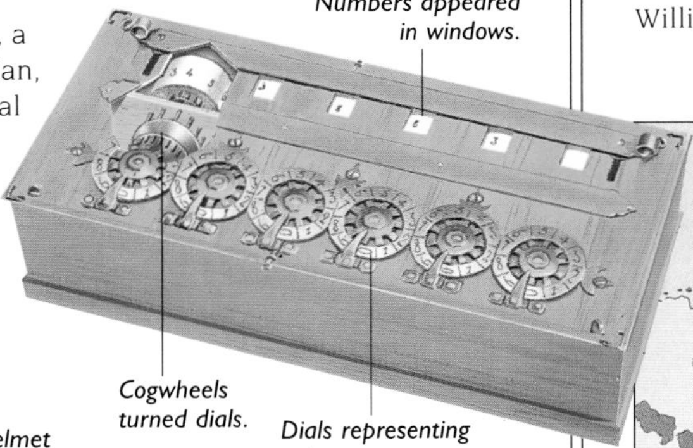

Pascal's mechanical adding machine

1642-48 English Civil War (see page 106).

Cogwheels turned dials.

Dials representing units

An English Civil War helmet

1643 Evangelista Torricelli (**1608-1647**), a Florentine, invents the barometer.

1643 The French beat the Spaniards at Rocroi. The start of French military superiority in Europe.

1643-1715 Reign of Louis XIV of France. Policy is controlled by first minister Cardinal Mazarin until **1661**.

1644 René Descartes, a French mathematician and philosopher, publishes his *Principles of Philosophy*.

1648 Peace of the Hague ends the Dutch Revolt (see page 77). Spaniards recognize the independence of the United Provinces. War continues between French and Spaniards.

1648-1653 Riots in Paris. A period of civil disorder in France known as the *Fronde*.

1649 Execution of English king, Charles I. Oliver Cromwell suppresses rebellions in Ireland and Scotland.

1649-1660 England is ruled by the Commonwealth (**1649-1653**), followed by the Protectorate (**1653-1660**), under Oliver Cromwell.

1652-1654 First Anglo-Dutch Trade War (see page 95).

c.1658 Robert Boyle (Irish) and Robert Hooke (English) design and build a new air pump to create a vacuum in a glass tube.

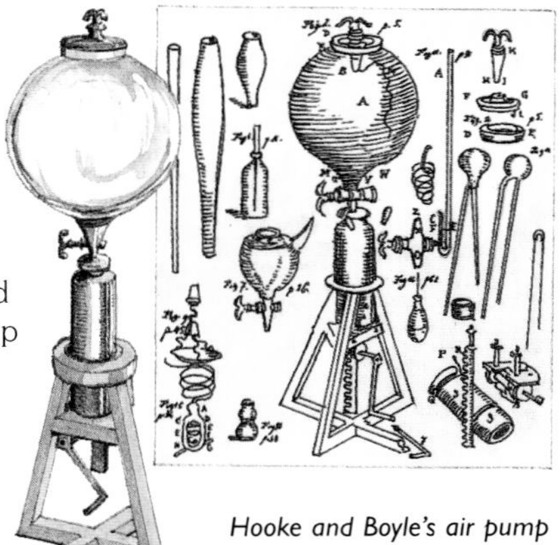

1659 Peace of the Pyrenees between France and Spain. Start of the rise of France and the decline of Spain.

Hooke and Boyle's air pump is used to research air pressure and to study how plants and animals breathe.

Northern and Eastern Europe

1640-1688 The state of Brandenburg-Prussia grows in importance under Frederick William, "the Great Elector".

Frederick William I

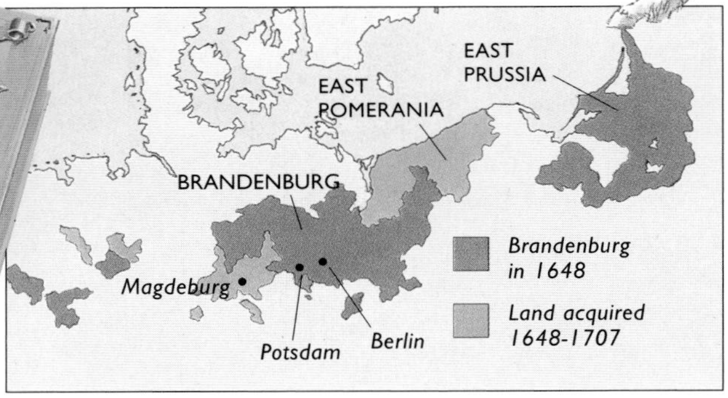

Map showing Brandenburg-Prussia 1648-1707

Map labels: EAST PRUSSIA, EAST POMERANIA, BRANDENBURG, Magdeburg, Potsdam, Berlin

Legend:
- Brandenburg in 1648
- Land acquired 1648-1707

1643-1645 War between Sweden and Denmark. Sweden becomes the major power in the Baltic.

1645-1659 War between Venice and the Turks leads to the conquest of Crete by the Turks.

1646 Swedes take Prague and invade Bavaria.

1648 Peace of Westphalia ends the Thirty Years' War.

1649 The Code of Laws marks the final establishment of serfdom in Russia.

1654 Queen Christina of Sweden abdicates and becomes a Catholic.

Gold horn which holds oil used to anoint a new ruler of Sweden

Queen Christina of Sweden

1654-1657 War between Russia and Poland. Russia acquires Smolensk and eastern Ukraine.

1654-1660 War between Sweden and Poland.

1657 The Elector of Brandenburg obtains the sovereignty of Prussia.

1658 Peace of Roskilde: the Danes give up all claims to southern Sweden.

Africa, India and the Middle East

1640 The English acquire the port of Madras, India.

1643 The French establish Fort Dauphin, Madagascar.

1644 Dutch settle in Mauritius.

1648 Arabs recapture Muscat from Portugal.

1650 Ali Bey makes himself hereditary governor of Tunis, North Africa.

1651 English occupy St. Helena.

1652 The Dutch found the Cape of Good Hope, South Africa.

A Cape Dutch farmhouse

1656 The Dutch displace the Portuguese in Ceylon (Sri Lanka).

1658-1707 Rule of Aurangzeb, the last great Mogul emperor. He defeats and deposes his father, Jahan, and conquers Kandahar, Kabul and the Deccan. The empire reaches its greatest extent, but decay sets in.

Indian emperors kept peacocks at their palaces.

Elephants dressed for a Mogul celebration

1659 French found trading posts on coast of Senegal.

The Far East and Australasia

1641 The Dutch seize Malacca, Malaya, from Portugal and dominate trade in the East Indies.

1641 Japan cuts itself off from the rest of the world until **1854**. Only the Dutch keep a trading post on an island off Nagasaki.

1642 Abel Tasman (Dutch) discovers Van Diemen's Land (Tasmania) and New Zealand.

1643 Abel Tasman discovers the Fiji islands.

1644 The Chinese Ming dynasty is overthrown by rebels. The Manchu dynasty is established in northern China and lasts until **1912**.

1644 Abel Tasman explores the north and west coasts of Australia.

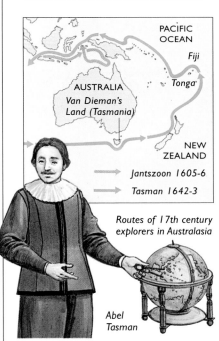

Routes of 17th century explorers in Australasia

Abel Tasman

1647 The Manchus take Canton, China.

1648 The Bering Strait is discovered by the Cossack explorer, Dezhnev.

1649 The Russians reach the Pacific Ocean and found Okhotsk in eastern Siberia.

1652 Most of China is united under Manchu control.

The Americas

1642 The French found Montreal, Canada.

The Canadian fur trade continues to grow. These are some of the animals hunted for their fur.

Stoat

Beaver

Otter

Native Americans hunted with traditional weapons, such as this Inuit bow.

1643 New Hampshire is founded.

1644 Rhode Island separates from the Massachusetts Bay Colony.

1648 The French establish settlements in the Caribbean islands of St. Martin, St. Bartholomew, St. Croix, The Saints, Maria Galante, St. Lucia and Grenada.

1648-1653 War between the Iroquois and the Huron and Algonquin tribes in North America.

c.1650 Settler population in the 13 North American colonies reaches about 60,000.

1651 Maine becomes part of the Massachusetts Bay Colony.

1654 First sugar cane plantations are established in the Caribbean islands by the English and French. Slaves are imported from West Africa to work on them.

1655 England acquires Jamaica from Spain.

The Mogul empire

The Mogul empire took its name from the Mongols. It began when Babar, Prince of Ferghana, in Afghanistan, a descendent of Tamerlane, defeated the Sultan of Delhi at the Battle of Panipat (**1526**).

The Muslim holy book, the Koran

The Khan, the ruler of the Mongols, bowing before Babar

Babar's grandson, Akbar (**1556-1605**), extended control over most of central and northern India. His reign was one of the great ages in Indian civilization, with a flowering in the arts, especially painting, poetry, and architecture. Akbar was a wise ruler, who attempted to unite India culturally, as well as by conquest. Although the Moguls were Muslims, Akbar won the support of his mainly Hindu subjects by allowing them to worship their Hindu gods and goddesses.

Shah Jahan and his wife Mumtaz Mahal

The Taj Mahal was built near Agra by Jahan in 1632-1653, as a tomb for his beloved wife, Mumtaz Mahal. It was designed in a mixture of Muslim and Hindu styles.

RISE AND DECLINE

Some of the finest works of Mogul architecture, including the Taj Mahal (below), were built during the reign of Akbar's grandson, Jahan (**1627-1656**). The empire reached its greatest extent under his successor, Aurangzeb (**1656-1707**). But decay set in after that. The Moguls began to persecute Hindus, which undermined their loyalty. They also brought in heavy taxes, provoking fierce resistance from the peasants.

The dome is hollow. It rests on a tower of bricks just above the ceiling of the tomb.

AFGHANISTAN
KASHMIR
Kabul
Kandahar
Lahore
PUNJAB
Delhi · Panipat
Fatepur Sikri · Agra
SIND
GUJERAT
BENGAL

DECCAN
· Goa
MARATHA STATES
Ceylon

Expansion of Mogul empire:

- under Babar 1526-1530
- under Akbar 1556-1605
- under Jahan 1627-1656
- under Aurangzeb 1656-1707

Relations grew worse with the Hindu Maratha princes, who had set up an independent kingdom in central India. They continued to grow in power and expand farther north. During the 18th century, although the Moguls were still nominally in control, India had become a collection of more or less independent states.

Sculptors carved hollows into the marble into which they slotted jewels.

The marble sarcophagi (tombs) of Mumtaz Mahal and Shah Jahan

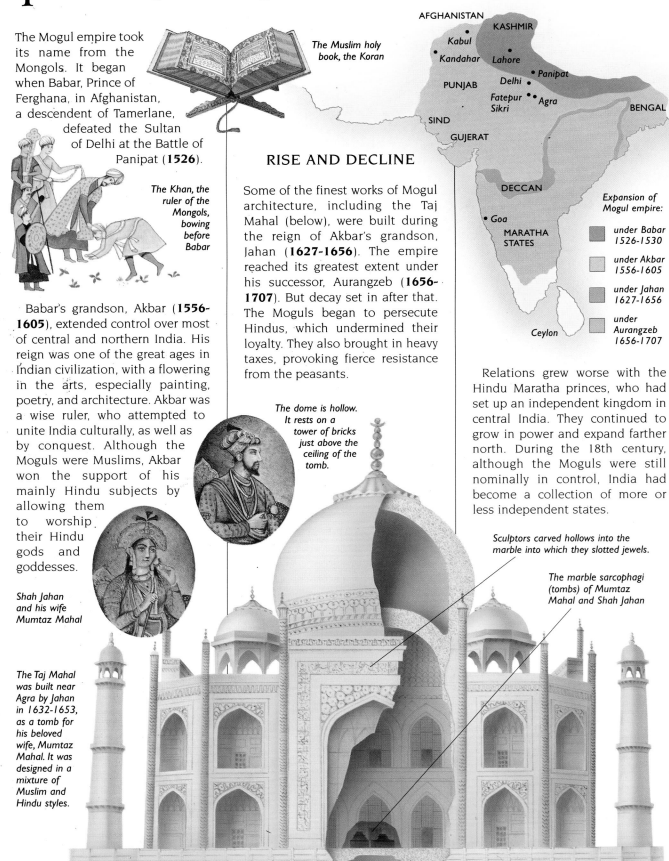

The decline of the Ottomans

In the 16th century, the Ottoman Turks possessed one of the most powerful empires in the world. They took control in Egypt and parts of North Africa, and occupied most of Syria, Lebanon, Israel, Iraq, the Yemen, as well as large parts of the Caucasus and the Balkan region of Eastern Europe.

Ottoman ceramics

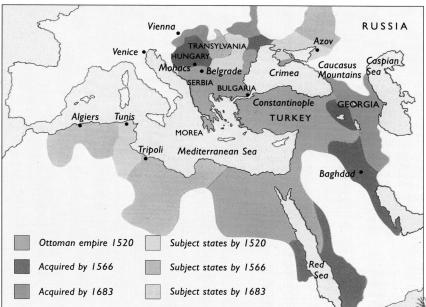

Ottoman empire 1520   Subject states by 1520
Acquired by 1566   Subject states by 1566
Acquired by 1683   Subject states by 1683

IMPORTANT DATES

1603 Turks lose Baghdad to Persia.

1618 Turks lose Georgia to Persia.

1638 Turks retake Baghdad.

1645-1649 War with Crete.

1656-1661 Grand Vizier Mohammed Koprülü saves the empire from decline.

1672-1676 War with Poland. Turks acquire Polish Ukraine.

1677-1681 War with Russia. Turks lose most of Ukraine.

1683 Turks besiege Vienna without success.

Turkish flags from the Siege of Vienna

1686 Austrians take Budapest from Turks.

1687 Battle of Mohacs: Turkish defeat. Hungary becomes a hereditary Hapsburg possession.

1689 Austrians take Belgrade.

1690 Turks drive Austrians from Bulgaria, Serbia and Transylvania, and recapture Belgrade.

1696 Russians seize Azov.

1699 Treaty of Karlowitz: Turks lose Hungary, Croatia, Transylvania, and Slavonia to Austria. Venice gets Morea and most of Dalmatia, and Podolia goes to Poland.

1717 Treaty of Belgrade: Turks take northern Serbia and Belgrade.

1743-1746 War with Persia.

1768-1774 War with Russia.

1783 Russia annexes Crimea.

From the end of the 17th century, however, Ottoman power began to wane. There were a number of causes. With many discontented Christian subjects, the empire had simply become too big to control, and there was a succession of weak rulers. Enemies on their borders, such as Russia and Austria, were growing in strength. As Muslims, the Ottomans came into conflict with Christian Europe, and there were clashes with their fellow Muslims, the Safavids of Persia.

Safavid warriors

THE LAST SIEGE OF VIENNA

In the 16th century, the Turks had posed a real danger to Western Europe, especially after their lengthy siege of Vienna in **1529**. But the threat is thought to have come to an end in **1683**, when the Ottomans besieged Vienna - unsuccessfully - for the last time. By now the Ottoman empire was well in decline, as the Turks had already had to concede territory to Persia, Poland and Russia.

A Janissary, a Christian slave who converted to Islam and was trained as a soldier

Southern and Western Europe

1660 Restoration of Charles II of England.

1661 Louis XIV of France takes control of government, aged 22.

1661 Robert Boyle (Irish) defines chemical elements.

Louis XIV dressed as a sun god

1665-1667 Second Anglo-Dutch Trade War ends in Peace of Breda.

1665 Portugal wins independence from Spain, with English help.

1665 Isaac Newton (English) discovers gravity.

An 18th century cartoon mocking Newton's Laws of Gravity

1665 The Great Plague in London.

1666 The Great Fire of London.

The Fire of London

1668 Treaty of Lisbon: Spain recognizes the independence of Portugal.

1668 War ends between France and Spain.

1668 Isaac Newton invents the reflecting telescope.

1670 Treaty of Dover: a secret treaty between Charles II of England and Louis XIV, supplying Charles with funds to fight the Dutch and restore Catholicism in England.

1672-1674 Third Anglo-Dutch Trade War.

1672-1678 War between France and Netherlands ends in Peace of Nijmegen.

1672-1702 William III of Orange is hereditary stadtholder (ruler) of the Netherlands.

1679 The Exclusion Crisis In England. A bill prevents the Catholic Duke of York from succeeding his brother as King of England. Charles II dismisses Parliament.

Northern and Eastern Europe

1660 Treaty of Oliva ends war between Sweden, Poland, Brandenburg and the Empire.

1660 Brandenburg acquires sovereignty over Prussia.

1660-1697 Reign of Charles XI of Sweden.

1661 First European bank-note issued by the Bank of Stockholm.

Early Swedish banknote

1663-1699 Turks attack central Europe.

1664 Turks invade and occupy Hungary.

1667 End of a 13-year truce between Russia and Poland. Kiev is ceded to Russia.

1669 Crete is ceded by Venice to the Turks, marking the end of Venice's colonial empire.

1670 A rebellion of Ukrainian Cossacks and peasants subject to Poland is crushed by the Polish leader, Jan Sobiewski.

Cossack soldiers dancing

1671 Turks declare war on Poland, in support of the Cossacks.

1672 Turks and Cossacks invade Poland. Poles give up Podolia and Ukraine.

1673 Poles defeat the Turks at the Battle of Khorzim.

1674 Jan Sobiewski is elected King of Poland.

1675 The Elector of Brandenburg defeats the Swedes at the Battle of Fehrbellin.

1676 Peace of Zuravno ends the war between Poland and Turkey. Turkey receives the Polish Ukraine.

1676 Swedes defeat the Danes at the Battle of Lund.

1677 Swedes defeat the Danes at Rostock and Landström.

1677 War between Russia and Turkey. At the Treaty of Radzin (**1679**), Russia gains most of Ukraine from Turks.

1678 War between Russia and Sweden.

1679 Peace between Sweden and Brandenburg.

Africa, India and the Middle East

c.1660-1670 The rise of the Bambara kingdoms of the Upper Niger, West Africa.

1662 Battle of Ambuila: the destruction of the Kongo kingdom by the Portuguese.

Carving from the Kongo kingdom

1662 Portuguese cede Tangier, North Africa to England.

1664 The French East India Company is founded.

1666-1668 Civil wars in India.

1668 English East India Company obtains control of Bombay, India.

1669 Aurangzeb bans Hinduism in India and persecutes Hindus.

1672 English Royal Africa Company (founded **1663**) merges with the Guinea Company. West African trade increases.

1674 The French establish a trading station at Pondicherry, India.

1674 Sivaji Bhonsla, leader of the Marathas, breaks away from Moguls and founds a Maratha state in India.

1676 Uprising of Sikhs, a reformed Hindu sect, in India.

The Sikh Golden Temple, Amritsar, rebuilt in 1766 after attacks by the Moguls

The Far East and Australasia

1661 Two Jesuit priests, John Grueber and Albert d'Orville, travel from Beijing, China to Agra, India and become the first Europeans to visit the city of Lhasa, in Tibet.

The Palace of Potala at Lhasa in Tibet, begun in the 17th century, the residence of the dalai lamas, the political and religious rulers of Tibet.

1661-1688 Rule of King Narai of Siam. He tries to resist Dutch attempts to monopolize trade by enlisting French help. This proves unpopular and his dynasty is overthrown, along with the French garrisons.

1662-1722 Rule of the powerful Manchu emperor, K'ang Hsi.

K'ang Hsi, Emperor of China

1663 French missionaries enter Vietnam.

1667 The Dutch extend their possessions in Java.

1679 War between Vietnam and Cambodia. Cambodia loses the Mekong river delta.

The Americas

1663 Europeans settle in Carolina.

1665 England gains New Netherlands (New York and New Jersey), as well as islands in the Caribbean from the Dutch.

1670 Hudson's Bay Company is founded in England to explore and acquire territory in the Hudson Bay area of Canada. They claim the fur trading area of Rupert's Land.

1673 Jacques Marquette and Louis Jolliet, French explorers, reach the headwaters of the Mississippi River.

1674 Plantations in Quebec become French royal colonies.

1675-1676 War between settlers and Native Americans in New England. Settlers win control of the North American seaboard.

1679 Robert de la Salle, a French explorer, explores the Great Lakes.

Map of the Great Lakes

Lake Superior
Lake Huron
Lake Ontario
Niagara Falls, explored by de la Salle
Lake Michigan
Lake Erie
Niagara Falls

Colonial expansion in the 17th century

In the 17th century, European trading companies, such as the East India Companies, were given monopolies by their governments, granting them the sole right to trade in an area. The companies set up trading stations overseas and acquired land, and this sometimes developed into a colony. So many early colonies were founded, not by nations, but by groups of traders or settlers.

English East India Company coat of arms

Much of South America was colonized by the Spaniards and Portuguese in the 16th and 17th centuries. But, as their power declined, the Dutch, English and French became major trading rivals in India and the Far East. The Dutch soon established a trading monopoly in the rich "spice islands" of the East Indies.

But it was North America and the Caribbean that attracted the greatest numbers of settlers, either in search of religious freedom or to find new land. Plantations were established, for crops such as sugar and tobacco. From about **1660** until the early 19th century, large numbers of slaves were shipped from West Africa to work on them.

Dutch East India Company base at Hugly in India

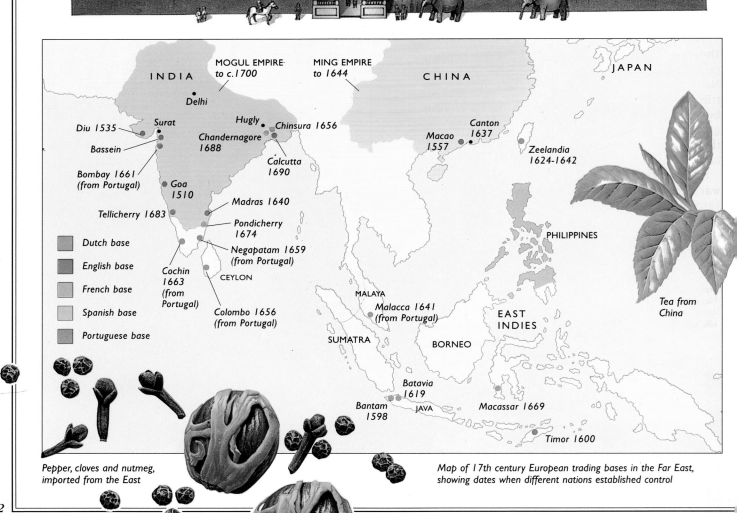

Map key

- Dutch base
- English base
- French base
- Spanish base
- Portuguese base

INDIA

MOGUL EMPIRE to c.1700

MING EMPIRE to 1644

CHINA

JAPAN

Delhi

Diu 1535
Surat
Hugly
Chinsura 1656
Chandernagore 1688
Bassein
Bombay 1661 (from Portugal)
Goa 1510
Calcutta 1690
Tellicherry 1683
Madras 1640
Pondicherry 1674
Negapatam 1659 (from Portugal)
Cochin 1663 (from Portugal)
CEYLON
Colombo 1656 (from Portugal)

Macao 1557
Canton 1637
Zeelandia 1624-1642

PHILIPPINES

MALAYA
Malacca 1641 (from Portugal)
SUMATRA

EAST INDIES
BORNEO

Tea from China

Batavia 1619
Bantam 1598
JAVA
Macassar 1669
Timor 1600

Pepper, cloves and nutmeg, imported from the East

Map of 17th century European trading bases in the Far East, showing dates when different nations established control

102

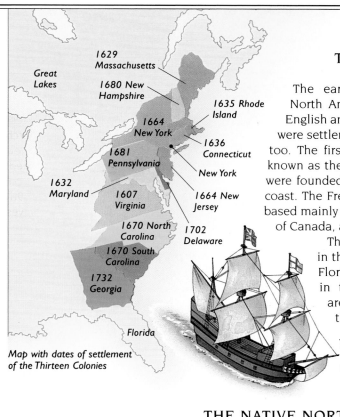

1629 Massachusetts
Great Lakes
1680 New Hampshire
1635 Rhode Island
1664 New York
1636 Connecticut
1681 Pennsylvania
New York
1632 Maryland
1607 Virginia
1664 New Jersey
1670 North Carolina
1702 Delaware
1670 South Carolina
1732 Georgia
Florida

Map with dates of settlement of the Thirteen Colonies

THE NORTH AMERICAN COLONIES

The earliest colonists in North America were mostly English and French. But there were settlers from other places too. The first English colonies, known as the Thirteen Colonies, were founded all along the East coast. The French colonists were based mainly in the eastern parts of Canada, and in Louisiana.

The Spaniards settled in the southwest and in Florida, and Germans in the central inland areas. The Dutch were the first to have a colony in New York (originally New Amsterdam). They also had a base in Guiana (in South America) and on the Caribbean island of Curaçao.

The Mayflower, which took the first Pilgrim colonists to Massachusetts in 1620

English   French
Spanish
Bermuda 1609
Antigua 1632
Haiti 1655
Martinique 1635
Jamaica
St. Christopher 1627
Nevis 1628
Curaçao   Montserrat 1632
Colonies in the West Indies
Guadeloupe 1635
Barbados 1625

THE NATIVE NORTH AMERICAN WARS

The earliest settlers lived peacefully alongside the Native North American tribes, but tensions built up as the rapid growth of colonies threatened their land and way of life.

There were major wars between the settlers and the Native Americans in the 17th and early 18th centuries - the Pequot War (**1636-1637**) and King Philip's War (**1675-1676**) - and uprisings in North and South Carolina (**1712-1716**). The settlers won many victories and destroyed important native settlements.

Despite frequent wars, the number of settlers continued to grow, and the Native Americans were gradually driven farther West. But, as settlers moved West, there was fighting there too. By **1810**, most Native American land in the eastern states was under settler control. Finally, from **1820** to **1840**, Native Americans were driven from their territory in the southern states too. As a result of wars and diseases, their numbers had been devastated. By **1890**, the surviving Native Americans were confined to areas of land called reservations set up by the U.S. government.

Early settlers

Native American eagle dance

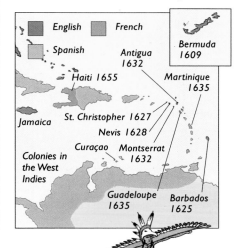

Traditional Native North American village life

Southern and Western Europe

1685 The revocation of the Edict of Nantes forces half a million Huguenots (French Protestants) to flee France.

1685 Catholic James II becomes King of England. A Protestant uprising on behalf of Charles's illegitimate son, the Duke of Monmouth, is defeated.

1686 League of Augsburg: HRE, Spain, Sweden, Saxony, Bavaria and the Palatinate ally against France.

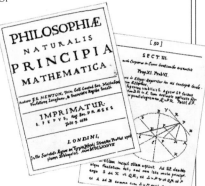

1687 Isaac Newton publishes the *Principia*, containing his three Laws of Motion and theory of gravitation.

Above: pages from Newton's book, the Principia
Left: device designed to demonstrate Newton's Third Law of Motion

1688-1689 Glorious Revolution in England: The House of Lords invites William of Orange to save England from Catholicism. James II flees to France. Reign of William III and Mary II (**1689-1702**).

William III and his wife Mary II, James II's daughter

1688-1697 War of League of Augsburg.

1689 Parliament confirms the abdication of James II. Declaration of Rights safeguards Parliament and bars Catholics from throne.

1690 Battle of the Boyne: Irish Catholic supporters of the exiled James II are defeated by English forces.

1692 Massacre of Scottish clan MacDonald at Glencoe by Campbell clansmen.

1697 Treaty of Rijswick ends the War of the League of Augsburg. France recognizes William III as the King of England and the Protestant succession of Queen Anne.

1698 England, France, United Provinces and HRE agree on the Spanish succession. Charles II of Spain makes a will, leaving his possessions to the Elector Prince of Bavaria.

1699 The death of the Elector of Bavaria.

Northern and Eastern Europe

1682 Sighting of Great Comet (named Halley's Comet) by Edmund Halley. The comet had also appeared in **1066**, before the Battle of Hastings, and in **1531** and **1607**.

Halley's Comet shown in the Bayeux tapestry, made after the Battle of Hastings

1682 Princess Sophia is regent of Russia.

1683 Ottoman Turks besiege Vienna and fail. The Turkish threat in Europe declines and Austrian power grows.

Battle plan of Vienna during the siege

1684 The Holy League (Holy Roman Empire, Poland and Venice) is formed by Pope Innocent XI to fight the Turks.

1687 Battle of Mohacs: Turks are defeated and Hungary becomes a hereditary Hapsburg possession.

1689-1725 Reign of Peter the Great of Russia. Russia becomes a major European power.

Peter the Great

1690 Turks take Belgrade, Serbia, in a counterattack against the Austrian empire.

1691 War continues between Austria and the Ottomans. The Turks are defeated at Zelankemen. The Hapsburgs conquer Transylvania, which is brought under their control.

1695-1706 Russo-Turkish War: Peter the Great fails to take Azov, a major fort on the Black Sea, and returns to Moscow.

1696 Russia captures Azov and Kamchatka, a peninsula at the easternmost end of the continent.

1697 Battle of Zenta: Prince Eugene of Savoy defeats the Ottoman Turks.

1699 Treaty of Karlowitz: the Austrians recover Hungary, Croatia and Transylvania from the Turks. Poland takes the Turkish Ukraine. Venice gains Peloponnese and Podolia.

Africa, India and the Middle East

1680 Death of Sivaji Bhonsla, great leader of the Hindu Marathas in India.

Sivaji Bhonsla

1680-1708 The French increase their trading activities in Madagascar and Nigeria.

1681 India: Prince Akbar leads an unsuccessful revolt against his father, Aurangzeb, and flees to the Deccan.

1686 Madagascar annexed by French East India Company.

1687 English East India Company transfers headquarters from Surat to Bombay.

c.1690 The Mogul empire reaches its greatest extent.

Map of India

- Kabul
- Kandahar
- Amritsar
- Delhi

I N D I A

- Surat
- Calcutta
- Bombay
- DECCAN
- Madras
- Pondicherry

Mogul empire in c.1690

Maratha territories in 1680

CEYLON

1690 The English establish a trading base in Calcutta, India.

1697-1712 Expansion of the Ashanti kingdom in West Africa.

The Ashanti were famous for their carving in gold.

The Far East and Australasia

1680 The Dutch join together their territories in the East Indies.

1683 Manchus conquer Formosa (Taiwan).

1683 Dutch traders are admitted to Canton, China.

1684 Dutch take control in Java.

1685 Chinese ports are opened to foreign trade.

1688 Death of King Narai of Siam. Siamese policies become isolationist until the **1850s**.

King Narai on an elephant

Subjects bowing down before the King

1688 William Dampier, an English adventurer who grew rich raiding Spanish New World settlements, explores Australia on a world trip.

1697 Chinese conquer western Mongolia.

1698 First French legation to China.

1699 Dampier leads a naval expedition to the Pacific, which increases European knowledge of the South Seas.

William Dampier, who may have been the inspiration for Daniel Defoe's novel, Robinson Crusoe

The Americas

1680 Portuguese establish the colony of Sacramento, Uruguay.

1681 William Penn, an English Quaker, is granted a charter to found colony of Pennsylvania.

1682 Robert de la Salle (French) founds St. Louis and takes the Mississippi Valley.

De la Salle exploring Mississippi River

1683 William Penn founds Philadelphia and the Quaker colony of Pennsylvania. Arrival of the first German immigrants. Penn makes a treaty with the Native Americans, which keeps Pennsylvania at peace.

The Native North Americans often smoked a peace pipe, like this one, after peace was made.

1684 Bermuda becomes an English Crown Colony.

1688 German Quakers in North America make the first protests against slavery.

1691 Massachusetts absorbs the Plymouth colony.

1691 The Carolinas are divided into North and South.

1691 The English found Kingston, Jamaica.

1699 French found Louisiana.

The English Civil War

The English Civil War (**1642-1649**) was the result of a growing rift between the English Parliament and the early Stuart kings, James I (**1603-1625**) and Charles I (**1625-1649**). Parliament felt that the kings were claiming too much power, and wanted more for itself. There were religious differences too. Many MPs were Puritans, while the Stuarts were suspected of having Catholic sympathies. Both kings increasingly tried to rule without the assistance of Parliament.

Charles I on horseback

Discontent grew after **1629**, when Charles I dissolved Parliament and ruled alone for 11 years (**1629-1640**). Fighting broke out between the two sides in **1642**.

The two sides in the Civil War

A Roundhead, supporter of Parliament

A Cavalier, or Royalist, supporter of the King

By **1646**, Parliament had won the Civil War, with the help of the New Model Army, established by Oliver Cromwell. Fighting began again between **1648-1649**, ending in the defeat and execution of Charles I.

Civil War helmet

Execution of Charles I, shown in a contemporary print

THE COMMONWEALTH

England was ruled by the House of Commons from **1649-1653**, a time known as the Commonwealth. During this period, there was an increase in the activities of religious sects and radical political groups, such as the Levellers and Diggers, who argued for greater democracy and a more equal distribution of the land. In **1653**, Oliver Cromwell took power as Lord Protector, but his death in **1658** left a political vacuum. The Stuarts were restored by Charles I's son, Charles II (**1660-1685**), whose reign is known as the Restoration.

The Crown Jewels date from the Restoration.

CIVIL WAR DATES

1640 Charles I calls Parliament to raise money to put down an uprising of Covenanters (Scottish Puritans).

1642 Edgehill: the first battle between King and Parliament.

1643 Alliance of Parliament and Covenanters against the King.

1644 Battle of Marston Moor: Parliament defeats King and occupies northern England.

1644 Battle of Lostwithiel: King wins control of southwest.

1644 Battle of Tippermuir: Scottish royalists defeat the Covenanters.

1645 Battle of Naseby: Parliament defeats King and wins control of the country.

1646 King surrenders to Scots.

1651 Charles II tries to regain the throne at Worcester, but is defeated and flees to France.

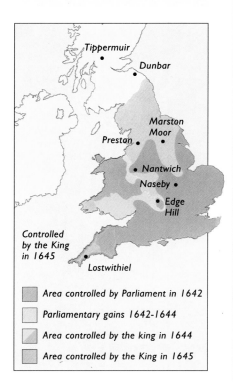

Controlled by the King in 1645

- Area controlled by Parliament in 1642
- Parliamentary gains 1642-1644
- Area controlled by the king in 1644
- Area controlled by the King in 1645

England, Scotland and Wales in the Civil War

France under Louis XIV

Under Louis XIV (**1643-1715**), France became the dominant power in Europe. Louis won a whole series of brilliant military victories, which extended France's boundaries. But many European powers feared his ambitions and formed leagues to fight him. Despite some major defeats at the end of his reign, France's power and prestige lasted for over a century. The economy was modernized under finance minister Colbert (**1619-1683**), and France extended her colonial empire in North America.

Louis XIV

Louis was able to control his nobles, and to exercise absolute power himself. He is famous for his claim: "*L'état, c'est moi.*" ("I am the state.").

Louis was nicknamed the "Sun King". This image is from his palace at Versailles.

Louis's autocratic rule set an example for other European rulers. He has been called the perfect absolute monarch. Absolutism is the belief that the power of the state is embodied in one person (the king), who does not have to answer to anyone. This idea was developed by theorists such as Thomas Hobbes (**1588-1679**) and Jean Bodin (**1530-1596**).

French influence on European culture was at its height during Louis's reign. Literature, music and drama all flourished, with writers such as Pierre Corneille (**1606-1684**), Jean Racine (**1639-1699**), Jean Molière (**1622-1673**) and Jean de la Fontaine (**1621-1695**). French became the official language of European diplomacy.

IMPORTANT DATES

1659 Peace of the Pyrenees between France and Spain. Louis marries Spanish princess.

1667-1668 War of Devolution against Spain.

1670 France occupies Lorraine.

1672-1678 War with UP (United Provinces).

1673 HRE, Lorraine, Spain and the UP ally against France.

1678 Peace of Nijmegen ends the war with Spain and UP. France acquires Franche-Comté.

1681 Strasbourg is annexed.

1682 HRE and Spain form a defensive league against France.

1684 France invades Spanish Netherlands and Luxembourg.

1686 The League of Augsburg forms (HRE, Sweden, Spain, Saxony, Bavaria and Palatinate).

1688-1697 War of the League of Augsburg: Louis takes Heidelberg and keeps Strasbourg.

1701-1714 War of the Spanish Succession.

The expansion of France map

BRABANT

SPANISH NETHERLANDS

• Cologne

Frankfurt •

• Luxembourg

French boundary 1714

• Paris

LORRAINE

• Strasbourg

FRANCE

FRANCHE-COMTÉ

SWISS CANTONS

French gains under Louis:
- 1659-1679
- 1643-1659
- 1679-1697

The expansion of France under Louis XIV

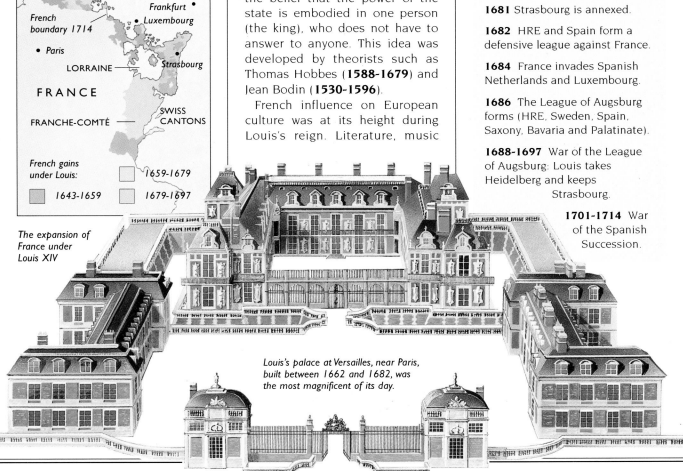

Louis's palace at Versailles, near Paris, built between 1662 and 1682, was the most magnificent of its day.

Japan - shoguns and samurai

From the 9th century, Japan was divided by civil wars between feuding families competing for power at court. In **1192**, Minamoto Yorikomo won control, taking the title *shogun* (hereditary military ruler). Although the emperors were revered as gods, from this time on they were honorary rulers only, delegating their authority to the shoguns. Between **1337** and **1573**, real power passed into the hands of the *daimyo*, local warlords who fought each other, and rebelled against the shoguns. This is known as the Ashikaga Period.

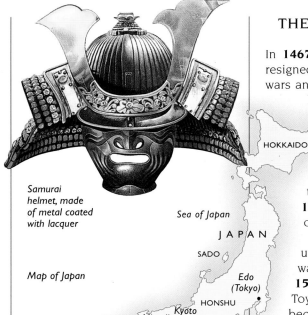

Samurai helmet, made of metal coated with lacquer

Map of Japan

HOKKAIDO

Sea of Japan

JAPAN

SADO

Edo (Tokyo)

HONSHU

Himeji Kyoto

Hiroshima Osaka

TSUSHIMA

SHIKOKU

GOTO Nagasaki

KYUSHU PACIFIC OCEAN

THE SAMURAI

Daimyos lived in fortified castle towns and employed huge armies. They inspired loyalty from the *samurai*, an elite caste of fierce professional warriors.

Samurai warriors

WEAPONS

Military specialists, known as *gunpaisha*, were taken on to study the art of warfare and improve weapons.

Samurai sword, scabbard and sword guard

THE PROVINCIAL WARS

In **1467**, the last Ashikaga shogun resigned, after a series of internal wars and peasant uprisings had left him powerless. This led to the Onin War (**1467-1477**) between rival clans. The Onin War was swiftly followed by a series of wars, known as the Provincial Wars (**1477-1568**), ending with the victory of Oda Nobunaga.

Nobunaga began a drive to unify the country. Although he was killed in a rebellion in **1582**, he was succeeded by Toyotomi Hideyoshi, who became the Emperor's chief minister and continued to work for national unity. From **1591**, until his death in **1598**, the country was under Hideyoshi's control.

Himeji Castle, taken over by Toyotomi Hideyoshi in 1577

Toyotomi Hideyoshi

JAPAN UNDER THE TOKUGAWAS

After Hideyoshi's death, there was a new struggle for power, and civil war broke out between the two main rivals. In **1600**, Ieyasu Tokugawa, a descendent of the Minamoto clan, won the Battle of Sekigahara. In **1603**, he became shogun and founder of the Tokugawa dynasty.

Part of a Japanese folding screen showing a siege at Osaka Castle in 1615

The Tokugawa family ruled Japan from their new capital, Edo (Tokyo), until **1867**. Under the Tokugawas, Japan was strictly organized into social classes. There was a new system of *daimyo* and *han* (fiefs), closely regulated by the shogun.

Japanese maple leaves

THE POLICY OF ISOLATION

After **1639**, Japan became virtually isolated from European contact until the **1850s**. This was a deliberate policy of the Tokugawas, who were afraid Japan would be invaded or influenced by a foreign power. The powerful ruler, Iemitsu Tokugawa (**1623-1651**), forbade all Japanese to travel abroad.

A wealthy Japanese woman parading new fashions, one of the great sights of Edo

At the same time, Iemitsu also expelled existing foreign merchants and missionaries, and banned others from setting foot in Japan. The only exceptions were Dutch and Chinese merchants, who were allowed to trade in Nagasaki Bay. But they were restricted to an island in the Bay, and were not allowed to enter the mainland.

During this period of peace and isolation, towns grew and trade flourished. By the 18th century, Edo had about a million inhabitants, and was possibly the largest city in the world at the time. By the early 19th century, Japan had developed into a literate, prosperous and well-governed society.

The Dutch traders' colony on an island in Nagasaki Bay

THE END OF THE DYNASTY

In **1853**, U.S. warships under the command of Commodore Perry forced Japan to open its ports to foreign trade. From this time on, European contacts with Japan increased. It was a period of weakness and unrest for the Tokugawas.

In **1868**, the Emperor, left Kyoto and took back power in Edo, replacing the last shogun. He started to modernize the country and set up a parliament in the western style. This is called the Meiji Restoration.

Japanese drawing of the white foreigners who appeared in their colony after 1853

The young Emperor leaving Kyoto and returning to Edo, to take back power from the shogun

Southern and Western Europe

1701-1714 War of the Spanish Succession (see page 120).

1702-1714 The reign of Queen Anne, the last of the Stuarts.

1704 England seizes Gibraltar from Spain.

Queen Anne

1704 The Battle of Blenheim. Victory for Anglo-Austrians, led by the Duke of Marlborough and Prince Eugene of Savoy, saves Vienna from the French and Bavarians.

1706 Thomas Newcomen, an English engineer, invents the first practical working steam engine for use in coal mining.

1707 The Union of England and Scotland. The British Isles become known as Great Britain.

The English flag (the St. George's cross, top) and the Scottish flag (the St. Andrew's cross, middle) are combined to make the Union Jack (bottom), which is adopted as the national flag.

1709 Bartolomeo Cristofori (Italian) builds the first piano.

1710 St. Paul's Cathedral in London is completed.

St. Paul's Cathedral, built by Sir Christopher Wren

1713-1714 Peace of Utrecht ends the War of the Spanish Succession. Sicily is given to Savoy.

1714-1727 Reign of George I of Great Britain, the first king of the German house of Hanover.

1715 Uprising in Scotland by Jacobites, supporters of James Edward, son of James II and pretender to the throne.

1718 Quadruple alliance is formed by Austria, Britain, France and Netherlands against Spain.

Northern and Eastern Europe

c.1700 Peak of great age of Baroque music in Europe.

The violin was especially popular in Baroque music.

For the orchestra 1750
Violins 12
Violas 6 } Strings
Cellos 6
Double Basses 6 }
Oboes 2
Bassoons 2 } Wind
Horns 2 }
Harpsichord 1 or 2 } Continuo
Also available ~ Trumpets and drums for festive occasions
Recorders for French and Venetian Opera
Trombones for Church music.

List of instruments in a Baroque orchestra

1700-1721 Great Northern War: a struggle for supremacy in the Baltic between Russia and Sweden. Swedes defeat Russians at Narva (**1700**) and invade Poland (**1701-1702**).

1701 Elector Frederick III of Brandenburg crowns himself Frederick I, "King in Prussia" (**1701-1713**).

1703 Peter the Great of Russia founds St. Petersburg.

Engraving of St. Petersburg

1703-1711 Hungarians revolt against Austria.

1706 Treaty of Altranstadt: Augustus II renounces the Polish throne and is replaced by Stanislaus Leszczynski.

1708-1709 Charles XII of Sweden invades Russia and is defeated at the Battle of Poltava (**1709**).

1710-1711 War between Russia and Turkey.

1710 Russia conquers Swedish Baltic provinces.

1716-1718 War between Turkey and Austria ends with Peace of Passarowitz: Turkey cedes Belgrade to Austria and Hungary is liberated from Austria.

1719 Russians invade Sweden. A coalition of Denmark, Sweden, Prussia and Britain is formed to oppose Russia.

Africa and India

c.1700-1712 West Africa: Ashanti kingdom continues to expand. Yoruba kingdom declines.

c.1700 East Africa: rise of the Bantu kingdom of Buganda.

Ashanti leather and brass shield, and gold cockerel

c.1700 Oman controls Zanzibar and extends its influence along the East African coast at Portuguese expense.

1705 Turkish rule is overthrown in Tunis and Hussain Ibn Ali establishes the Hussainid dynasty.

1707 Mogul empire disintegrates after the death of Aurangzeb.

1708 English East India Company possessions are divided into Bengal, Madras and Bombay.

1708 Revolution in Ethiopia.

1711 Tripoli becomes independent from Turkey.

1712-1755 West Africa: growth of Bambara kingdoms of the Upper Niger.

1714 Ahmed Bey sets up Karamanli dynasty in Tripoli.

1714-1720 The Marathas increase their territory in northern India.

Maratha soldier

1715 French take control in Mauritius.

Asia and Australasia

1700 English East India Company establishes a base in Borneo.

1700 William Dampier, an English navigator, discovers the north coast of New Guinea.

1707 Last eruption of Mount Fujiyama in Japan.

1709-1711 Afghans rise against their Persian overlords and set up an independent Afghan state.

1714-1733 Reign of King Taninganway Min of Burma. Flourishing period of Burmese culture and power.

1715 China conquers Mongolia and East Turkestan.

1715 British East India Company builds first factory at Canton, China.

The port of Canton in the 18th century

1716 Emperor K'ang Hsi prohibits the teaching of Christianity in China.

1716-1745 Rule of Shogun Yoshimune of Japan.

1717 The Bugis from Selangor extend their influence in Johore.

The Americas

1701 French set up base at Detroit to control the trade in Illinois.

1701 Yale College is founded in New Haven, Connecticut.

1701 Peace treaty between French and Native Americans in New France (Canada).

A lacrosse stick and ball, a game adopted from the Native Americans. The name is said to have come from the resemblance between a lacrosse stick and the cross carried by a bishop.

1703 Delaware becomes a colony.

1709 First German settlers arrive in North America.

1713 Britain acquires Nova Scotia, Hudson Bay and Newfoundland from France.

1714-1716 War between French and Native North Americans in New France (Canada).

1718 French found New Orleans.

THE SLAVE TRADE

From the early 18th century until the early 19th century, millions of slaves were shipped from West Africa to work on sugar and cotton plantations in America and the Caribbean. Conditions on board ship were cramped, unhealthy and hot, and more than a million died en route.

Diagram of a slave ship, showing the cramped conditions

A head of cotton

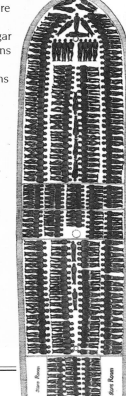

The Enlightenment

The Enlightenment is a term used to describe a change in philosophy and outlook which came about in Europe between **c.1650-1750**. Its base was in France, although contributions also came from Britain, Italy, Germany and the U.S.A. The Enlightenment was made up of many different elements. At its heart was an optimistic belief in the powers of reason, or rational thought, and human progress, and an intense curiosity to find out about new things, both through science and exploration.

Royal Society coat of arms

Forms of life new to 18th century European explorers

Breadfruit

Butterfly fish

One of the greatest achievements was the vast *Encyclopédie*, compiled by Denis Diderot in France from **1751-1776**. It set out to record the total stock of knowledge at the time.

Engraving of a canal lock from the Encyclopédie

The idea that people could themselves discover more about the world posed an important challenge to the authority of the Church, which felt threatened. Although most major philosophers and scientists were devout Christians, some key figures, such as Galileo, were imprisoned. Others, including Descartes, had their books banned.

However, a number of European rulers, in particular the so-called "enlightened despots", supported the new ideas. They introduced reforms, such as religious toleration, and founded universities, scientific societies and other institutions. In Britain, the Royal Society was set up in **1662**, as a forum for ideas. Its members were mainly doctors, philosophers, and writers. In **1666**, the Académie Royale des Sciences was founded in France. Closely run by the king, its members were all salaried scientists.

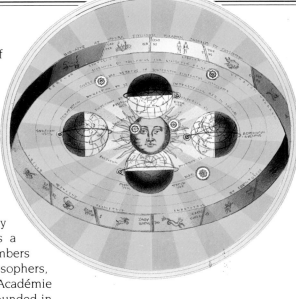

Diagram demonstrating Kepler's view of how planets move around the Sun (see page opposite)

IMPORTANT ENLIGHTENMENT PEOPLE

René Descartes (**1596-1650**), French mathematician and philosopher, who stressed reason and logic. Seen as the founder of modern philosophy.

Galileo Galilei (**1564-1642**), Italian mathematician, astronomer and physicist. He was the first to suggest the use of a pendulum to measure time.

Reconstruction of Galileo's pendulum escapement, inside a mechanical clock

Immanuel Kant (**1724-1804**), German philosopher, who explored the role of reason in human experience and the limits of knowledge.

Johannes Kepler (**1571-1630**), German-born astronomer, who defined three laws of planetary movement.

Pendulum swing

Isaac Newton (**1642-1727**), English physicist, philosopher, astronomer and mathematician.

Thomas Paine (**1737-1809**), American political pamphleteer and author of *The Rights of Man* and *The Age of Reason*.

Jean-Jacques Rousseau (**1712-1778**), French writer and philosopher, who influenced the ideas of the French Revolution.

Adam Smith (**1723-1790**), Scottish economist whose writings formed the basis for modern economics.

Voltaire (**1694-1778**) (François Marie Arouet), French writer and philosopher. Clashed with both Church and State over his criticism of intolerance and tyranny.

Bust of Voltaire

A louse illustrated in Hooke's 'Micrographia'

SCIENTIFIC DISCOVERIES IN THE 17TH AND 18TH CENTURIES

The Enlightenment stimulated scientific thought, which resulted in inventions and discoveries in all areas of science. Here are some of the most important ones.

1605 Johannes Kepler (German) discovers the principle of the telescope.

1609 Galileo Galilei (Italian) works on the motion of falling bodies and the pendulum.

1609-1619 Kepler formulates his laws on the movement of planets. He shows that planets move around the Sun in ellipses, not circles.

1610 Galileo publishes *The Starry Messenger*, concerning observations of stars and planets with his telescope.

1614 John Napier (Scottish) invents logarithms and works on decimals.

1628 William Harvey (English) publishes his book *De motu cordis*, on the circulation of the blood.

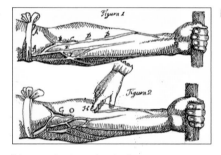

Diagram showing valves in the veins from Harvey's book

1637 René Descartes (French) does important work on analytical geometry. His major scientific work *Principles of Philosophy* is published in **1644**.

1642 Blaise Pascal (French) designs an adding machine.

1643 Evangelista Torricelli (Italian) invents the mercury barometer, used for measuring atmospheric pressure.

Torricelli with his barometer

1656 Christian Huygens (Dutch) builds the first pendulum clock, based on Galileo's ideas.

1661 Robert Boyle (Irish) publishes his book *The Sceptical Chymist*, concerning the properties of gases and defining chemical elements.

1665 Robert Hooke (English) publishes drawings made with the help of new microscopes.

1666 Isaac Newton (English) defines the laws of gravity, which he publishes in his book *Principia* in **1687**.

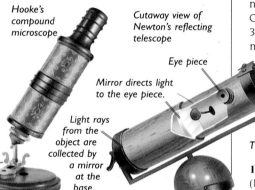

Hooke's compound microscope

Cutaway view of Newton's reflecting telescope

Eye piece

Mirror directs light to the eye piece.

Light rays from the object are collected by a mirror at the base.

1668 Isaac Newton builds a new reflecting telescope, which reduces blurring.

1718 Gabriel Fahrenheit (German) invents the mercury thermometer.

1735 Carolus Linnaeus (Swedish) compiles a classification of nature in his *Systema Naturae*.

1742 Anders Celsius (Swedish) invents the centigrade thermometer.

An early Celsius thermometer

1752 Benjamin Franklin (American) invents the lightning conductor.

1766 Henry Cavendish (English) identifies the gas hydrogen.

1771 Karl Scheele (Swedish) discovers oxygen.

1777 James Watt (Scottish) designs a steam engine, which leads to the use of steam power in industry.

Watt's steam engine

1779 Antoine Lavoisier (French) shows that air consists of oxygen and nitrogen. He publishes *Methods of Chemical Nomenclature* in **1789**. This lists 33 elements, and introduces the modern system for naming them.

1783 Pilâtre de Rozier and the Marquis d'Arlandes (French) make the first ascent in a hot-air ballon built by Joseph and Jacques Montgolfier.

The Montgolfier balloon

1791 Luigi Galvani (Italian) publishes the results of his experiments on dead frogs. They show that fluids in the frog can carry an electrical current between two pieces of metal, although Galvani mistakenly believes the electricity has come from the frog itself.

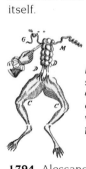

Engraving showing Galvani's experiments with a frog's leg

1794 Alessandro Volta (Italian) builds the first battery.

Southern and Western Europe

1720 The South Sea Bubble: South Sea Company fails in Britain, causing financial panic.

1720 John Law's Mississippi Company collapses in France. This leads to national bankruptcy.

1721-1742 Robert Walpole becomes the first Prime Minister of Great Britain.

Robert Walpole

1725 Treaty of Vienna between Philip V of Spain and Charles VI of Austria. Philip guarantees the Pragmatic Sanction, allowing for the succession of Charles VI's daughter, Maria Theresa.

1726 Russia allies with Austria.

1727-1729 War between Spain and Britain over Gibraltar.

c.1730 Rococo, a highly decorative style applied to architecture and interiors, often including scrolls and shells, reaches the height of its popularity.

Some examples of Rococo furniture and ornaments

1733 Pact between French and Spanish Bourbons.

1733 John Kay (British) invents the flying shuttle loom, which improves weaving.

1734 France invades Lorraine.

1734 Spain takes the kingdom of Naples.

1737 Death of the Grand Duke of Tuscany marks the end of the rule of the Medici in Florence.

1739 John and Charles Wesley found the Methodist movement in Oxford, England. John travels all over the country preaching, especially to the poor.

1739 War of Jenkins' Ear between Britain and Spain, named after a Captain Jenkins who claimed that Spaniards had boarded his ship and cut off his ear.

Centurion, a British battleship used in the war against Spain

Northern and Eastern Europe

1720 Treaty of Stockholm between Sweden, Prussia, Hanover, Denmark, Savoy and Poland.

1721 Peace of Nystadt ends war between Russia and Sweden. Russia makes great gains (Estonia, Livonia and part of Karelia) and ends Swedish domination of the Baltic. Peter the Great is proclaimed Emperor of all the Russias.

Peter the Great's Summer Palace, outside St. Petersburg

1722-1723 War between Russia and Turkey. Russia makes gains on the Caspian Sea.

1725 Treaty of Hanover: alliance between Britain, France, Prussia, Sweden, Denmark and the Netherlands.

1725-1727 Czarina (Empress) Catherine I rules Russia, after the death of her husband, Peter the Great.

Catherine I of Russia

1732 Frederick William I of Prussia introduces military and administrative reforms.

1733 Death of Augustus II, Elector of Saxony and King of Poland.

1733-1738 War of the Polish Succession. France and Sweden support Stanislaus Leszczynski. Austria and Russia support Augustus II's son. Treaty of Vienna ends the war and Augustus III succeeds to the throne.

1735-1739 War between Russia and Turkey. Russia obtains the port of Azov and expands to reach the Black Sea.

Africa and India

1721 The French annex Mauritius.

1723 British Africa Company acquires land in Gambia.

1724 Hyderabad wins independence from the Moguls.

1726 France establishes a settlement on the Seychelle Islands.

1727 The death of Mulai Ismail in Morocco is followed by a period of anarchy.

1729 Portugal loses Mombasa, capital of Portuguese East Africa since **1593**, to the Arabs.

1731-1743 West Africa (northern Nigeria): war between Kano and Bornu. Sultan of Bornu becomes overlord of Kano.

Bornu horsemen

1735 French East India Company sets up sugar industry on Mauritius.

1737 The Marathas extend their power in northern India.

1737-1739 Nadir Khan of Persia occupies northern and western India and attacks Delhi. He takes Jahan's peacock throne back to Persia.

1739 Anglo-Maratha Treaty allows the British to trade in the Deccan.

Asia and Australasia

1720 China conquers Tibet.

Pandas, native to northwest China and Tibet

1721 China suppresses a revolt in Formosa (Taiwan).

1721-1722 Jacob Roggeveen (Dutch) discovers Samoa, the Solomons and Easter Island.

Statues on Easter Island

1722-1730 Afghans invade Persia, bringing an end to Safavid rule. The Afghans are expelled in **1730**.

1727 Treaty between Russia and China settles borders.

1736-1747 Persia is ruled by Nadir Khan.

1736-1796 China is ruled by the powerful emperor, Ch'ien Lung, who reorganizes the empire and reduces European influence. During his reign, China prospers and the population increases.

1737-1747 Nadir Khan occupies Afghanistan.

The Americas

1726 Spanish first settle in Montevideo, Uruguay.

1727 Coffee is planted in Brazil.

1727 Quakers (a Christian sect founded in **c.1650**) demand the abolition of slavery.

1728 Vitus Bering, a Danish navigator, discovers the Bering Straits between Russia and America.

Detail of map drawn by Bering

Wolf and polar bears, native to the region

1729 North and South Carolina become British crown colonies.

1730 First sugar cane refinery is established in New York. The success of sugar cane plantations in the Caribbean, worked by slaves imported from Africa, leads to the expansion of the trade in sugar.

1733 Georgia, the last of the 13 Colonies, is founded.

1737 Founding of Richmond, Virginia.

Sugar cane and sugar plantation

Peter the Great

Peter the Great was one of the greatest rulers in Russian history. From **1682**, at the age of 10, he was joint czar with the regent, Princess Sophia. He became sole ruler in **1689** when he was 17, until his death in **1725**. Peter was responsible for the start of Russia's rise to greatness. By the end of the 18th century, it had become one of the major European powers.

Peter the Great

Map of Russia under Peter the Great

Russia in 1689

Expansion 1689-1725 (under Peter)

Expansion by the end of the 18th century

The Winter Palace at St. Petersburg. The building of the city began in Peter's reign and continued under his successors, the empresses Anna, Elizabeth and Catherine II.

MILITARY SUCCESS

Peter founded a navy, built up a strong army, and won brilliant victories against both Turkey and Sweden (in the Great Northern War: **1700-1721**).

Dragoon officer in Peter's army

This extended Russia's boundaries, making her stronger and safer. Russia moved into the mainstream of European politics, and Swedish domination of the Baltic came to an end.

Cathedral of St. Peter and Paul, St. Petersburg

BUILDING A MODERN STATE

Although his methods were often ruthless and cruel, Peter forced through reforms which helped to modernize and strengthen the country. He improved education, and introduced new industries and foreign craftsmen.

His aim was to turn Russia into a strong, westernized European power. He built St. Petersburg, a new city on the Baltic Sea, to give himself a "window on the West", and moved the capital there from Moscow in **1703**.

Despite all this, most people in Russia continued to live as serfs (landless peasants), in a society that stayed conservative and rural, without a strong urban middle class.

To enforce western styles, Peter ordered long beards to be cut, as shown in this cartoon.

The rise of Prussia

At the beginning of the 17th century, Prussia was a weak duchy under the overlordship of Poland, ruled by the Elector of Brandenburg, who held scattered territories within the Holy Roman Empire. Yet in a little over 200 years, Prussia rose to become the nucleus of a great German state.

THE GREAT ELECTOR

The rise began under Frederick William, the Great Elector (**1640-1688**). He built up a powerful army and increased his territory. His successor, Frederick III, was granted the title "King in Prussia" by the Emperor, and crowned himself Frederick I in **1701**. All his territories,

Prussian foot soldier

including Brandenburg, became known as Prussia. The country began to develop into a strong military state under his son, Frederick William I (**1713-1740**).

FREDERICK THE GREAT

Frederick William's son, Frederick II, known as "the Great" (**1740-1786**), was a brilliant soldier. In the first year of his reign, he invaded Silesia and provoked war with Austria. By **1772**, he had joined together the Prussian territories, making Prussia the strongest German state after Austria.

Frederick was also a talented musician and was interested in the ideas of the Enlightenment (see page 112-113). Although he was an absolute ruler (who kept power

Crown decorating the throne of Frederick II

firmly in his own hands), he also tried to modernize the country, and to provide strong but efficient government in the interests of his people. He promoted education, agriculture and industry, brought in a fairer legal system, abolished torture and censorship, and declared religious freedom.

Prussia in 17th and 18th centuries

Map key:
- Territory ruled by Brandenburg in 1648
- Territory acquired 1648-1740
- Territory acquired by Frederick II

(Map labels: EAST PRUSSIA, WEST PRUSSIA, Berlin, Potsdam, SILESIA, BRANDENBURG)

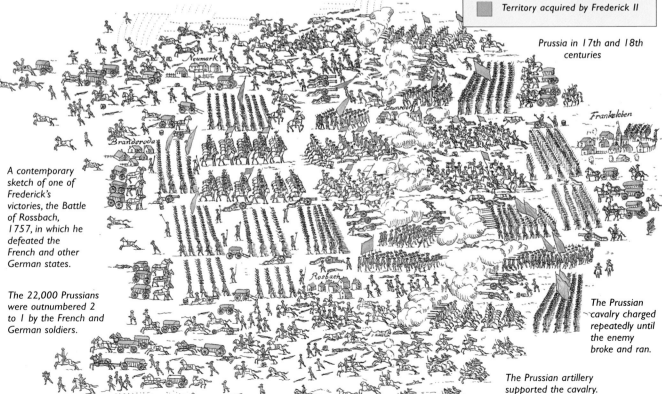

A contemporary sketch of one of Frederick's victories, the Battle of Rossbach, 1757, in which he defeated the French and other German states.

The 22,000 Prussians were outnumbered 2 to 1 by the French and German soldiers.

The Prussian cavalry charged repeatedly until the enemy broke and ran.

The Prussian artillery supported the cavalry.

Southern and Western Europe

1740 Death of Charles VI of Austria and succession of his daughter, Maria Theresa (**1740-1780**), leads to the War of the Austrian Succession (**1740-1748**).

1744 War breaks out between France and Britain in Europe, India, North America and the West Indies and lasts intermittently until **1815**.

1744 Sighting of the most-tailed comet on record, the De Chéseaux comet. It had at least six bright tails.

The De Chéseaux comet of 1744

1745 Second Jacobite uprising in Scotland attempts to put Charles Edward Stuart (Bonnie Prince Charlie) on the throne of England and Scotland. Jacobites are defeated by the English at Culloden (**1746**).

Bonnie Prince Charlie (1720-1788)

1746 France seizes the Austrian Netherlands (Belgium). They are restored to Austria in **1748**.

1748 Georges de Buffon (French) publishes 36 volume survey of natural history. He suggests fossils provide evidence of extinct species.

1748 Peace of Aix-la-Chapelle ends War of the Austrian Succession.

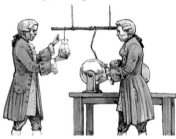

Fossil of a trilobite, an extinct sea creature

1750-1777 Reign of José I of Portugal. The chief minister, the Marquis de Pombal, is virtual military dictator from **1775**.

1755 Corsicans rise against Genoese rule.

1755 Earthquake destroys Lisbon, Portugal.

1756 Joseph Black (Scottish) produces carbon dioxide by heating chemicals.

1756 Alliances formed between Austria and France; and Britain and Prussia.

1756-1763 Seven Years' War caused by rivalry between Austria and Prussia in Europe and Britain and France in America.

French Royal Navy Commander 1763

1759 Spain joins the Franco-Austrian alliance.

Northern and Eastern Europe

1740 Frederick II of Prussia invades Silesia.

1741 Ivan VI of Russia is deposed and replaced by Empress Elizabeth (**1741-1762**), Peter the Great's daughter. German influence and the power of the nobles increase.

1741 French, Bavarian and Saxon troops occupy Prague. Charles Albert of Bavaria is recognized as King of Bohemia.

1744 Frederick II of Prussia invades Bohemia, but is repelled by Austrians and Saxons.

1745 Ewald von Kleist, a German priest, invents the Leiden jar, an instrument that stores electricity.

A Leiden jar being charged with static electricity from a generator

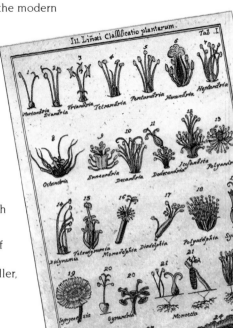

French playing card c.1750 showing a demonstration of static electricity

1746 Russia and Austria ally against Prussia.

1747 Sweden allies with Prussia. Russia allies with Britain.

1749-1832 Life of Johann Wolfgang von Goethe, German poet, novelist and playwright.

1753 Carl von Linné, also known as Linnaeus, a Swedish botanist, publishes his system for classifying plants, the starting point for the modern classification of species.

A page from Linnaeus's Systema Naturae

1757 Russia joins the Franco-Austrian alliance and invades East Prussia. Prussian victory at Rossbach and Leuthen.

1759-1805 Life of Johann Christoph Friedrich von Schiller, German poet, playwright and historian.

Africa and India

c.1740 Lunda kingdom of Kazembe is established in Central Africa.

1740-1756 Bengal becomes independent of the Mogul empire.

Bengal tiger

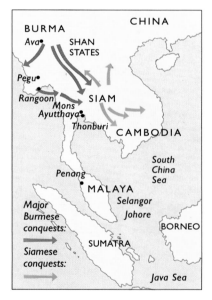

1746 The French take Madras from the British.

1746 East Africa: Mazrui dynasty in Mombasa becomes independent of Oman.

1747-1748 West Africa: Yoruba conquer Dahomey, Benin.

1748 British retake Madras: start of intense Anglo-French rivalry in India.

1751 Robert Clive defeats the French at Arcot: the end of French influence in Madras.

1756 Black Hole of Calcutta: Nawab of Bengal puts 146 British people into a tiny prison and many die.

1757 Clive captures Calcutta and defeats the Nawab of Bengal at Plassey: the start of British supremacy in India.

Indian ivory chess pieces in the form of British and Indian soldiers

1758 The Marathas seize the Punjab and take Lahore.

Asia and Australasia

1743 Mataram, Java becomes a Dutch subject state.

1751-1759 China overruns Tibet, Dzungaria and the Tarim Basin.

1752 The Mons people conquer Upper Burma. The Burmese leader, Alaungpaya, rebels and proclaims himself king. He gains control of most of Upper Burma.

1753 Alaungpaya takes the capital, Ava, and the Shan states.

1755 Alaungpaya seizes Dagon (renamed Rangoon) from the Mons in Lower Burma.

Map showing Burmese and Siamese conquests

1755 Dutch East India Company holds supremacy in Java after war with Javanese Mataram kingdom.

1756 Alaungpaya takes Pegu and now controls all Burma. His dynasty rules until **1885**.

1757-1843 China reduces European influence by restricting foreign trade to Canton.

1758 The Bugis people of Johore recognize Dutch tin trade monopoly.

1758-1759 China conquers East Turkestan.

The Americas

1742 Russians explore Alaska.

Alaskan wildlife

1742 Venezuela becomes a separate province inside the Spanish South American empire.

1744-1748 King George's War, between Britain and France in North America.

1745 Vitus Bering, a Danish navigator, discovers the Aleutian Islands.

1745 Canada: British capture French fortress of Louisbourg.

1748 British return Louisbourg to France, as a part of the peace settlement in Europe.

1750 Boundary commission fails to settle British-French boundary disputes in North America.

1752 Marquis Duquesne is appointed governor of Quebec.

1752 Benjamin Franklin, a publisher and politician from Boston, Massachusetts, shows that lightning is caused by electricity.

1755 French and Native Americans fight against the British in North America.

1759 British troops, led by General Wolfe, capture Quebec from France.

North American trading fort

The War of the Spanish Succession

Shields of the claimants to the Spanish throne, Philip V (top) and Charles III

The War of the Spanish Succession was fought by the major European countries to decide who would inherit the kingdom of the childless Hapsburg king, Charles II of Spain. With land in Italy and the Spanish Netherlands, and rich colonies in America, it was an important prize. There were claims both by the French Bourbons and the Austrian Hapsburgs.

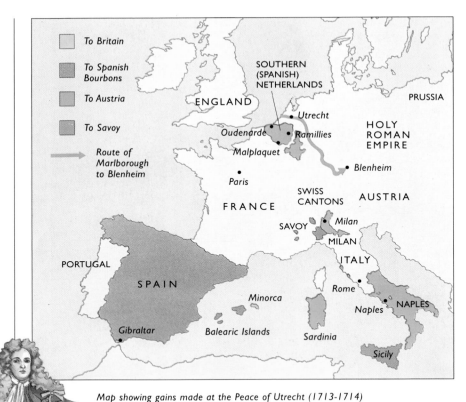

Map showing gains made at the Peace of Utrecht (1713-1714)

THE GRAND ALLIANCE

When Charles II died in **1700**, Louis XIV of France proclaimed his grandson Philip V of Spain. The English and Dutch felt Louis already had too much power and were unwilling to see France and Spain ruled by the same family. In **1701**, they formed an alliance to support Charles, son of Emperor Leopold I. They were joined in **1703** by Portugal and Savoy and won a series of brilliant victories, led by Eugene, Prince of Savoy, and John Churchill, the Duke of Marlborough.

The Duke of Marlborough

Blenheim Palace, near Oxford, England, built for the Duke of Marlborough and named after one of his victories

In **1711**, Charles became Charles VI, of Austria. As this altered the balance of power, the English and Dutch switched support to Philip, on condition that Spain and France should never unite.

By the Peace of Utrecht (**1713-1714**), Philip became Philip V of Spain, and separation between France and Spain was guaranteed. Britain made gains from the French in North America (Nova Scotia, Hudson Bay and Newfoundland), won Gibraltar and Minorca from the Spaniards, and the sole right to supply slaves to Spanish colonies in America. Austria won Spanish land in the Netherlands and Italy, and the Elector of Brandenburg was given the title King of Prussia.

MAJOR BATTLES

1704 Battle of Blenheim: Prince Eugene of Savoy and the Duke of Marlborough defeat the French and Bavarians.

1706 Battle of Ramillies: Duke of Marlborough wins control of the Southern Netherlands.

1708 Battle of Oudenarde: the French are forced to withdraw from the Southern Netherlands and Italy.

1709 Battle of Malplaquet: Prince Eugene and Duke of Marlborough defeat the French.

Maria Theresa

In **1740**, Charles VI of Austria died, leaving his possessions to his 23-year-old daughter, Maria Theresa, who became Archduchess of Austria and Queen of both Bohemia and Hungary (**1740-1780**).

Maria Theresa

Palace of Schönbrunn, Vienna

Although the empire she inherited was decaying and bankrupt, and her title and lands were coveted by other countries, she emerged as one of the greatest rulers in modern history. She not only kept her throne, but also built Austria into a strong, stable power.

MILITARY SUCCESS

Frederick II of Prussia took the opportunity of Charles's death to seize the rich Austrian province of Silesia. Then, Charles Albert of Bavaria (a rival claimant) refused to recognize a woman as Empress. France backed him, hoping to rid Europe of a strong central power, and so ensure French domination.

Austria under Maria Theresa

This led to the War of the Austrian Succession (**1740-1748**). Maria Theresa successfully fought this, and the Seven Years' War (**1756-1763**), to preserve the Austrian empire for the Hapsburgs.

Lipizzaner horse from the Spanish Riding School in Vienna

The School was founded by Charles VI in 1735.

Both these conflicts were wide-reaching, involving Franco-British colonial rivalry in Asia, Africa and America, as well as in Europe. In **1748**, Maria Theresa's husband, Francis of Lorraine, was crowned Emperor Francis I. After his death in **1765**, she ruled alongside her son, Joseph II (**1765-1790**).

THE FLOWERING OF VIENNA

Maria Theresa is remembered not only for Austria's revival as a great political power, but for her magnificent court and palaces. During her long reign, Vienna became one of the cultural capitals of Europe. Painting, architecture and especially music flourished. Musicians who played at her court in Vienna included the six-year-old Wolfgang Amadeus Mozart.

Augarten Park in Vienna, where many concerts were held

Dancing a serenade

Southern and Western Europe

1761 Portugal is invaded by Spain for refusing to close its ports to British ships.

1762 Britain declares war on Spain.

1763 The Peace of Paris ends the Seven Years' War.

1767 James Hargreaves (British) invents Spinning Jenny.

1768 France buys Corsica from Genoa.

The Spinning Jenny, a hand-powered loom

1769 Richard Arkwright (British) invents the water frame, a water-powered spinning machine.

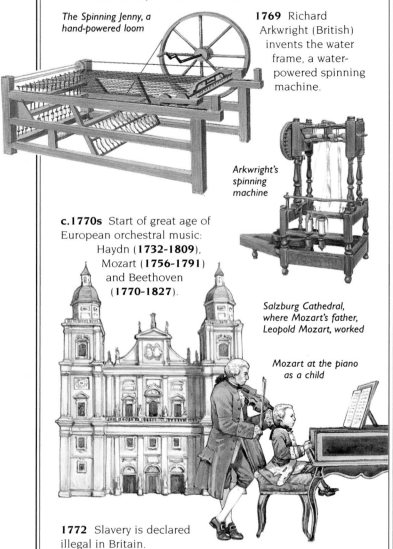

Arkwright's spinning machine

c.1770s Start of great age of European orchestral music: Haydn (**1732-1809**), Mozart (**1756-1791**) and Beethoven (**1770-1827**).

Salzburg Cathedral, where Mozart's father, Leopold Mozart, worked

Mozart at the piano as a child

1772 Slavery is declared illegal in Britain.

1773 Pope Clement XIV suppresses the Jesuit order.

1774 Joseph Priestley, a British scientist, isolates oxygen, which he calls "dephlogisticated air".

1778 France and Holland declare war on Britain in support of the American colonists.

1779 Antoine Lavoisier, a French scientist, confirms the existence of "dephlogisticated air" and names it oxygen.

1779 France and Spain unsuccessfully besiege Gibraltar.

Northern and Eastern Europe

1762-1796 Reign of Catherine II ("the Great") of Russia. A German princess, she marries the heir to the throne, Peter III, and is a party to his murder. Under her rule, Russia extends its boundaries, Russian culture develops and St. Petersburg becomes a magnificent city. She introduces reforms in government and allows religious freedom.

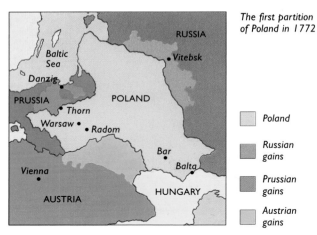

Catherine II's crown

A brooch showing Catherine II

1768-1774 War between Russia and Turkey.

1769 Austria seizes the Polish territories of Lvov and Zips.

1771-1792 Reign of Gustavus III of Sweden.

1772 First partition of Poland by Russia, Prussia and Austria. Russia makes modest gains. Prussia annexes most of the territory between Pomerania and Eastern Prussia. Austria annexes a large area north of Hungary.

The first partition of Poland in 1772

RUSSIA
Baltic Sea
Danzig
Vitebsk
PRUSSIA
POLAND
Thorn
Warsaw • Radom
Bar
Balta
Vienna
HUNGARY
AUSTRIA

Poland

Russian gains

Prussian gains

Austrian gains

1772 Gustavus III of Sweden forces through a new constitution giving himself greater power.

Marquee built for Gustavus III in Haga Park, Stockholm

1773-1775 Peasant uprisings in Russia, led by Cossack Pugachev.

1774 Treaty of Kuchuk-Kainarji ends Russo-Turkish war. Russia gains Black Sea ports and the right to represent Christians in the Ottoman empire.

Africa and India

1761 British capture Pondicherry and destroy French power in India.

1761 Battle of Panipat: the Afghans defeat the Marathas.

1761-1790 The rise of Sikh power in India.

1764 Robert Clive is appointed governor and commander-in-chief in Bengal (**1764-1767**).

1769-1772 James Bruce, a Scottish explorer, visits Ethiopia.

1774-1785 Warren Hastings becomes first governor-general of British India.

East India Company official and servants

1775-1782 British and Marathas at war in India.

c.1775 The Masai expand in East Africa, reaching the Ngong Hills.

Masai cattle herders

Asia and Australasia

1767 Burmese invade Siam, destroy the capital, Ayutthaya, and take control of most of the country.

1767-1769 China invades Burma and war breaks out between them. Burma becomes a Chinese dependency.

1768 Taksin, a Siamese general, forms an army and drives out the Burmese. He defeats various local rulers and becomes the new King of Siam. His capital is at Thonburi.

COOK'S TRAVELS

James Cook, a British navigator, reached the Pacific island of Tonga and New Zealand in **1769**, and the east coast of Australia (which he claimed for Britain) in **1770**. He named the spot where he landed Botany Bay, because of the abundant plant life. Further trips (**1772-1774** and **1776-1779**) took him to New Hebrides and Hawaii.

James Cook (1728-1779) and Australian budgerigar

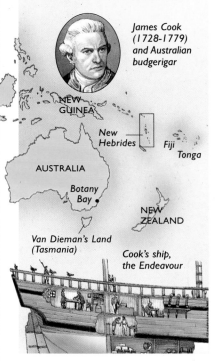

NEW GUINEA

New Hebrides

Fiji

Tonga

AUSTRALIA

Botany Bay

NEW ZEALAND

Van Dieman's Land (Tasmania)

Cook's ship, the Endeavour

The Americas

1760 Britain takes Montreal and controls St. Lawrence River.

The wreck of an 18th century boat, used on the St. Lawrence River for the fur trade and for military operations

1762 Britain captures Grenada and St. Vincent.

1763 The Peace of Paris ends Anglo-French rivalry in North America, establishing British supremacy.

1763 The capital of Brazil is moved to Rio de Janeiro.

1763 The Proclamation Line in North America defines the limits of settler expansion. All land to the west of it is reserved for Native North Americans.

1766 Britain occupies the Falkland Islands.

1767 New British import taxes imposed on goods to North America upset the colonists.

1770 The Boston Massacre.

1773 The Boston Tea Party.

1775-1783 The American War of Independence (see page 128).

Officer from Virginia

1776 American Declaration of Independence.

1776 Spaniards found San Francisco.

1778 France and Spain ally with the Americans against Britain.

1779 James Cook is killed in Hawaii.

The British in India

British power in India grew at an enormous pace during the 18th century. The Mogul empire, which had once controlled almost the entire subcontinent, was in decline. Instead, local rulers asserted their independence.

Sivaji Bhonsla, leading his Maratha warriors against the Mogul empire

The Moguls faced growing threats from warlike groups, such as the Marathas in Central India, and the Sikhs in the Punjab, as well as invasions by hostile rulers such as the Persians and Afghans, who invaded Delhi in **1757**. The lack of any central power encouraged the Europeans to extend their trading bases and settlements, partly as a protection against increasing disturbances and unrest.

Afghans

KASHMIR

SIND

Maratha Confederacy

Sikhs

Ceded to the British East India Company by 1805

PUNJAB

Rajputs

• Meerut
• Delhi

OUDH

Lucknow • GHAZIPUR

BIHAR

Benares • River Ganges

BENGAL ASSAM

Plassey 1757 • Calcutta

GAIKWAR

ORISSA Bay of Bengal

Bombay • PESHWA

MARATHA CONFEDERACY

NORTHERN SARKARS

HYDERABAD

Goa (Portuguese) •

Map of British territory in India by 1805

MYSORE

ARCOT Madras •

Coromandel Coast

CARNATIC • Pondicherry

Malabar Coast

CEYLON

THE ANGLO-FRENCH STRUGGLE

19th century British Indian Army soldier

Britain's growing influence in India was also the result of a successful struggle for power against the French. In periods of war, such as during the Seven Years' War (**1756-1763**), they often attacked each other's colonial possessions.

In India, the British East India Company proved stronger than that of the French. The French Company established control of the Carnatic coast in **1750**. But, in **1751,** a young clerk named Robert Clive, later known as "Clive of India", led a small force of 500 to victory against the French at Arcot. The final blow to the French was the capture of Pondicherry in **1761**. This marked the collapse of French power in India.

British East India Company fort on the Coromandel Coast, 1693

Shah Alam, who handed over control of Bengal to the British East India Company

VICTORY OVER BENGAL

At the Battle of Plassey in **1757**, Clive's small force defeated the much larger army of the ruler of Bengal. This victory gave the British East India Company effective control of Bengal, the richest area of India, and the capital, Calcutta, the major port.

From then on, the Company's prosperity grew steadily, operating from its bases at Calcutta, Madras and Bombay. Land and privileges were obtained from wealthy native rulers, in return for support and protection. A series of wars brought more territory, as well as recognition of British sovereignty.

India became so important to Britain that the government took control of the political administration in **1784**. This was a significant step toward colonization. In **1803**, the Mogul emperor accepted British protection. But the British victory in the Third Anglo-Maratha War (**1813-1823**) removed the most serious threat to British supremacy.

Meanwhile, the British continued to acquire new territory. They conquered Sind (**1843**) and the Punjab (**1849**), extending the frontiers in the northwest. Several self-governing but dependent states, such as Oudh, were also absorbed.

THE INDIAN MUTINY

In **1857-1858**, there was a series of uprisings against the British, which became known as the Indian Mutiny. It began in Meerut as a protest by Bengali soldiers in the British army,

A Bengal tiger, traditionally hunted by India's rulers

but soon spread throughout northern India. Although the mutineers held out for over a year, the British managed to restore their authority.

A 19th century picture of an Indian woman waving a British flag

THE JEWEL IN THE CROWN

In response to the Mutiny, the British government took complete control in **1858**, and the East India Company lost all its governing powers. India became the keystone of the British empire and the focus for European colonial rivalries, especially after the Russians began to expand into Central Asia. In **1877**, Queen Victoria was proclaimed "Empress of India", and a viceroy was appointed to represent her. Railways were built all over the subcontinent, modern industries were developed, and foreign trade increased.

The relief of Lucknow by British troops, March 19, 1858, which brought an end to the Mutiny. British residents had been trapped in the Residency and under siege for months.

Southern and Western Europe

1781 Joseph II of Austria (**1780-1790**) introduces religious toleration and major reforms, including abolition of serfs.

1782 James Watt (Scottish) invents rotary steam engine.

1784 William Pitt the Younger becomes British Prime Minister and dominates politics for 20 years.

1784 Power struggle in Holland between the stadtholder, the Estates-General, and the Patriot party.

1785 Edmund Cartwright (British) invents the power loom, which mechanizes weaving.

1789 Revolt in Austrian Netherlands (Belgium) against centralizing policy of Joseph II. Proclamation of a Belgian Republic (**1790**), which is later reconquered by Austria.

1789 The French Revolution (see page 132).

The storming of the Bastille, a famous prison in Paris, an event which marked the start of the French Revolution

1791 Wilberforce's bill for abolition of slavery is passed.

1792 France declares war on Austria and Prussia.

1793 Execution of Louis XVI of France. France declares war on Britain, Netherlands and Spain.

1793-1794 Reign of Terror in France.

The guillotine, used for executing all those thought to oppose the Revolution

1794 France occupies the Netherlands, renamed the Batavian Republic (**1795-1806**).

1795 European coalition forms against France.

1796 Edward Jenner, a British doctor, introduces vaccination against smallpox.

1796-97 French troops, led by Napoleon Bonaparte, conquer much of Italy.

1798 French invade Rome and Switzerland and set up Roman and Helvetic republics.

1798 Failed rebellion against the British in Ireland, led by Irish Protestant Wolfe Tone.

The blade fell quickly when the rope was pulled.

The person's head was secured between two pieces of wood.

Northern and Eastern Europe

1781 Austro-Russian alliance against Turkey.

1783 Russia annexes the Crimea.

1787-1791 Russia goes to war with Turkey and gains the Black Sea Steppes.

1788 Austria declares war on Turkey and overruns Moldavia.

1788 Gustavus III of Sweden declares war on Russia.

Swedish soldier

1790-1792 Reign of Emperor Leopold II.

Leopold II of Austria

1791 The King of Poland adopts a new constitution to protect the country from Russian interference. Catherine II invades at the request of the nobles, destroys the constitution and divides large areas of Poland between Russia and Prussia.

1792 Gustavus III of Sweden assassinated at a masked ball.

1793 Second partition of Poland. Russia takes the eastern territory inhabited by Ukrainians and White Russians. Prussia gains Danzig, Thorn and Posen and expands its eastern frontier.

1794 Polish uprising suppressed by Russia.

1795 Poland disappears after the third partition. Prussia takes Warsaw, Austria takes West Galicia, and Russia gains the remaining territory, including Lithuania.

Poland ▢ Russian gains ▢ Prussian gains ▢ Austrian gains ▢

The 2nd partition of Poland in 1793

The 3rd partition of Poland in 1795

Africa and India

1784 India Act: British government takes control of political affairs in British India.

1786 Ottoman Turks send a fleet to restore control in Egypt, after a period of unrest.

1787 British establish a colony for freed slaves in Sierra Leone.

c.1790 East Africa: Buganda kingdom expands its frontiers.

1795-1797 West Africa: Mungo Park, a British explorer, reaches Segu and the River Niger.

Mungo Park

A sextant, a navigational instrument used by early explorers

1795-1796 British take Cape of Good Hope, South Africa, and Ceylon (Sri Lanka) from the Dutch.

1798-1799 Napoleon invades Egypt. Defeated by British at Battle of the Nile (**1798**), but defeats the Turks at Aboukir Bay (**1799**).

1799 British control South India. Tippoo, ruler of Mysore (**1750-1799**), is killed fighting the British.

Tippoo's tiger, a musical toy showing a tiger attacking a European, from Seringapatam, capital of Mysore

Asia and Australasia

1782 Siam: Taksin is deposed and executed after a rebellion. Prince Chakri seizes the throne and becomes Rama I, first king of the Chakri dynasty. He moves the capital to Bangkok. Siam grows in prosperity, the only Southeast Asian country to remain uncolonized by Europeans in the 19th century.

1783-1823 The Burmese capital is moved to Amarapura.

1785 François de la Pérouse leaves France for the Pacific, in search of the Solomon Islands.

1786 British East India Company establishes a base in Penang, Malaysia: the first British settlement in Southeast Asia.

1787 Severe famine and rice riots in Edo (Tokyo), Japan.

City of Edo in the 18th century

1788 François de la Pérouse lands on the coast of New South Wales, Australia, a day after the British had established a colony there.

1788 Convicts are transported from Britain to Sydney, the first British settlement in Australia.

1791-1792 China and Tibet at war.

1794 Aga Muhammed founds the Qaja dynasty in Persia, which lasts until **1925**.

1795 Matthew Flinders and George Bass (British) make the first inland trip from the east coast of Australia.

The Americas

1780 British capture Charleston.

1780-1783 Tupac Amara, the last of the Incas, leads the Peruvian Indians in an unsuccessful revolt against the Spaniards.

A jaguar, native to South America

1781 British General Cornwallis surrenders at Yorktown.

1783 Treaty of Paris: Britain recognizes the independence of the 13 Colonies, renamed the United States of America. Britain gives Florida to Spain.

1787 A new constitution is drawn up in the United States by Thomas Jefferson.

A bald eagle, used on the seal of the United States

1789 George Washington becomes first President of the United States (until **1797**).

1791 The Canada Act: Canada is divided into English and French-speaking territories.

1791 Slave revolt in Haiti against the French, led by Toussaint L'Ouverture. He becomes Lieutenant Governor in **1796**.

Toussaint L'Ouverture

1797 Britain takes Trinidad from Spain.

1798 Spaniards found Los Angeles.

America - Independence to Civil War

Hudson Bay

HUDSON BAY
COMPANY
(British)

CANADA

QUEBEC
(British 1763)

Quebec •

St. Lawrence River

THE
GREAT
LAKES

Lexington
• Concord
Bunker Hill

• Saratoga

(British
1774)

Philadelphia

Mississippi
River

Ohio River

UNITED STATES OF
AMERICA
(1783)

Yorktown

THE
THIRTEEN
COLONIES

LOUISIANA
(Spanish
1763)

INDIAN
RESERVE
(1763)

• Charleston

• New
Orleans

FLORIDA
(Spanish 1783)

United States of America after
the treaty of Paris, 1783

British (Canada)
after 1783

Spanish after
1783

*Map of the United
States in 1783*

For example, Britain declared all land west of the Proclamation Line of **1763** to be an Indian Reserve. Settlers in colonies such as Virginia regarded the **1774** Quebec Act, extending Quebec's boundaries over an area south of the Great Lakes, as another threat.

Anti-tax protests erupted into violence in Boston in **1770**, when British troops fired on protesters, and in the **1773** "Boston Tea Party", when Bostonians threw chests of tea into the sea.

In **May 1775**, representatives from the colonies met at the Philadelphia Congress. In **June**, an army was set up under George Washington. On **July 4, 1776**, Congress signed the Declaration of Independence.

The Americans found allies in France and Spain, who had their own reasons for disliking British influence in America. In **1778**, France declared war on Britain, followed by Spain in **1779**. But the colonists won most of the major battles without help from their allies. After a fierce fight, the war ended in victory for the Thirteen Colonies. Britain recognized their independence at the Treaty of Paris, **September 1783**.

IMPORTANT DATES

1775 Battles of Lexington and Concord, won by the colonists. British victory at Bunker Hill.

1776 British troops forced out of Boston. American Declaration of Independence.

1777 British defeated at Battle of Saratoga.

1780 British capture Charleston.

1781 British under Cornwallis surrender at Yorktown.

1783 Treaty of Paris: Britain recognizes American independence.

1787 New American constitution is drawn up.

1789-1797 George Washington becomes first President of the United States of America.

In **1775**, the American colonies began a rebellion against British rule. The relationship had been deteriorating since the Seven Years' War (**1756-1763**). The settlers increasingly resented British interference, particularly in trade, such as the imposition of import taxes in **1767**. They also saw other British policies as damaging to their interests.

Paul Revere riding to warn fellow Americans that British troops were coming on April 18, 1775

Signing the Declaration of Independence 1776

THE CIVIL WAR

By the middle of the 19th century, the northern and southern states of the U.S.A. were growing apart. The North was richer and more industrialized, while the South, with its economy based on huge plantations of cotton and sugar, was dependent on slavery.

As the movement for the abolition of slavery grew in strength, bitter rows developed in Congress. In **1860**, an anti-slavery candidate, Abraham Lincoln, was elected President.

Abraham Lincoln, who led the Unionist North against the breakaway South. He was assassinated, just as the war ended, in 1865.

The Battle of Gettysburg, July 3, 1863.

Lincoln's election prompted the southern states to break away and form the Confederate States of America in **1861**. The northern Unionists wanted to preserve the unity of the U.S.A. This provoked a bloody civil war, which lasted from **1861-1865**.

In the first two years of the War, the Confederates, led by generals Robert E. Lee and "Stonewall" Jackson, won many important battles. But the Unionists had more soldiers, factories to make weapons, and railways to transport them. After bitter fighting, and the loss of 635,000 lives, they defeated the southern Confederates. Slavery was officially abolished in **1863**.

Map showing how the States were divided in the American Civil War

IMPORTANT DATES

1861 Fort Sumter, South Carolina, is captured by Confederates. First Battle of Bull Run: a high point for the South.

1862 Confederates, under Robert E. Lee, win victories at Richmond and Fredericksburg.

1863 War turns against South after Unionist victories at Vicksburg and Gettysburg. "Stonewall" Jackson is killed.

1864 Ulysses S. Grant becomes Commander of Unionist Army. Unionist General Sherman marches through Georgia, destroying the land.

March 1865 Confederates are defeated: Lee surrenders at Appomattox.

WASHINGTON TERRITORY

OREGON

NEBRASKA TERRITORY

MINNESOTA

WISCONSIN

MICHIGAN

VERMONT MAINE

NEW HAMPSHIRE

MASSACHUSETTS

RHODE ISLAND

CONNECTICUT

NEW JERSEY

NEW YORK

PENNSYLVANIA

NEVADA

UTAH TERRITORY

IOWA

ILLINOIS INDIANA OHIO

Gettysburg

Washington

Bull Run

DELAWARE

MARYLAND

WEST VIRGINIA VIRGINIA

Appomattox

CALIFORNIA

NEW MEXICO TERRITORY

KANSAS

MISSOURI

KENTUCKY

TENNESSEE

NORTH CAROLINA

SOUTH CAROLINA

Fort Sumter

INDIAN TERRITORY

ARKANSAS

ALABAMA GEORGIA

Vicksburg

MISSISSIPPI FLORIDA

TEXAS

LOUISIANA

Union states

Slave states that stayed in the Union

Confederate states

Territories not yet states, but administered by the Union

Asia

Opium poppies

1800 British traders begin importing opium from India into China.

1801 Russia takes Georgia.

1801 British East India Company takes Tanjore and the Carnatic coast, India.

1802 Siam (now Thailand) annexes Battambang, Cambodia.

1802 Wars in the Deccan lead to the supremacy of the British East India Company in India.

1802 Ceylon (now Sri Lanka) becomes a Crown Colony.

1809-1824 Reign of King Rama II of Siam. Start of contacts with Europe after a period of isolation.

Fath Ali of Persia attacking a Russian

1811-1813 British occupy Dutch Java.

1811 War between Russia and Persia.

1817 Expansion of Burmese in Assam.

1817-1818 British East India Company defeats the Marathas and becomes effective ruler of India.

1818 Java is restored to the Dutch.

1819 Singapore is founded.

RAFFLES AND SINGAPORE

Singapore was founded in **1819** by Sir Stamford Raffles, as a base for the British East India Company, to rival the Dutch port of Malacca. Raffles negotiated with the island's ruler and established a colony. Strategically situated at the opening of the Malacca Straits, but disease-ridden and virtually uninhabited, Singapore grew to become the largest and most prosperous port in the region. It also played a large part in the expansion of British influence in Asia.

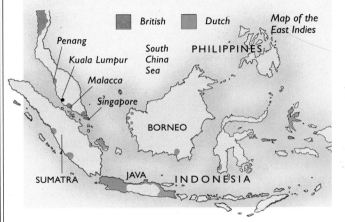

British   Dutch   *Map of the East Indies*

Penang
Kuala Lumpur
South China Sea
PHILIPPINES
Malacca
Singapore
BORNEO
SUMATRA   JAVA   INDONESIA

Africa and Australasia

1802-1803 The Australian coast is surveyed by English navigator, Matthew Flinders.

1802 Trutor and Somerville, British explorers, explore Bechuanaland (now Botswana).

1804 Hobart, Tasmania, is founded.

1805 Mungo Park, a Scottish doctor, sets out to explore the River Niger.

1805-1848 Mehemet Ali massacres the ruling Mamelukes and is installed as *pasha* (viceroy) of Egypt. His dynasty rules until **1952**.

Mungo Park 1771-1806

Mehemet Ali at his palace in Alexandria. During his reign, Egypt was opened to European influences.

1806 The Cape of Good Hope, South Africa, becomes a British colony (officially recognized in **1814**).

1807 English politician William Wilberforce passes a law banning British ships from taking part in slavery.

1807 Sierra Leone and Gambia become British Crown Colonies.

1808 Import of African slaves into the U.S.A. is prohibited.

1810 Britain takes Mauritius from France.

Zulu warriors fighting

1810 West Africa: the Yoruba kingdom breaks up.

1818 The Mfecane, or time of troubles, in southern Africa. Shaka the Great (**c.1787-1828**) organizes an army of 40,000 men into uniformed regiments called *impi*. He founds the Zulu empire which extends over much of southern Africa and many local tribes are driven north.

Western Europe

1801 Act of Union unites Britain and Ireland.

1804 Richard Trevithick, a British engineer, builds first steam train.

Trevithick's steam train

1804 Napoleon crowns himself Emperor of France. First Empire period (**1804-1815**).

1805 Battle of Trafalgar. British, led by Admiral Nelson, defeat French.

Statue of Nelson

1808-1814 Peninsular War (see page 133).

1809 Jean de Lamarck, a French zoologist, publishes his theories on the changes in living things, based on a study of fossils.

1814 Napoleon is forced to abdicate. Louis XVIII is restored.

Crown of Louis XVIII

Standard from one of the divisions of Napoleon's Army

1815 The Hundred Days: Napoleon escapes from Elba and retakes power, but is finally defeated at the Battle of Waterloo.

Northern and Eastern Europe (and Italy)

1800 Alessandro Volta, an Italian, invents the battery.

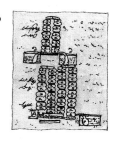

A sketch from Volta's notebook showing his battery, known as a voltaic pile.

1806 Napoleon dissolves the Holy Roman Empire.

1809 Russia gains Finland from Sweden.

1810 Napoleon's general, Jean Bernadotte, is made heir to the Swedish throne.

1812 Napoleon invades Russia.

The retreat of the Grand Army from Moscow

Napoleon's army was ill-prepared for the harsh winter. Of 600,000 men, only about 30,000 returned.

1815 The Congress of Vienna meets to settle post-war boundaries and other problems, led by Austrian statesman, Prince Metternich.

The Americas

1803 The Lousiana Purchase: U.S. buys French land in North America.

1803 Britain acquires British Guiana, Tobago and St. Lucia.

1808 Uprisings against the Spaniards begin in New Spain.

1808-1825 Wars of independence from Spanish and Portuguese colonial rule in South and Central America. Argentina (Provinces of Rio de la Plata) declares independence in **1810**, Paraguay and Venezuela in **1811**, Colombia in **1813**, Uruguay in **1814** and Chile in **1816**.

VENEZUELA
BRITISH GUIANA
NEW GRANADA
COLOMBIA
DUTCH GUIANA
ECUADOR
FRENCH GUIANA
PERU
BRAZIL
PACIFIC OCEAN
BOLIVIA
PARAGUAY
CHILE
URUGUAY
ARGENTINA
FALKLAND ISLANDS

☐ *Great Colombia 1819-1830*

☐ *Provinces of the Rio de la Plata*

South America in the 19th century

1812-1814 Trade war between the U.S.A. and Britain.

1816 Argentina receives formal independence from Spain.

1818 A boundary is established between the U.S.A. and Canada.

1818 Chile becomes independent.

1819-1830 The state of Great Colombia is set up under Simon Bolivar. It becomes independent from Spain in **1822**.

1819 Spain loses Florida to United States.

The French Revolution

On **May 5th**, **1789**, faced with mounting debts and growing unrest, Louis XVI of France called a meeting of the Estates-General. This was a national parliament, consisting of representatives from the three Estates - Nobility, Clergy and Commoners - which had not met since **1614**. On **June 17th**, the Commoners decided to form their own National Assembly. This move marked the start of the French Revolution.

Reports swept Paris that the King was about to dissolve the Assembly, and on **July 14th** an angry mob stormed and destroyed the infamous Bastille prison. Revolution spread throughout France: there were uprisings of peasants in rural areas, and many nobles fled abroad for safety.

The storming of the Bastille on July 14, 1789

THE FRENCH REPUBLIC

In **1790**, Louis had to accept a new constitution, based on the abolition of feudal rights, and a limited monarchy. The Catholic Church was also under attack. In June **1791**, the King tried to flee, but he was discovered and taken back to Paris, and forced to agree to an even more radical constitution.

Stripes of red, white and blue, known as the tricolore, became the French national symbol.

In **1792**, the National Assembly was replaced by the National Convention. The monarchy was abolished and France was declared a Republic. Power passed to a political group, the Girondins, and, in **1793**, Louis was executed for treason.

The execution by guillotine of Louis XVI

A poster showing the revolutionary slogan: Liberty, Equality and Fraternity

THE REIGN OF TERROR

By **1793,** power had passed to a more extremist group, the Jacobins, controlled by Maximilien Robespierre. All those even suspected of betraying the revolution were sentenced to death by guillotine. This period of terror lasted until the fall and execution of Robespierre himself in **July 1794**.

From **1795-1799**, France was ruled by a group called the Directory, which became increasingly dependent on a brilliant young officer, Napoleon Bonaparte. From **1792-1815**, France was almost continually at war. Other European powers felt threatened, first by the spread of revolution, and later by the ambitions of Napoleon. The revolution inspired egalitarian movements and unleashed new nationalist forces (see pages 140-141) all over the continent.

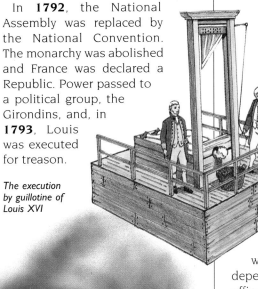

The rise of Napoleon

A young Corsican general named Napoleon Bonaparte rose to power in France after winning a dazzling reputation on campaigns in Italy (**1796-1797**) and Egypt (**1798-1799**). In **1799**, Napoleon appointed himself First Consul (effectively military dictator) and disbanded the by then corrupt and ineffective Directory. In **1804**, he crowned himself as Emperor Napoleon I.

Austria to abandon the title of Holy Roman Emperor and then reorganized the German states. He had members of his family installed as rulers in Spain, Italy and Westphalia.

By **1812**, he had most of Western Europe under his control.

Napoleon as a young man

Napoleon also proved to be a successful statesman and administrator. He introduced the *Code Napoléon* (**1804**), confirming the property rights granted to peasants during the Revolution.

In **1805**, a new coalition of Britain, Austria, Russia and Sweden allied against France. Napoleon won important victories, against Austria and Russia at Austerlitz (**1805**), Prussia at Jena (**1806**), and Russia at Friedland (**1807**). He forced Francis II of

Contemporary sketch showing Napoleon crowning himself

Napoleon's imperial crown

Napoleon crossing the Alps, by the French painter Jacques Louis David

Napoleon's army occupying Vienna

But France's enemies continued to oppose his ambitions. Britain supported a resistance movement against the French in Spain (the Peninsular War **1808-1814**), which ended in French defeat. In **1812**, Napoleon invaded Russia, with disastrous results. Badly equipped and ill-prepared for the harsh winter, of 600,000 men, only about 30,000 returned.

Napoleon's empire in 1812

In **1813**, joint Austrian, Prussian and Russian forces won a series of major victories in Germany. This brought about the collapse of the Napoleonic system in Germany, Italy and Holland. The British then invaded France itself and, in April **1814**, the allies reached Paris. Napoleon was exiled to the island of Elba, and replaced as ruler of France by King Louis XVIII.

THE HUNDRED DAYS

Duke of Wellington, British commander at Waterloo

In **1815**, Napoleon made a dramatic escape from Elba and retook power for a brief period known as the Hundred Days. He was decisively defeated the same year, by Prussian and British forces at the Battle of Waterloo, and he died in **1821**, in exile on the island of St. Helena.

Napoleon's defeat ended for good the threat of French domination of Europe. British supremacy at sea was assured, and Russia and Austria became the major powers on the continent.

Asia

1821 Siam invades the Malay state of Kedah.

1824-1826 First Anglo-Burmese War. British take Lower Burma and Assam.

1825-1830 Java War: Indonesians revolt against the Dutch.

1826-1828 War between Persia and Russia. Russia gains Armenian provinces.

1830 British East India Company takes Mysore.

1831-1840 Syria and Lebanon are occupied by Egypt.

1833 British East India Company trade monopoly with India and China is abolished.

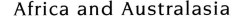

Map of Southeast Asia

A clipper, a ship developed in the USA in the 1820s, for trade with the East

1838 War between the British and Afghans.

1839 Britain takes Aden.

1839-1842 Opium War between Britain and China.

THE OPIUM WAR

In **1838**, Emperor Tao-kuang of China sent an official, Lin Tse-hsu, to Canton to prohibit the importation and use of Indian opium. Lin burned 20,000 chests of opium and drove the British traders out of Canton to Hong Kong. This attempt to ban the trade in opium led to the outbreak of war in **1839**. The British fleet blockaded the Chinese coast and defeated the Chinese. By the Treaty of Nanking of **1842**, the Chinese were forced to open five ports to British trade. Britain also acquired Hong Kong.

Indians carrying an opium chest. British traders used the opium to pay for Chinese goods.

Africa and Australasia

1820-1821 Egypt conquers the Sudan.

1822 The U.S.A. founds Liberia, West Africa, as a colony for freed African slaves.

1823 William Wilberforce helps found the Anti-Slavery Society, which campaigns to abolish slavery. Slavery is abolished in the British empire in **1833**.

1823-1831 War between the British and Ashanti (Ghana).

1824 René Caillié, a French explorer, sets out for Timbuktu in West Africa.

1826 The Black War in Tasmania between settlers and aborigines (the native people).

1829 Swan River Settlement is founded in Western Australia.

1830 French forces conquer Algiers. Start of French colonization of Algeria.

Aborigine

Aboriginal bark painting

1834 British settlement at Port Philip Bay (Melbourne).

1835 Tripoli becomes an Ottoman province.

1835-1837 The start of the Great Trek of Boers (Dutch settlers) from the Cape of Good Hope, South Africa.

1838 Boers defeat Zulus at Battle of Blood River, Natal.

1839 Dutch settlers found the Republic of Natal.

1839 New Zealand is proclaimed a British colony.

European occupation by 1850

Grey kangaroo (left) and rainbow lorikeet (above), two of the unusual animals Europeans found in Australia

Western Europe

1820 Revolutions in Spain and Portugal.

1825 First passenger railway, from Stockton to Darlington, England.

1826 J-N Niepce (France) takes the world's first photograph.

1829 George and Robert Stephenson, British engineers, build the *Rocket*, a steam engine.

1829 English Metropolitan Police Force is founded by Sir Robert Peel.

1830 Belgium wins independence.

1830 July Revolution in France installs Louis Philippe as king.

1832 Reform Act in Britain gives the middle classes the vote.

1834 Tolpuddle Martyrs, six English workers, are sent to Australia for trying to set up a Trade Union.

1834-1839 Carlist Wars in Spain: Don Carlos, the pretender, attempts to gain the throne.

1834-1871 Charles Babbage designs an analytical engine, the first computer, helped by Ada Lovelace who designs the programs.

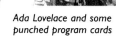

Ada Lovelace and some punched program cards

1836 Chartists in England demand the vote for all adult males.

1837-1901 Reign of Queen Victoria.

1837 First electric telegraph invented by W. Cooke and C. Wheatstone.

Early telegraph machine

1838 First practical photographic process is produced by Louis Daguerre (French).

Northern and Eastern Europe (and Italy)

1820 Hans Oersted, a Danish scientist, shows that an electric current has a magnetic effect on a compass needle.

1821-1829 Greek War of Independence against Turkey (see page 141).

1827 Battle of Navarino: Greece's allies destroy the Turkish fleet.

The Battle of Navarino

British, French and Russian ships fought for the Greeks.

1829 Treaty of Adrianople. Russia makes gains in the Balkans. Turks agree to Greek independence.

1831 Michael Faraday, an English scientist, produces an electric current from a moving magnet, using a device called a disc dynamo.

Faraday's disc dynamo, used to produce an electric current

Michael Faraday

The Americas

1821 Mexico is proclaimed independent. Agustin Iturbide becomes Emperor Agustin I in **1822**.

1822 Haiti is independent.

1822 Brazil declares independence and is ruled by King Pedro I.

1823 Monroe Doctrine in U.S.A.: President Monroe warns Europeans not to interfere in U.S. affairs.

1823 Formation of the United Provinces of Central America.

The United Provinces of Central America

1823-1824 Agustin I is overthrown and Mexico becomes a republic.

1828 Uruguay, part of Argentina since **1816**, becomes a republic.

c.1830s U.S. settlers move West, driving many Native North Americans from their homes.

Native North American tepee

1830 Colombia, Venezuela and Ecuador become republics.

1833 Britain takes possession of the Falkland Islands.

1836 American rebels massacred by Mexican forces at the Alamo mission station. Texas breaks away from Mexico and forms a republic.

1839-1840 El Salvador, Honduras, Nicaragua, Guatemala and Costa Rica become independent republics.

The Industrial Revolution

In the early 18th century, Britain was already richer than many other nations, with fertile and well-farmed land, a flourishing cloth industry, and rapidly expanding overseas trade. Between **c.1750-1850**, this wealth increased, as a result of the development of new industries, which were transformed by the invention of machinery powered by steam and water. The series of changes that produced this is known as the Industrial Revolution.

The Industrial Revolution was more than just a collection of new inventions. Improved agriculture played a part, and the development of banking, foreign trade and transportation (road, canal and rail) made the movement of goods cheaper and more efficient.

Hargreaves' Spinning Jenny led to important developments in cloth production.

THE INDUSTRIAL DIVIDE

During the 19th century, more and more European countries began building industries along similar lines. Germany expanded rapidly, encouraged by the development of railways from the **1840s**, and the dismantling of internal customs barriers after the unification of the country in **1871**. The United States, and later Japan, followed suit. As the industrialized nations became richer, a gap widened between them and the undeveloped areas of the rest of the world.

KEY DATES IN THE INDUSTRIAL REVOLUTION

1698 Thomas Savery invents the first steam engine, used to pump water from flooded coal mines.

1712 Thomas Newcomen improves the design of the steam engine by fitting a piston.

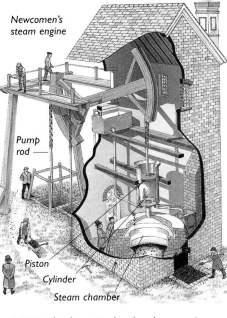

Newcomen's steam engine

Pump rod

Piston

Cylinder

Steam chamber

1713 Abraham Darby develops an iron smelting process.

1733 John Kay invents the "flying shuttle", which improves weaving.

1759-61 The Bridgewater Canal, the first entirely man-made canal, is built.

1767 James Hargreaves invents the "Spinning Jenny", which can spin up to eight threads at a time.

1769 Richard Arkwright builds a water-powered spinning machine which produces stronger thread.

Life in an industrial town

1776 Adam Smith publishes *Wealth of Nations*, which promotes free trade and private enterprise.

1777-79 The world's first iron bridge is built at Coalbrookdale, Shropshire.

Iron bridge, Coalbrookdale

1779 Samuel Crompton's "Spinning Mule" improves spinning.

1782 James Watt builds a rotary steam engine, which becomes the main source of power in British textile mills.

1784 Henry Cort improves iron production with his "puddling" process.

1785 Edmund Cartwright introduces a mechanically-driven loom.

1793 Eli Whitney (U.S.) invents the cotton gin, a machine for separating cotton from seeds.

1804 Richard Trevithick builds the first steam train to run along a track.

1825 Britain's first public railway opens from Stockton to Darlington.

George Stephenson's Locomotion pulling the first passenger train from Stockton to Darlington

1829 George Stephenson's steam train, the *Rocket*, reaches a top speed of 30 miles per hour.

Stephenson's Rocket pulling a passenger carriage

Passenger carriage

Tender carried coal and water.

1838 Steamship service across the Atlantic is started, with the launch of *Great Western*, designed by Isambard Kingdom Brunel.

1851 The Great Exhibition is held in London.

1856 Henry Bessemer invents a steel converter, which enables steel to be produced in large quantities.

1858 The steamship *Great Eastern* is launched, designed by Brunel, to sail between England and Australia.

Isambard Kingdom Brunel

The Great Eastern, Brunel's largest ship

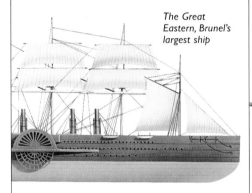

1860 Etienne Lenoir, a Belgian engineer, builds the first internal combustion engine.

Lenoir's gas (internal combustion) engine

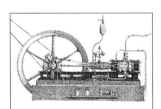

Iron fire box

Piston driven by steam

1863 The Metropolitan line, the first underground railway, opens in London.

A steam train used on the Metropolitan line

1876 Nikolaus Otto, a German engineer, builds a four-stroke engine, the basis for motor car engines.

1879 Ernst von Siemens, a German engineer, runs the first electric train.

1890 The Forth Bridge is built in Scotland, the first bridge to be built entirely of steel.

The Forth Bridge

1890 The first electric underground railway is opened in London.

1890 First motor car company set up by German engineer Gottlieb Daimler.

1897 *Turbinia*, first ship to be powered by a steam turbine engine, is launched.

Chimney for exhaust gases

Asia

1841 Egypt loses Syria to Turkey.

1842 Britain takes Labuan, Borneo.

1843 The British conquer and take Sind.

1845-1846 First Anglo-Sikh War. The British gain control of the Punjab.

1847 French expedition to Cochin China.

1848-1849 Second Anglo-Sikh War. The British add the Punjab to their territory in India.

1850-1864 Taiping Rebellion in China against the decaying Manchu dynasty.

1852 Second Anglo-Burmese War.

1853 Richard Burton, a British explorer, reaches holy city of Mecca in Arabia, which was forbidden to non-Muslims.

Early 19th century Indian sword with the East India Company crest

Bedouin camp

Burton went in disguise as an Arab doctor, as travel in Arabia was unsafe for non-Muslims.

1853 United States gunboats force Japan to open its ports to foreign trade. European contacts increase. A time of growing unrest and weakness for Tokugawa dynasty.

1856 British East India Company takes Oudh.

1856-1860 Second Opium War between Britain and China.

1857-1860 Anglo-French forces occupy Beijing.

Lakshimbai, Queen of Jhansi, who joined the Indian Mutiny

1857 The Indian Mutiny: uprisings against the British in northern India.

1858 Relief of Lucknow ends the Indian Mutiny. The British government takes over and administers India directly, through a viceroy (governor). The Mogul emperor is deposed and the dynasty comes to an end.

1858 Treaty of Tientsin: 11 Chinese ports are opened to European trade.

1859-1865 Mandalay is the capital of Burma.

Africa and Australasia

1840 Treaty of Waitangi: Maori chiefs give sovereignty over New Zealand to Britain.

1840 Captain Wilkes, an American explorer, discovers the Antarctic coast.

1841 David Livingstone, a Scottish missionary, makes his first journey of exploration in Africa.

1842 Boers establish the Orange Free State, South Africa.

1842-1843 Wars between Boers and British in Natal. Natal becomes a British colony.

1844 War between France and Morocco.

1844-1848 Unsuccessful uprisings by Maoris (natives of New Zealand) against the British.

1844-1845 Charles Sturt, an English explorer, leads an expedition into central Australia.

1846-1847 British defeat Bantus (Africans) in South Africa.

1847 Liberia becomes independent.

1848 Otago, New Zealand, is founded.

1851 Gold is discovered at Bathurst, Victoria.

1853-1854 Gold rush in Victoria, Australia.

1854 The Orange Free State recognized as a Boer republic.

1855 Livingstone discovers Victoria Falls, southern Africa.

1856 Pretoria becomes the capital of the Transvaal.

1858 John Speke, a British explorer, reaches Lake Victoria in East Africa, the source of the Nile.

Maori Warrior, and sword

Sturt's desert pea, found in the Australian outback

Ptolemy's map of c.AD150 (right) had correctly proposed two lakes feeding into the Nile.

Speke at Lake Victoria

1858-1864 Livingstone explores the River Zambezi.

1859-1869 Suez Canal is built in Egypt.

1859 Queensland, Australia, becomes a separate colony.

Western Europe

1840 The first postage stamp, the Penny Black, issued in Britain.

Penny Black, showing the head of Queen Victoria

1845-1848 Great famine in Ireland leads to mass emigration to U.S.A.

1847 Civil war in Switzerland.

1848 Revolutions affect most of Europe. The Second Republic is declared in France (**1848-1851**).

1848 *Communist Manifesto* is issued by Karl Marx (**1818-1883**) and Friedrich Engels (**1820-1895**).

1851 The Great Exhibition, an international trade fair, is held in London.

Crystal Palace, designed by Joseph Paxton to house the Great Exhibition

1852-1870 Second Empire in France: reign of Napoleon III.

1859 Charles Darwin, an English naturalist, publishes *On the Origin of the Species by Natural Selection*, outlining his theory of evolution.

Contemporary cartoon mocking Darwin's claim that humans evolved from apes

Beetles collected on Darwin's expeditions

Northern and Eastern Europe (and Italy)

1848 The Year of Revolutions.

1849 Austria wins back her Italian possessions, after defeating Piedmont-Sardinia.

1849 Guiseppe Garibaldi marches to Rome, but his revolt is crushed.

1854-1856 The Crimean War.

1859 Italian uprising against Austria, led by Piedmont-Sardinia.

THE CRIMEAN WAR

In **1853**, Russia demanded the right to use the Dardanelles Straits for her ships, and to protect Turkish Christians. Turkey, France and Britain felt this would give the Russians too much power and declared war. After much bloodshed on both sides, Russia was defeated and forced to make concessions at the Treaty of Paris in **1856**.

Florence Nightingale, a famous nurse in the Crimean War

Map showing battles of the Crimean War

The Charge of the Light Brigade at the Battle of Balaklava

The Americas

1840 Upper and Lower Canada are united. They are given self-government under the British monarch in **1841**.

1843 New telegraph code is designed by Samuel Morse (U.S.A.), replacing the one used by Cooke and Wheatstone.

1845 Texas and Florida become states of the U.S.A.

1845-1848 War between Mexico and U.S. over boundaries. Mexico loses California, New Mexico, Arizona, Utah and Colorado.

1848-1849 Gold is discovered in California. This leads to a huge rush to the West by settlers in search of gold.

American settlers in the Gold Rush

1851 Isaac Singer (U.S.A.) produces the first practical sewing machine.

1857 Civil war in Mexico.

1859 Oil is discovered in Pennsylvania, which leads to the start of the modern oil industry.

The year of revolutions - 1848

During **1848**, a wave of revolutions swept through Europe. There were many reasons for this. In France and Austria, there had been growing opposition to their conservative rulers, as well as economic difficulties, such as food shortages and rising prices. In Hungary and Italy, nationalist feeling was forming out of an increasing resentment of foreign rule. In Germany and Italy, there were calls to join together the separate states to found new nations.

A rioter in Paris

The retaking of the Panthéon, Paris, by government troops June 1848

Title page of the Communist Manifesto, written by Karl Marx and Friedrich Engels, first published in 1848

Karl Marx (1818-1883), German-born founder of communism

Despite this, the events of **1848** had seriously shaken the establishment, giving a boost to nationalists and liberals. It also inspired radical new movements such as communism, which aimed for a classless society, based on the common ownership of property and industry.

PARIS AND VIENNA

In February **1848**, an uprising in Paris forced King Louis Philippe to abdicate. He was replaced by the Second Republic (**1848-1852**), with Louis Napoleon, Napoleon's nephew, as the first president. Europe's rulers looked on in fear and anticipation. An uprising in Vienna followed in March, and Emperor Ferdinand was forced to abdicate. These events encouraged rebellions against Austrian rule in Italy, Bohemia and Poland, and in **1849** in Hungary. And there were revolts in many German states too.

Prince Louis Napoleon

THE RESULTS OF 1848

In the end, however, the rebellions were unsuccessful and short-lived, except in France. After temporary panic, the old regimes managed to reassert themselves. In England, the Chartist movement, which had been demanding the vote for all adult males since **1836**, finally collapsed. By **1849**, the Austrians had recovered their position in Italy and in Eastern Europe. Attempts at German unification had also failed.

1848 UPRISINGS

12 January Revolution in Sicily.

21-24 February Paris revolution.

12 March Revolution in Venice.

13-15 March Vienna revolution.

18-19 March Berlin revolution.

22 March Revolution in Milan.

23 March Sardinia declares war on Austria and leads movement for Italian unification.

April England: troops brought in to crush the Chartists.

23 April Uprising in Warsaw.

15 May Communist riot in Paris.

17 June Czech revolt in Prague.

Nationalism

Nationalism is the name given to the assertion of national identity by people with a common language or culture. In the 19th century, it was the major political force, and was often linked with liberalism, and the desire for democracy.

Illustration from a Polish pamphlet calling for freedom from Russian domination

In many countries, nationalism took the form of a struggle for independence from foreign rule. There were nationalist protests and uprisings in Italy, Hungary, Poland, Belgium, the Balkans and Norway. The first effective nationalist struggle began in **1821**, in the Greek provinces of the Ottoman empire.

Greek nationalist soldiers

Russia, Austria and Britain backed Greece, because the break-up of the Ottoman empire would affect the balance of power. The Turks were forced to accept Greek independence in **1827**, and in **1832**, Prince Otto of Bavaria became the first king.

The **1848** rebellions also shook the Austrian Hapsburg empire. In **1867**, the Hungarians demanded and were granted self-government.

ITALY AND GERMANY

In the early 19th century, Italy and Germany did not exist: they were each made up of separate states. In both countries, movements began which aimed at uniting them into single nations. However, their eventual unification owed less to national feeling than to the expansionist ambitions of two of the states and their chief ministers: Piedmont-Sardinia, led by Camillo Cavour, and Prussia, led by Prince Otto von Bismarck.

Map showing when different states joined the Italian kingdom

Venice 1866
Lombardy 1859
Piedmont
Romagna 1860
Parma 1860
Modena 1860
Lucca 1860
Tuscany 1860
Papal states 1860-1870
Naples 1860
Sardinia
Sicily 1860

Italian patriot Giuseppe Garibaldi

His flag, a symbol of unity, later became the Italian national flag.

In **1859**, Piedmont beat Austria at Magenta and Solferino and gained Lombardy. In **1860**, most of northern Italy voted to join Piedmont. In southern Italy, a revolution led by Garibaldi joined it to the Italian kingdom. The first Italian Parliament opened that year in Turin and, in **1861**, Victor Emmanuel II of Piedmont-Sardinia became first king of a united Italy.

Kaiser Wilhelm II, third emperor of a united Germany

Economically, Prussia was already the strongest of the German states. Under Bismarck's direction, it gained political control as well. He won Schleswig-Holstein from Austria in **1866**, and incorporated the northern states into a North German Confederation in **1867**. Prussia's victory over France in **1870** convinced the South that it should join too. In **1871**, the King of Prussia became emperor of a united Germany.

SCHLESWIG
HOLSTEIN
PRUSSIA
• Berlin
WESTPHALIA
BAVARIA
• Vienna

▮ Prussia 1815

▢ North German Confederation boundary 1867

▮ Incorporated into the German empire by 1871

Asia

1860 British and French forces burn down the Summer Palace, Beijing. Second Opium War between Britain and China comes to an end. China cedes Kowloon to Britain.

1861-1862 France goes to war with Cochin-China (South Vietnam) and establishes a protectorate over the province by **1867**.

1862-1908 Dowager Empress Tz'u-hsi rules China, on behalf on her baby son.

1863 France establishes a protectorate in Cambodia.

1865 Russia expands in Central Asia, taking the khanate of Tashkent.

Map showing expansion of Russia into Central Asia in the 19th century
Left: Bukharan gold coins

1868 Russia takes the khanate of Bukhara.

1868 The major clans in Japan organize opposition to the Tokugawas. The last shogun, Kei-ki, abdicates after a coup d'état and the emperor's power is restored under a new government (the Meiji Restoration **1868-1912**). A period of growth and modernization.

1873 Russia acquires Khiva and other provinces of Central Asia.

Queen Victoria

1874 Annam (now part of Vietnam) is opened to French trade. Tonkin is made a French protectorate in **1883**.

1876 Korea is declared independent by China.

1877 Queen Victoria of Britain is proclaimed Empress of India.

1878-1880 War between Britain and Afghanistan. British India makes frontier gains and British influence in Afghanistan grows.

Africa and Australasia

1860 The French begin expansion in West Africa.

1860-1861 Robert Burke and William Wills, British explorers, cross Australia.

Witchetty grub

Australian aborigines ate grubs and lizards like these.

Goanna

Burke leading the expedition across Australia

1860-1864 War between Maoris (native peoples) and settlers in New Zealand.

1863 Gold rush in New Zealand.

1868 Transportation of convicts to Australia begins.

1869 Diamond rush begins in South Africa.

1869 Tunisia is controlled by Britain, France and Italy.

1869 The opening of the Suez Canal in Egypt.

1871 Ujiji, East Africa: Sir Henry Stanley, a journalist, meets David Livingstone, who has been missing four years.

1872 British take over Dutch forts on Gold Coast (Ghana).

1873-1874 British and Ashanti at war.

Benjamin Disraeli

1874-1877 Stanley explores the Congo.

1875 British Prime Minister Disraeli buys majority shares in the Suez Canal, ensuring control of the sea route to India.

A 19th century illustration of the Suez Canal in Egypt

1876 Britain and France control Egypt's finances.

1877 Transvaal is annexed by Britain.

1879 Britain and France control Egypt.

1879 Zulus defeat British at Isandlhwana (Natal) but are defeated at Ulundi.

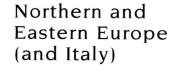

Western Europe

1863 The world's first underground railway is built in London.

1864 Red Cross Society is founded in Geneva, to provide care for war casualties.

1865 Louis Pasteur publishes his germ theory of disease.

Louis Pasteur (1822-1895), a French chemist, and his flask and microscope

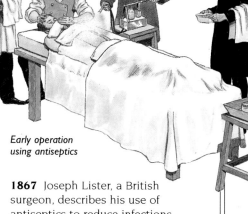

Early operation using antiseptics

1867 Joseph Lister, a British surgeon, describes his use of antiseptics to reduce infections.

1867 Second Reform Act extends the right to vote in Britain.

1867 Karl Marx publishes *Das Kapital*, outlining his theories.

1870 Irish Land Act gives Irish tenants compensation for eviction.

1870-1871 War between France and Prussia. Prussians overthrow Second Empire. A revolution sets up the Third Republic (**1870-1940**).

1871 The Paris Commune (a revolutionary group) is crushed.

1872-1874 Civil war in Spain.

1873 Home Rule League is founded to promote Irish self-government.

Northern and Eastern Europe (and Italy)

1860 Parma, Modena, Tuscany, and Sicily join the Italian kingdom. The Papal States are absorbed too, but the Pope keeps Rome.

1861 Victor Emmanuel, King of Piedmont-Sardinia, becomes King of a united Italy.

1861 Alexander II of Russia frees the serfs (landless peasants).

1866 War between Austria and Italy. Italy gains Venice.

1866 Gregor Mendel, a Bohemian botanist, publishes his laws of inheritance.

Mendel performed experiments on sweet pea plants.

1867 The Austrian empire is renamed Austro-Hungarian empire.

1867 Prussia forms Confederation of North German states.

1870 Rome falls to the Italian kingdom and becomes the capital.

1871 Wilhelm I of Prussia becomes Kaiser (emperor) of a united Germany.

1873 Alliance of 3 emperors: Russia, Germany and Austria-Hungary.

1874 Iceland becomes independent.

1877-1878 Russo-Turkish War ends in Congress of Berlin. Romania, Montenegro and Serbia win independence from Turkey.

1879 Dual Alliance between Germany and Austria-Hungary.

The Americas

1860s -1870s Wars with settlers lead to huge reduction in population of Native North Americans.

An Apache spear

1860 Abraham Lincoln becomes U.S. President.

1861-1865 American Civil War.

1864 France installs Archduke Maximilian of Austria as Emperor of Mexico. He is shot in **1867**.

1865 Slavery is abolished in the U.S.A. Lincoln is assassinated.

1866 First transatlantic cable.

1867 United States purchases Alaska from Russia for $7 million.

1867 Canada becomes a dominion.

1868-1878 Cuba loses war of independence against Spain.

1869 First U.S. trans-continental railroad built.

1876 Battle of Little Big Horn (also known as Custer's Last Stand): Sioux and Cheyenne warriors defeat U.S. army, led by Colonel George Custer.

1876 The telephone is patented in the U.S.A. by Alexander G. Bell.

A Bell telephone in use

Edison's electric light bulb

1877 Thomas Edison, a U.S. inventor, invents the record player.

1877-1911 Rule of Porfirio Diaz, Mexican dictator. He establishes order, wealth and prosperity.

1879 Edison invents a light bulb, a year after Joseph Swan (English).

1879-1884 Chile wins territory after war with Bolivia and Peru.

The Scramble for Africa

At the beginning of the 19th century, most of Africa was still unknown to Europeans. There was a handful of British and French settlements on the west coast, but these were mainly just trading stations. The only established colonies were the Portuguese coastal colonies of Angola and Mozambique, the Cape Colony (which passed from Dutch to British control in **1814**) and, from **1830**, the French colony in Algeria.

But between **1877** and **1914** most of the continent was colonized by European powers. The process was so rapid it became known as "the Scramble for Africa".

Once the movement started, it took on a momentum of its own. Despite determined resistance from people such as the Zulus in southern Africa, and the Muslim kingdoms in the north, the only permanent European defeat was in **1898** in Ethiopia.

Guineas, named after Guinea, in West Africa, where the gold was mined

TRADE AND EMPIRE

There were a number of reasons for the Scramble. The French had long been trying to extend their influence in North Africa and on the west coast. Industrialization in Europe, and the expansion of world trade, produced a demand for new markets and materials. The activities of explorers and the development of railways opened up previously impenetrable regions.

To a large extent the Scramble came about as a result of land-grabbing by men on the spot, such as Cecil Rhodes, who founded De Beers and the British South Africa Company. He

Le drapeau français arboré à Tombouctou

Soldiers raising the French flag in Timbuktu

was interested in mining gold and diamonds, but also hoped to unite South Africa under British rule. But it was also a question of rivalry between European nations, and the prestige of having a colonial empire. Africa was the last great continent to be opened up, and new nations such as Germany, Italy and Belgium looked to it to provide them with an empire.

Zulus, fierce warriors who defeated the British at Isandhlwana, South Africa, 1879

19th century print of British troops at Isandhlwana

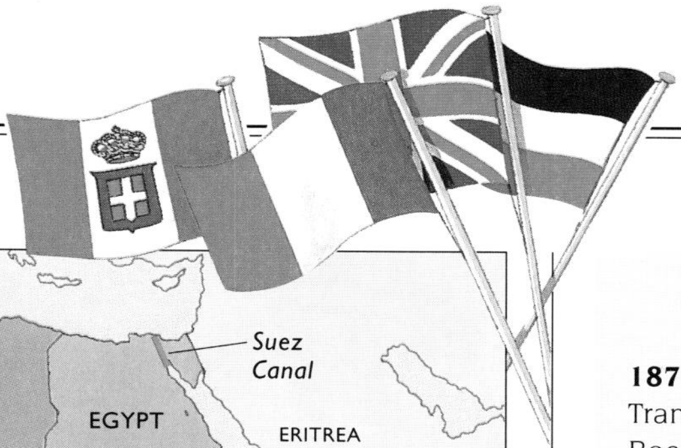

19th century Italian, French, British and German flags

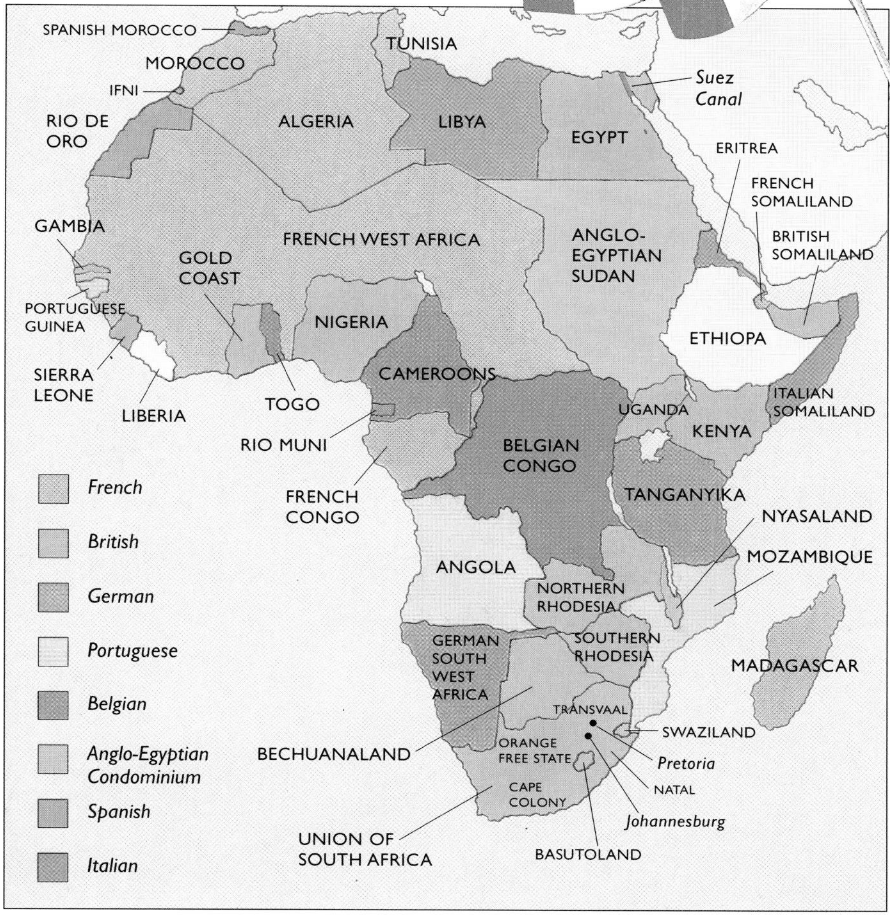
SPANISH MOROCCO
MOROCCO
IFNI
RIO DE ORO
TUNISIA
ALGERIA
LIBYA
EGYPT
Suez Canal
ERITREA
FRENCH SOMALILAND
BRITISH SOMALILAND
GAMBIA
GOLD COAST
FRENCH WEST AFRICA
ANGLO-EGYPTIAN SUDAN
PORTUGUESE GUINEA
NIGERIA
ETHIOPA
SIERRA LEONE
LIBERIA
TOGO
CAMEROONS
UGANDA
ITALIAN SOMALILAND
KENYA
RIO MUNI
BELGIAN CONGO
FRENCH CONGO
TANGANYIKA
NYASALAND
MOZAMBIQUE
ANGOLA
NORTHERN RHODESIA
GERMAN SOUTH WEST AFRICA
SOUTHERN RHODESIA
MADAGASCAR
TRANSVAAL
SWAZILAND
BECHUANALAND
ORANGE FREE STATE
Pretoria
NATAL
CAPE COLONY
Johannesburg
UNION OF SOUTH AFRICA
BASUTOLAND
French
British
German
Portuguese
Belgian
Anglo-Egyptian Condominium
Spanish
Italian

Map showing colonization of African countries before the First World War

THE ANGLO-BOER WARS

There were two wars in southern Africa between the British and Boer (Dutch-speaking) settlers: **1880-1881** and **1899-1902**. Relations between them had been tense from the start. When Britain took over the Cape Colony in **1814**, it prompted a mass exodus of Boer farmers into the interior, where they set up two republics: the Transvaal and the Orange Free State.

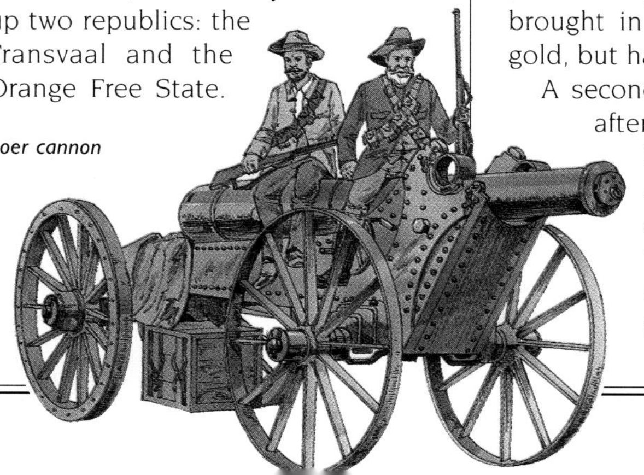

Boer cannon

The discovery of a gold reef in the Transvaal in **1886** provoked tensions between the Boers, led by President Paul Kruger, and the mainly English-speaking workers who had been brought in to mine the gold, but had no political rights.

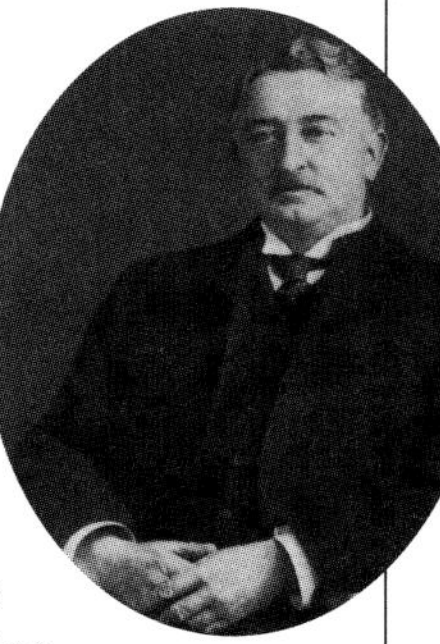

Cecil Rhodes

A second war became inevitable after the disastrous Jameson Raid in **1895**, in which a group led by Dr. Jameson, an associate of Rhodes, tried unsuccessfully to overthrow the Transvaal government.

KEY DATES

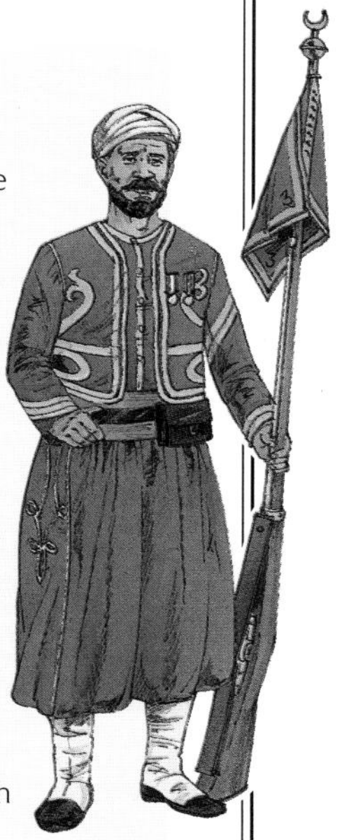

French Saharan soldier

1877 Britain annexes the Transvaal. Leads to First Boer War (**1880-1881**). Britain recognizes Transvaal independence.

1880-1900 French empire grows in the Sahara region.

1881 Tunisia is a French colony.

1882 Britain occupies Egypt (colony in **1914**).

1884 Britain takes British Somaliland. Germany takes South West Africa, Cameroons and Togo.

1885 Britain takes Bechuanaland; Germany, Tanganyika; Italy, Eritrea; Belgium, Belgian Congo; Spain, Rio de Oro and Spanish Guinea.

1886 Lagos (on Nigerian coast) becomes a British colony. Royal Niger Company is given control of British territories in Nigeria. Kenya becomes a British colony.

1888-1889 Rhodesia becomes a British colony.

1889 French take Ivory Coast. Italians take Italian Somaliland.

1894 French annex Dahomey.

1895 British take Uganda.

1896 French annex Madagascar.

1899 British goverment takes over territories in Nigeria. Sudan is under Anglo-Egyptian control.

1899-1902 Second Anglo-Boer War: Britain annexes Transvaal and Orange Free State.

1901 Britain joins Ashanti kingdom to Gold Coast colony after Ashanti wars (**1873-1874**, **1893-1894**, **1895-1896**).

1910 Britain forms Union of South Africa. French Congo is renamed French Equatorial Africa.

1912 Italians take Libya.

Asia

1883 Annam becomes a French protectorate.

1883-1884 The French expand in Southeast Asia.

1884 Russia takes Turkmenistan.

1884 Cambodia is annexed by France.

1885 The founding of the Indian National Congress.

1885-1886 The British attack and annex Ava in Burma.

Indian army troops fighting in Upper Burma

1887 France establishes an Indo-Chinese Union.

1890-1897 Armenian revolutionary movement is formed against Turkey.

1894-1895 War between Japan and China. Japan gains Formosa. Korea becomes independent of China.

1896 Britain sets up the Federated Malay States.

1896 Rebellion against the Spanish in the Philippines.

1897 Anglo-Siamese agreement on Malaya-Siam boundary.

1898 War between Spain and the U.S.A. over the Philippines. Spain cedes Philippines to the U.S.A.

1898-1909 Reactionary and repressive rule in China under Empress Tz'u-hsi. Attempts at liberal reforms are crushed.

19th century Siamese king

Summer Palace, Beijing, rebuilt by Empress Tz'u-hsi

Africa and Australasia

1880-1881 First Anglo-Boer War. Boers defeat British at Majuba Hill. Britain recognizes Transvaal.

1881 Nationalist revolt in Egypt.

1882 British forces occupy Egypt and Sudan, in order to suppress anti-European riots.

1884 Anti-British uprising in the Sudan, led by the Mahdi, a religious leader. General Gordon is sent to Khartoum.

1885 The Mahdi takes Khartoum and Gordon is killed.

1886 Gold found in Transvaal. Johannesburg is founded.

1888-1889 Expansion of British influence in Rhodesia (Zimbabwe) by Cecil Rhodes's British South Africa Company. Salisbury (Harare) is founded.

Map of Sudan and (above) General Gordon

1889 Italy claims a protectorate over Ethiopia.

1891 Emperor Menelik of Ethiopia denounces the Italian protectorate. Italians invade in **1895**, but are forced to recognize Ethiopian independence.

1893 Women in New Zealand become the first in the world to be given the vote.

1895-1896 Jameson Raid in South Africa: a failed attempt by Cecil Rhodes to take over the Transvaal.

1898 The Fashoda Crisis: French soldiers advancing north confront British soldiers advancing south at Fashoda, Sudan. It ends in French withdrawal.

1898 Battle of Omdurman: the British, led by Lord Kitchener, defeat Sudanese nationalists. Sudan comes under Anglo-Egyptian rule (**1899**).

1899-1902 The Second Anglo-Boer War.

Queen Victoria's South Africa Medal, awarded to British soldiers who fought in Boer War.

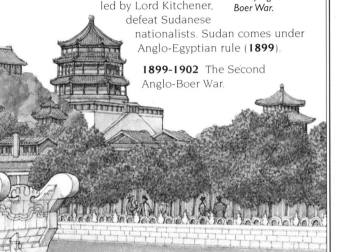

Western Europe

1880-1885 Unrest in Ireland.

1884 Reform Act in Britain gives the vote to all males over 21.

1886 Gladstone's First Home Rule Bill for Ireland is defeated.

1889 The Eiffel Tower is built for the **1889** Paris Exposition.

A lift on the Eiffel Tower

1890 Luxembourg becomes independent from Holland.

1890s Art Nouveau style is popular in Europe.

Art Nouveau lamppost in Paris

1893 The Independent Labour Party is founded in Britain by Keir Hardie.

1893 France allies with Russia.

1894 Dreyfus Affair in France. Alfred Dreyfus, a Jewish army officer, is expelled for treason. Many believe he is innocent and it leads to a political battle. (He is cleared in **1906**.)

1898 Pierre and Marie Curie, French scientists, observe radioactivity and isolate radium.

Caricature of Pierre and Marie Curie

Northern and Eastern Europe (and Italy)

1881 Czar Alexander II of Russia is assassinated. Repression follows under Alexander III.

1883 Russian Marxist Party is founded. Unrest follows.

1885 Karl Benz, a German engineer, builds the first motor car.

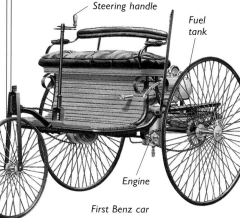

Steering handle

Fuel tank

Engine

First Benz car

1888-1918 Kaiser Wilhelm II rules Germany.

1891-1896 Otto Lilienthal, a German engineer, makes over a thousand flights in his gliders, which inspire the Wright brothers (see page 151).

Lilienthal's glider

1892-1903 Modernization and industrial growth in Russia under Sergei Witte (finance minister).

1893 Franco-Russian alliance.

1894-1897 Greeks in Crete rise against the Turks. Crete is united with Greece in **1897**.

1895 Guglielmo Marconi, an Italian physicist, invents the wireless.

1895 Sigmund Freud, an Austrian psychiatrist, publishes his first work on psychoanalysis.

1895 Wilhelm Röntgen, a German physicist, discovers x-rays.

The Americas

1880 Start of the construction of the Panama Canal.

1887 Emile Berliner (**1851-1929**), a German who emigrated to the U.S.A., patents the gramophone.

Horn

Needle

Berliner's gramophone

1889 Pedro II of Brazil is deposed and a republic set up.

1890 Battle of Wounded Knee: last Native American uprising in the U.S.A. by the Sioux people. The Native Americans are defeated and their weapons taken away.

A ghost shirt. Many Sioux warriors wore these, believing they could protect them from the settlers' bullets.

Sioux ghost dancers

Many tribes were rounded up and taken to live on special areas of land called reservations.

1893 Hawaii becomes a U.S. protectorate.

1898 Spanish-American War. Cuba becomes independent under temporary American control.

Asia and Australasia

1900 Boxer Rebellion in China against foreign influence is crushed by an international force.

A dragon, ancient symbol of China

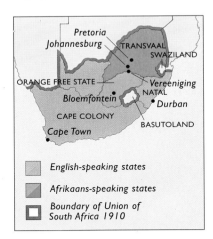

1900 New Zealand takes the Cook Islands. Papua is transferred from Britain to Australia. Britain annexes Tonga.

1901 The Commonwealth of Australia is established.

1901 British company in Persia is granted the right to search for oil. Oil is found in **1907.**

1904 Russia and Japan at war over Manchuria and Korea.

1905 Japan destroys Russian fleet at Tsushima. Treaty of Portsmouth gives Japan a protectorate over Korea and territory in China.

Japanese print showing the Battle of Tsushima

1907 New Zealand is given dominion status.

1908-1909 Ahmed Shah seizes power in Persia.

1909 Anglo-Siam Treaty: Siam recognizes British control over Malayan states.

1909 China attacks Tibet. The Tibetan ruler, the Dalai Lama, flees to India.

The 8-spoked wheel, an important Buddhist symbol

Tibetan monk playing a trumpet at a festival

1910 Malayan states of Trengganu and Perlis accept British protection.

1910 China: uprising in Yunnan province.

1910 Nationalist movement in Burma led by Buddhist monks.

1910-1945 Korea is a Japanese colony.

1911 Chinese Revolution: a government is set up in Nanking under Sun Yat-sen.

1912 Chinese Manchu dynasty is overthrown and a republic is established. This is followed by a period of great unrest and local rule by warlords.

Africa and the Middle East

1900 British win victories over the Boers and annex the Orange Free State and Transvaal. The Anglo-Boer War ends with the Peace of Vereeniging (**1902**).

Map of South Africa 1910

1908 The Belgian government takes over the Congo from King Leopold.

1908 A revolution in Turkey by the Young Turks, a group of army officers, including Mustafa Kemäl. The Sultan introduces a liberal constitution and promises reforms. A period of instability follows.

Map labels: Pretoria, Johannesburg, TRANSVAAL, SWAZILAND, ORANGE FREE STATE, Vereeniging, NATAL, Bloemfontein, Durban, CAPE COLONY, BASUTOLAND, Cape Town

English-speaking states
Afrikaans-speaking states
Boundary of Union of South Africa 1910

1909 The Sultan of Turkey is deposed by the Young Turks.

1910 Union of South Africa becomes a British dominion.

1911 Italy and Turkey at war over Tripoli. Italians take Libya in **1912.**

1914-1915 Britain and France conquer all German colonies, except German East Africa.

1914-1922 Egypt is a British protectorate.

1916 Arab nationalists in the Hejaz, Saudi Arabia, rise against the Ottomans. Further uprisings follow.

1916 Colonel T.E. Lawrence explores the Hejaz area of Saudi Arabia.

Colonel T.E. Lawrence

1917 The Balfour Declaration: Britain supports Zionism and a Jewish home in Palestine, on condition that Arab rights are respected.

Dome of the Rock, Jerusalem, an Arab mosque built on the site of an ancient Jewish temple

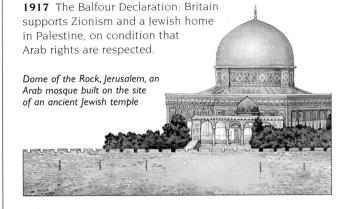

1918 Syria proclaims independence. Not recognized by France or Britain. French forces take control in **1919.**

1918 Ottoman empire collapses: Allies control Istanbul.

Southern and Western Europe

1901 Death of Queen Victoria and accession of Edward VII.

Queen Victoria

1902 Britain allies with Japan: the end of a long period of Japanese isolation.

1903 French minister Delcassé visits London. Growing Anglo-French friendship.

1904 *Entente Cordiale*: friendship pact between Britain and France.

1910 Revolution in Portugal: the King is deposed. A republic is declared in **1911**.

1911 Ernest Rutherford (N.Z./U.K.) shows that atoms have a nucleus.

Rutherford's model of an atom

Electron

Nucleus

1914 -1918 The First World War.

1915 Italy joins the Allies.

1916 Easter Rising in Dublin: Irish nationalists rise against the British.

1916 British are first to use tanks.

1918 Britain: the vote is given to women over 30.

Suffragettes fighting for votes for women

Northern and Eastern Europe

1903 King and Queen of Serbia are murdered.

1905 Revolts in St. Petersburg and other Russian cities.

1905 Norway becomes independent from Sweden.

1905 Albert Einstein (Switzerland) publishes his Special Theory of Relativity.

Albert Einstein

1908 Austria-Hungary takes Turkish provinces of Herzegovina and Bosnia. International tension follows. Bulgaria wins independence.

1912 First Balkan War: Bulgaria, Greece, Serbia and Montenegro unite and defeat Turkey.

1913 Second Balkan War: Turkey, Romania, Serbia and Greece defeat Bulgaria.

1914 Murder of Archduke Franz Ferdinand in Sarajevo starts the First World War.

1917 The Russian Revolution.

Rifle used in the Russian Revolution

Red flag, a symbol of revolution

1918 March: Treaty of Brest-Litovsk: Russia is defeated and makes peace with Germany.

1918-1919 New nations win independence: Latvia, Estonia, Lithuania, Czechoslovakia and Yugoslavia.

1918 Revolution in Berlin. The Kaiser flees and the Weimar Republic is set up (**July 1919**).

1918 Emperor Charles of Austria-Hungary abdicates.

The Americas

1903 Revolution in Panama. Panama gains independence from Colombia as a U.S. protectorate.

1903 First wireless transmission from U.S.A. to England.

1903 Orville and Wilbur Wright (U.S.A.) make the first successful powered and controlled flight.

Wright brothers' plane, Flyer I

Wooden propeller

Flexible but strong wooden frame

The pilot's hand controls

1908-1918 Unrest in Haiti.

1910-1911 A revolution in Mexico overthrows Porfirio Diaz. Followed by disorder and the rise of dictators.

1912 Roald Amundsen (Norway) is the first to reach the South Pole.

1912-1913 Henry Ford (U.S.A.) begins the mass production of motor cars.

Cutaway to show the engine inside

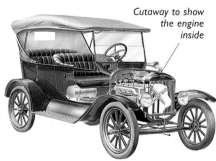

Ford Model T, the first mass-produced car

1914 Opening of Panama Canal.

1917 A number of U.S. passenger ships are sunk by German U-boats (submarines). U.S.A. declares war on Germany, joined by other South American states and Cuba.

The First World War

The First World War, or Great War, was mainly a European war, fought across Europe and the Middle East to solve European disputes. But it was called a "world war" because so many other nations, particularly the colonies, became directly involved. The governments claimed it would be short and glorious, but it dragged on for four years, killing 17 million - more than in any other conflict in history.

Since the **1870s**, various alliances had been made to preserve the

Aircraft, like this German Fokker Dr-I flown by ace pilot Manfred Von Richthofen ("the Red Baron"), flew over enemy lines. It was the first war in which planes were regularly used in combat.

The Kaiser by William Nicholson

balance of power. By **1914** there were two armed camps: on one side, Germany and Austria-Hungary; on the other, France, Russia and Britain. These alliances were so delicately balanced that an attack on one country would automatically involve its allies and lead to war.

ASSASSINATION AT SARAJEVO

There were many issues that might have led to war. Britain, France and Russia were alarmed at the speed of Germany's growing military strength, and Russia and Austria disagreed over who should have control in the Balkans. Rivalry over colonies abroad also provoked tensions.

But the incident which actually triggered the conflict was the assassination of Archduke Franz Ferdinand, the heir to the Austrian throne, by a Serbian nationalist at Sarajevo in **June 1914**. Austria decided to strike back, giving Serbia an ultimatum.

WAR IS DECLARED

The ultimatum ran out and Austria declared war on **July 28**. Within weeks, fighting had broken out between the two sides. Germany and Austria (the Central Powers) were joined by Turkey (**1914**) and Bulgaria (**1915**). France, Russia and Britain (Entente, or Allies) were joined by Italy (**1914**), Greece (**1915**), Portugal (**1916**), the U.S.A. and Romania (**1917**).

The British Dreadnought, the most powerful ship in the world at the time

Funnel for moving bombshells for firing

Boiler room and coal stores

Steam engine

Prison cells for sailors who didn't follow orders

Archduke Franz Ferdinand, in Sarajevo on the day he was assassinated

Map of the two sides during the First World War

Central Powers

Allies

Neutral countries

Gas masks were introduced in 1915 to protect soldiers from poison gas attacks.

TRENCH WARFARE

The Germans made advances at first, but were soon checked by the Allies in northern France. Both sides dug trenches and strengthened their positions. But trench warfare made it very difficult for either side to advance. By **1915,** there was a stalemate on both the western and eastern fronts. The ill-equipped and often half-starved Russians suffered huge casualties and loss of morale, which helped contribute to the Russian Revolution (see page 154).

German helmet

Map of Europe in 1919, showing the new nations formed from the break-up of the old empires

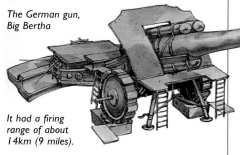

The German gun, Big Bertha

It had a firing range of about 14km (9 miles).

The U.S.A. joined the Allies in **April 1917**, after persistent attacks by German submarines, known as U-boats, on American passenger liners. American entry made a crucial difference to the War. By **1918,** Germany was exhausted and facing revolution at home. Final surrender came in **November 1918.**

POSTWAR EUROPE

The outcome of the war changed Europe forever; the old empires of Russia, Austria and the Ottomans broke up, and new nations emerged. But the terms placed on Germany at the Peace of Versailles (**1919**) - loss of territory, no armies in the Rhine, and crippling reparation payments - left problems which would take another major war to settle.

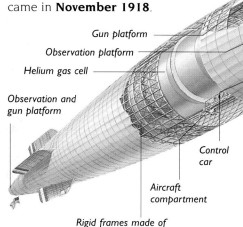

Gun platform
Observation platform
Helium gas cell
Observation and gun platform
Control car
Aircraft compartment
Rigid frames made of lightweight metal

During the War, airships like this were converted into bombers which carried out air raids on London and other cities.

IMPORTANT BATTLES

August-September 1914 Germans advance through Luxembourg and Belgium. Invasion of France is halted by Allies at the Battle of the Marne.

April 1915 British, French, Australian and New Zealand forces land at Gallipoli, Turkey, but are massacred by Turks. The Allies retreat.

February-June 1916 Battle of Verdun: the longest battle of the war, lasting 300 days, ends in stalemate.

July-November 1916 Battle of the Somme ends in stalemate after 1,250,000 casualties.

July-Nov. 1917 Third Battle of Ypres (also known as Passchendaele): British offensive fails. Stalemate continues

March-April 1918 The German Spring Offensive, led by General Ludendorff, breaks through Allied lines in northern France.

July-August 1918 Battle of the Marne: The German Spring Offensive is broken by the Allies.

Poppies that grew on the battlefields of the Western Front became a symbol of remembrance of the War.

Asia and Australasia

1919 India: British soldiers under the command of General Dyer fire on protesters at a peaceful political meeting in Amritsar. This leads to a rise in Indian nationalist feeling. General Dyer is sacked.

Mao Zedong

1920 Mohandas (Mahatma) Gandhi forms the Indian National Congress: a non-violent campaign for independence. First Indian Parliament meets in **1921**.

1921 Mao Zedong (Mao Tse-tung) and Li Ta-chao form the Chinese Communist Party in Beijing.

1923 An earthquake and fire destroys much of Tokyo, Japan.

Tokyo after the earthquake

1924-1925 Reza Shah seizes power in Persia.

Japanese imperial flag, known as "the Rising Sun"

1925 China: Sun Yat-sen dies. He is succeeded by Jiang Jie Shi (Chiang Kai-shek), who campaigns against the warlords.

1926 Hirohito becomes Emperor of Japan.

1927 Jiang Jie Shi, leader of the Kuomintang (Chinese Nationalists), breaks with the Communist Party. Civil war follows. The Communists set up bases in remote areas.

1927 Canberra becomes the federal capital of Australia.

1928 Jiang Jie Shi becomes President of China.

1929 Gandhi demands Indian independence and begins a campaign of civil disobedience.

Gandhi

Africa and the Middle East

1919 War begins between Britain and Afghanistan.

1919 German African colonies are mandated to the Allies by the League of Nations.

1919 Egypt: nationalist revolt against British protectorate.

1920 Feisal I becomes King of Syria. Transjordan is separated from Syria.

1920 Abdullah becomes King of Iraq.

1921 Moroccan Berbers led by Abd-el-Krim defeat Spaniards at Anual.

1922 Mustafa Kemäl, known as Atatürk, seizes power in Turkey. The Greek army is expelled and the last Ottoman emperor deposed. A Turkish republic is proclaimed and a period of reform and modernization follows.

Turkish flag

Mustafa Kemäl, Atatürk

1922 Britain recognizes Egyptian independence.

1922 France gains League of Nations mandate over Syria.

1923 Ethiopia joins the League of Nations.

1923 Southern Rhodesia (now Zimbabwe) is formally annexed as a British colony.

1924 Moroccan independence movement grows, but is crushed by Spanish and French forces in **1926**.

1926 Ibn Saud becomes King of Hejaz and Nejd. In **1932** they unite to form Saudi Arabia.

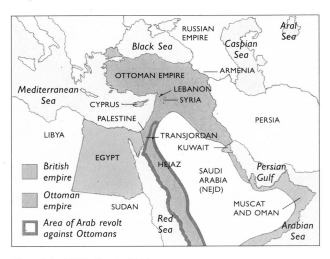

Map of the Middle East in 1914

1926 A republic is proclaimed in the Lebanon.

1927 Britain recognizes independence of Iraq and position of Ibn Saud as ruler of Saudi Arabia.

Southern and Western Europe

1919 Peace of Versailles between Germany and the Allies. League of Nations is set up to preserve peace.

1919 Benito Mussolini establishes the Fascist movement in Italy.

Benito Mussolini

Fascism comes from the Latin word fasces, a bundle of sticks tied around an axe, which was a symbol of power in ancient Rome.

1919 Ernest Rutherford (N.Z./U.K.) splits the atom.

1919-1921 Disorder in Ireland.

1920 The six northern counties separate from the rest of Ireland, and set up parliament in Belfast.

1921 Irish Free State is recognized as a dominion within the British empire.

1922 Michael Collins, Irish nationalist leader, is assassinated.

1922 Mussolini marches on Rome. He is appointed Prime Minister and forms a Fascist government.

1923 Revolution in Spain. De Rivera becomes dictator.

1925 Mussolini bans all political parties in Italy except the Fascists.

1926 Britain: 9-day General Strike.

1928 Alexander Fleming (Scottish) discovers penicillin, the first antibiotic.

Penicillin seen under microscope

Northern and Eastern Europe

1919 Solar eclipse confirms Einstein's theories.

Stages in a total solar eclipse, when the Moon passes in front of the Sun

1919 Finland becomes a republic.

1921 Lenin introduces the New Economic Policies in Russia.

1923 Russia is renamed Union of Soviet Socialist Republics (U.S.S.R.).

1923 Germany: strike in the Ruhr Valley, in protest against post-war payments leads to massive inflation.

1923 Failed uprising of the Nazis in Germany, led by Adolf Hitler.

1924 Lenin dies and is replaced by three leaders. Josef Stalin wins supreme power and remains leader until his death in **1953**.

1924 The Greek monarchy is replaced by a republic.

1924 Ahmed Zogu seizes power in Albania.

1925 Treaty of Locarno: European powers agree on frontiers and demilitarization of the German Rhineland.

1925 Hitler publishes his ideas in his book *Mein Kampf.*

Adolf Hitler

1926-1935 Józef Pilsudski takes control in Poland.

1928 The first Five Year Plan is launched in the U.S.S.R.: a period of rapid growth and industrialization.

The Americas

1920 The U.S. Senate votes not to join the League of Nations. Prohibition of alcohol and women's suffrage are introduced in the U.S.A.

1923 Edwin Hubble (U.S.) proves the existence of other galaxies.

1927 *The Jazz Singer*, the first talking picture, or movie, is made in U.S.A.

1927 Charles Lindbergh makes the first solo flight across the Atlantic.

1929 Hubble shows galaxies moving away from each other. Forms the basis of the Big Bang Theory.

1929 The Wall Street Crash: U.S. stock market collapses. The beginning of the Depression.

THE DEPRESSION

From **1929** until the mid **1930s**, nearly every country in the world experienced an economic crisis, known as the Depression. There was falling production, declining incomes and mass unemployment. The U.S.A., Germany, Eastern Europe and many places in Africa, Asia and Latin America were worst affected.

LINE FOR
1¢ RESTAURANT

20 MEALS FOR 1¢
DONATIONS WANTED
HELP FEED THE HUNGRY
I WILL FEED 20
1¢ RESTAURANT
107 W 43ᴿᴰ ST

Soup kitchens sold cheap food to the many who had lost their jobs.

Chrysler Building, New York, built 1928-1930

The Russian Revolution

At the start of the 20th century, the Russian empire covered one sixth of the earth's surface, but it was one of the most backward regions in Europe. Aristocrats lived in grand palaces, while most of the population scratched a living as peasants in extreme poverty and hardship.

Easter eggs designed by Carl Fabergé and commissioned by the Russian imperial family

Growing discontent with the oppressive and autocratic rule of the Russian czars came to a head with the outbreak of the October Revolution* in **1917**, one of the most important dates in 20th century history.

PLOTTING FOR CHANGE

In the late 19th century, different revolutionary groups - democrats, anarchists and socialists - met in secret to discuss reform. In **1898**, the Russian Social Democratic and Labour Party was formed. In **1903**, it split into the Bolsheviks and the Mensheviks. The Bolsheviks were led by Vladimir Ilyich Ulyanov, later known as Lenin (**1870-1924**). They followed the ideas of Karl Marx, who wanted to create a socialist society. Lenin was frequently imprisoned and exiled for his views.

The ancient fortress of the Kremlin at the heart of the city of Moscow. After the Revolution, the capital was moved back to Moscow from St. Petersburg.

THE 1905 REVOLUTION

A disastrous war with Japan in **1904-1905** and anger about living conditions sparked off mutiny in the army and riots at home. In **January 1905**, a group marched to the Winter Palace in St. Petersburg to demand changes. Troops fired into the crowd without warning, killing many.

This increased the pressure for change. Czar Nicholas II set up a *duma*, an elected advisory council, and tried to reform the economy by allowing peasants to own land. But the dumas had little real power: the first two were closed within weeks for criticizing the Czar.

Cartoon of Rasputin, a monk who was said to have a mysterious hold on the unpopular Czarina Alexandra

THE FEBRUARY REVOLUTION

Russian involvement in World War I brought defeats, huge loss of life, and starvation. Riots broke out in St. Petersburg (renamed Petrograd because of anti-German feeling) and workers' councils, called Soviets, were formed. Realizing that his position was impossible, the Czar abdicated, and a provisional government was set up, led by the Mensheviks.

Cathedral of the Archangel Michael and the Ivan the Great Bell Tower

Nicholas and Alexandra and their children

RED OCTOBER

German politicians thought they could remove Russia from the War by encouraging political disorder at home. So, in **April 1917**, they helped Lenin return to Russia from exile in Switzerland in a protected train.

As a result of this, Bolshevik influence increased rapidly. On **October 24, 1917**, Lenin and a group of supporters stormed the Winter Palace and seized power, with little resistance. The new government acted through a Congress of Soviets. It centralized control of the land, including that of the Church. Lenin got rid of all his opponents, including the Czar and his family, who were murdered in **1918**.

Lenin

Although the Bolsheviks were popular in the cities, they had less support in rural areas. But they succeeded in holding onto power through a campaign of fear, known as the "Red Terror".

CIVIL WAR

From **1918** to **1920**, there was civil war between the Bolshevik Red Army and the Whites (anti-revolutionaries), and between Russians and non-Russians in the old empire.

This civil war propaganda poster asks "Have you joined the Red Army?"

Map showing areas of influence during the Civil War

Barents Sea
NORWAY
White Sea
SWEDEN FINLAND
Petrograd (St. Petersburg)
Baltic Sea
BALTIC STATES
Moscow
EASTERN EUROPE
BOLSHEVIK RUSSIA
Caspian Sea
Black Sea
TURKEY PERSIA

Bolshevik control 1918
White forces
Soviet territory 1921

Despite support for the Whites from foreign powers anxious to stop the spread of revolution abroad, the Reds won because they were better organized.

THE BIRTH OF THE SOVIET UNION

War was followed by drought and famine in **1921**, leaving millions of people dead and the economy in ruins. In an attempt to tackle this, Lenin introduced the New Economic Policy (NEP), which allowed for a limited return to capitalism. In **1922**, the country was renamed the Union of Soviet Socialist Republics (U.S.S.R.).

IMPORTANT DATES

1900 In exile Lenin develops the philosophy of Marxism-Leninism.

1903 Lenin leads the Bolsheviks.

March* 13, 1917 February Revolution: Nicholas II abdicates and a provisional government is set up.

November* 8, 1917 October Revolution: Lenin and Trotsky control the Petrograd Soviet and overthrow the government.

July 1918 Czar and family are shot.

1919 The Comintern, a Communist international organization, is formed.

1921 The New Economic Policy stimulates trade and industrial growth.

December 1922 Russia is renamed the Union of Soviet Socialist Republics (U.S.S.R.), or Soviet Union.

Peasant farmers awaiting deportation from their village in 1930, holding banners protesting against Stalin's treatment of them

STALIN

When Lenin died in **1924**, he was succeeded by the ruthless Josef Djugashvili, who became known as Stalin, meaning "man of steel".

Josef Stalin

Stalin succeeded in turning a backward agricultural nation into an industrial giant. But the people paid a heavy price. In **1928**, he announced the first Five Year Plan, setting huge targets for growth. All Soviet factories were brought under state ownership, and millions of peasants were forced to work on collective farms.

Posters, like this one, made peasant life look happy and heroic.

Land-owning peasants, or kulaks, who opposed this, were executed, or exiled to the harsh region of Siberia. Stalin also disposed of anyone else he saw as a threat. This included intellectuals and those who just didn't meet the goals of the Five Year Plans.

In **1932**, millions starved to death in the Ukraine, while the state exported their food abroad. From **1934** to **1939**, about 7 million were arrested in "purges", and executed or sent to prison camps called gulags. It is thought that up to 15 million may have died as a result of Stalin's policies.

The Soviet flag

The October Revolution actually took place in November, and the February Revolution in March. Russia still followed Julius Caesar's calendar, which was 13 days behind the one used in the rest of Europe since 1592.

Asia and Australasia

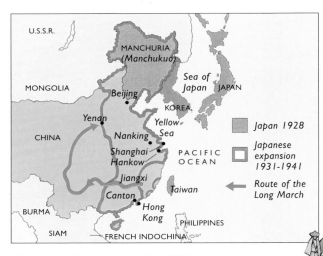

Amy Johnson's plane

1930 Amy Johnson (U.K.) flies from London to Darwin, Australia, the first woman to fly solo across the world.

1931 Mao Zedong proclaims a Chinese Soviet Republic in the remote Jiangxi province.

1931 Japanese occupy Manchuria. In **1932**, they set up Republic of Manchukuo, with Chinese ex-emperor Pu Yi as President.

Map showing the Japanese invasion of China

1934 Rapid military and naval rearmament begins in Japan.

1934-1935 The Long March to northern China by Chinese Communists led by Mao Zedong. Driven from their stronghold in Jiangxi by Jiang Jie Shi, they are forced to make a 8000km (5000 mile) journey to Yenan, a mountainous region in northwest China. They set up government and plot to take over the whole country.

The Communist Long March of 1934-1935, led by Mao Zedong

1935 Persia is renamed Iran.

1937 Burma is separated from British India and ruled as an individual colony.

1937-1945 The Japanese attack China. They take Shanghai and Nanking (**1937**), Canton and Hankow (**1938**).

Africa and the Middle East

1930 A revolution in Ethiopia establishes Ras Tafari (**1892-1975**) as Emperor. He takes the name Haile Selassie.

Emperor Haile Selassie

1932 Kingdom of Saudi Arabia is established by Ibn Saud.

1932 Harry Philby crosses the Rub' al-Khali Desert in Arabia, known as the Empty Quarter, probably the first European to do so.

1933 Britain limits the number of Jews allowed into Palestine, to try to stop Arab unrest.

Harry Philby and camel

1935 Italy invades Ethiopia, disobeying the terms of the League of Nations.

1936 Anglo-Egyptian alliance ends the British protectorate over Egypt, but gives Britain control over the Suez Canal for 20 years. British troops garrison the Suez Canal zone.

1936 Italian troops capture Addis Ababa, the capital of Ethiopia, and annex the country. Haile Selassie appeals for League of Nations support. Britain and France agree to impose limited sanctions on Italy.

1936 Arab revolt in Palestine against Jewish immigrants, in an attempt to stop the establishment of the state of Israel.

1938 Mussolini declares Libya part of Italy.

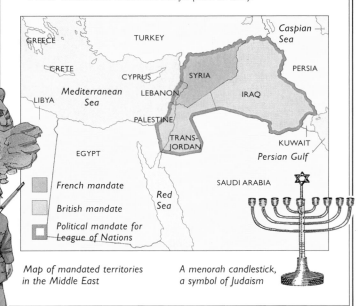

Map of mandated territories in the Middle East

A menorah candlestick, a symbol of Judaism

156

Southern and Western Europe

1931 Growth of republican feeling in Spain. King Alphonso XIII leaves the country and a republic is set up. A period of disorder follows.

1931 Statute of Westminster defines the rights of British dominions: an important step in the founding of the Commonwealth.

1932 Antonio Salazar becomes Prime Minister and virtual dictator of Portugal until **1968**.

1936 King Edward VIII of Britain abdicates to marry Mrs. Simpson.

1936-1939 The Spanish Civil War. General Franco, leader of the Nationalists, rebels against the Republican government. Germany and Italy give military aid. The U.S.S.R. supports the Republicans. Franco becomes dictator until his death in **1975**.

Spanish flag

Republican soldiers in the Spanish Civil War

1937 Southern Ireland becomes the sovereign state of Eire.

1939 Mussolini seizes Albania.

1939-1945 Second World War (see pages 158-159).

Northern and Eastern Europe

1930 A period of terror begins in the U.S.S.R. Stalin enforces the collectivization of agriculture. Millions of kulaks, peasant farm owners who oppose this, are suppressed and murdered.

1933 Hitler becomes Chancellor of Germany. The Berlin parliament, the *Reichstag*, burns down.

The Reichstag fire was probably started by the Nazis themselves, to justify granting themselves greater powers.

1934 Hitler is appointed *Führer* (leader) of a one-party Germany.

1934-1939 Stalin crushes all political opposition in Soviet Union.

1935 The Saar territory votes to join Germany. Germany increases its military strength.

1935 Nuremberg Laws: start of persecution of German Jews.

The Star of David, which German Jews were forced to wear (top), and Nazi officer's badge (bottom)

1936 Germans occupy Rhineland.

1936 German-Italian Axis Pact.

1938 Germany takes Austria and is granted Sudetenland (German-speaking Czech territory) at Munich.

1939 Hahn and Strassman (German) discover nuclear fission.

1939 Germany invades Poland.

The Americas

1930 Getulio Vargas seizes power in Brazil and becomes President.

1932 War between Peru and Colombia.

1932-1935 War between Paraguay and Bolivia over disputed Chaco region.

Peruvian textiles and bowl

ATLANTIC OCEAN

MEXICO Gulf of Mexico CUBA Caribbean Sea
BELIZE
GUATEMALA HONDURAS GUYANA
EL SALVADOR
NICARAGUA VENEZUELA
COSTA RICA COLOMBIA
PANAMA SURINAM FRENCH GUIANA
PACIFIC OCEAN ECUADOR
BRAZIL
PERU
BOLIVIA
CHILE PARAGUAY
URUGUAY
ARGENTINA

1933 Sanchez Cerro is elected President of Peru, and assassinated by a member of the opposition.

1933-1945 F. D. Roosevelt is U.S. President. He introduces New Deal policies to deal with the Depression. The end of Prohibition.

mid 1930s Fierce winds in the U.S. plains destroy farms and wreck the landscape. The area becomes known as "the Dust Bowl".

1936 Jesse Owens, an African American, wins 4 gold medals at the Berlin Olympics.

U.S. and German flags, and a stopwatch used at the Olympics

1938 Unsuccessful Nazi plots in Chile and Brazil.

1938-1945 Getulio Vargas is dictator of Brazil.

1939 Igor Sikorsky (U.S.S.R./ U.S.) designs the first modern helicopter.

The Second World War

In the **1930s**, it looked increasingly unlikely that peace in Europe would last. The treaties that followed the First World War had failed to solve the political and economic rivalries that had started it. The economic difficulties of the Depression led to the rise of an extremist political ideology called fascism. Fascist parties came to power in Germany (the Nazis), Italy (Mussolini's Fascists) and Spain (the Falange).

Hitler sponsored the Volkswagen Beetle (the "people's car") to boost the car industry.

THE RISE OF GERMANY

German military strength increased rapidly during the **1930s** under Adolf Hitler. In **1936**, German troops re-occupied the Rhineland, breaking the terms of the Treaty of Versailles.

By **1938**, Hitler was ready to begin his plans for a Greater Germany. In **March**, he marched into Austria and joined the two countries under the *Anschluss*, or "union". Then he demanded that Germany be allowed to annex the Sudetenland, the German-speaking territory of Czechoslovakia.

From 1933-1938, annual meetings of the Nazi Party were held at Nuremburg, including military parades and mass rallies.

At the Munich conference in **September 1938**, Britain and France tried to appease Hitler by agreeing to his plans for the Sudetenland, on the condition that he advance no farther. But within six months he had taken over the whole country. Seeing too late that his promises were worthless, they then agreed to help Greece, Poland or Romania, if any of those countries were attacked. In **August 1939**, Germany made a secret pact with the U.S.S.R., to divide Poland between them.

Machine guns in the wings fired out of gun holes.

The Swastika, symbol of the Nazi Party

BLITZKRIEG

On **September 1, 1939**, Hitler invaded Poland. Two days later, Britain and France declared war. Little happened for the first six months. But, from spring **1940**, Hitler's troops swept through Europe. By **June**, they had taken over Poland, Norway, Denmark, Belgium, Luxembourg and Holland, as well as much of France. They moved with tanks and planes at incredible speed, using a method known as *Blitzkrieg*, or "lightning war".

Grerman motorcyclist with French soldiers surrendering

German Messerschmitt 109E fighter plane (far left) and British Vickers Supermarine Spitfire 1A fighter plane (left), which fought in the Battle of Britain

THE BATTLE OF BRITAIN

Hitler then planned to invade Britain, beginning with a series of air attacks by the *Luftwaffe*, the German air force. During the Battle of Britain (**Aug.-Dec. 1940**), the *Luftwaffe* attacked airports, factories and cities. But, despite heavy losses, the British Royal Air Force won a decisive victory. After this, the Germans changed tactics and began bombing British cities. The regular night attacks that ran from **September 1940** to **May 1941** were known as the *Blitz*. From **1941**, Britain responded by bombing German cities, with even more devastating results. Some cities, such as Dresden and Düsseldorf, were virtually wiped out.

Gas masks, issued to civilians during the War, in anticipation of attacks by poison gas

Map of the two sides during the War

Legend:
- Axis territory before September 1 1939
- Axis satellites
- Neutral countries
- Allied countries
- Allied occupied countries
- Axis occupied countries

British troops returning from action in Crete

THE EASTERN FRONT

In **June 1941**, the Germans launched a massive invasion of the Soviet Union, in an operation codenamed "Barbarossa". The invasion was at first a great success, but it was to be Hitler's greatest mistake. It committed large numbers of troops to the Eastern Front and drained German resources. By **December**, they had almost reached Moscow, but the bitterness of the winter and strength of the Soviet resistance forced them to retreat.

THE FINAL SOLUTION

Hitler believed Jews, gypsies, homosexuals and the mentally ill had no place in the German *Reich* (empire). From **1941**, the Nazis built vast concentration camps in German-occupied countries. Hitler used them to carry out his plan: from **1941-1945**, over 12 million people, including over six million Jews, were murdered in these camps. This terrible destruction is known as "the Holocaust".

During the War, pigeons were used to deliver messages carried in a message tube on the pigeon's leg.

WAR IN THE PACIFIC

Japan signed a pact with Germany and Italy in **September 1940**. In **December 1941**, the Japanese attacked the U.S. fleet at Pearl Harbor, in Hawaii, bringing the Americans into the War. By **April 1942**, Japan controlled much of Southeast Asia and the Pacific.

THE TIDE TURNS

From **1942**, the Allies began to reverse the earlier successes of the Axis powers. U.S. naval victories at Midway, Philippine Sea and Coral Sea put an end to Japanese supremacy in the Pacific. There were also major Allied victories in North Africa at El Alamein (**1942**)

and in Russia at Stalingrad (**1943**). In **1943**, the Allies occupied much of Italy, which resulted in the downfall of Mussolini.

On **June 6, 1944** (D-Day), Allied forces landed in Normandy, taking the Germans by surprise. Pushing from the opposite direction Soviet troops met the Allies in Berlin on **April 1945**. Faced with defeat, Hitler committed suicide on **April 30**, and on **May 8** (VE Day), the Germans finally surrendered. In spring **1945**, Japan suffered defeats in the Far East. On **August 6** and **9**, Nagasaki and Hiroshima were devastated by atomic bombs. Japanese surrender came on **September 2, 1945**.

Churchill, Roosevelt and Stalin, the leaders of Britain, U.S.A. and U.S.S.R., at a meeting at Yalta on the Black Sea in February 1945, to make plans for a postwar settlement

Asia and Australasia

1940 Friendship treaty between Siam and Japan.

1941 Neutrality pact between the Soviet Union and Japan.

Pacific albatross (left) and Southeast Asian kingfisher (right)

1941-1942 The Japanese occupy much of Southeast Asia and the islands of the Pacific.

1942 Battle of Midway: U.S. halts Japanese expansion.

1944 The U.S. seizes Saigon and launches bombing raids against Japan.

1945 U.S. destroys Japanese fleet at Okinawa and drops atomic bombs on Japan. Japanese surrender on **August 14**.

This atomic bomb, named "Fat Boy", was dropped on Nagasaki, Japan.

Inside was a substance called plutonium. All the atoms in the plutonium split, releasing huge amounts of energy.

Stabilizing fin

1945 U.S.S.R. and U.S.A. administer Korea.

1945 Ho Chi Minh forms a government in Hanoi, Vietnam. French attempts to reassert control lead to a war of independence in Indochina (**1946-1954**).

1945-1951 The Allies occupy and administer Japan.

1946-1949 Civil war between nationalists and communists in China leads to communist victory. Nationalists set up state of Nationalist China in Taiwan.

1947 India becomes independent and is divided into Hindu India and Muslim Pakistan. Massacres take place as people migrate to different parts of the subcontinent.

People migrating to different parts of India

1948 Mahatma Gandhi is assassinated.

1948 Terrorism leads to a state of emergency in Malaya.

1948 Two republics in Korea: a pro-communist regime in North Korea and a pro-western regime in South Korea.

1949 Siam is renamed Thailand.

1949 Japan: the U.S. launches a scheme to improve the Japanese economy.

Africa and the Middle East

1940 Italy invades Egypt, but is driven back by the British, who occupy Libya.

1940 Many French African colonies support General de Gaulle's Free French Forces.

1941 General Erwin Rommel leads a German counterattack against the Allies in North Africa.

Rommel's troops after capture in 1941

1941 Italians expelled from Somalia, Eritrea and Ethiopia.

1942 Rommel is defeated by the British under General Montgomery at El Alamein, Egypt.

1943 Germans surrender in Tunisia: the end of German involvement in Africa.

1945 Formation of the Arab League in Cairo.

1945 Uprising against the French in Algeria.

1946 Transjordan wins independence under King Abdullah, and is renamed Jordan.

1947 Partition of Palestine into Arab and Jewish states is agreed by UN, but opposed by the Arabs. There is fighting after the British withdraw.

Map of Israel and Palestine 1947-1948

Jewish areas 1947
Arab areas 1947
Israel's border 1948

LEBANON
SYRIA
Jerusalem
Dead Sea
PALESTINE
JORDAN
SINAI PENINSULA
SAUDI ARABIA

1948 Nationalist Party is elected in South Africa on a policy of *apartheid* (separate development for blacks and whites). *Apartheid* is introduced in **1949**.

1948-1949 Arab League goes to war with Israel, but fails to stop the establishment of the state.

Palestinian refugees leaving Israel

Southern and Western Europe

1940 Battle of Britain: air battle between Britain and Germany ends in British victory.

British plane

1940 Germans take France. De Gaulle sets up Free French Forces (FFL) to continue fighting.

1940-1945 Coalition government in Britain, led by Sir Winston Churchill.

Sir Winston Churchill

1943 Italy surrenders. Germans occupy North Italy and Rome.

1944 Allied advances on all fronts. France is liberated on **June 6** (D-Day). De Gaulle sets up a government in Paris in **August**.

1945 French women are given the vote for the first time.

1946 The King of Italy abdicates and a republic is proclaimed.

1946 Italian women are given the vote for the first time.

1947 Belgium, Netherlands and Luxembourg form a Customs Union. The start of the movement for European unity.

1947-1958 Fourth Republic in France.

1948 Organization for European Economic Cooperation (OEEC) is established.

1949 U.K. Labour government begins a policy of nationalization.

1949 Eire leaves the British Commonwealth.

The Irish flag

Northern and Eastern Europe

1941 Operation Barbarossa: Germans invade U.S.S.R.

1942 Wernher von Braun, a German scientist, launches the V-2, the first long-range jet rocket.

The V-2 war rocket

Warhead

Radio control

Nitrogen bottles

This fuel tank contains a mixture of ethyl alcohol and water.

This fuel tank contains liquid oxygen to speed up burning of fuel.

The two fuels are forced by pumps into the combustion chamber. The mixture is then ignited by gunpowder.

Exhaust fumes escape at supersonic speed.

1944-1949 Civil war in Greece.

1945 Germany surrenders on **May 8** (VE Day). It is split into French, British, U.S., and Soviet occupation zones.

1945-1946 War trials of Nazi leaders at Nuremburg, Germany.

1946 Hungary, Albania and Bulgaria become republics.

1947 Romania becomes a republic.

1948 Communists seize power in Czechoslovakia, Hungary, Romania, Bulgaria and Poland.

1948-1949 Berlin Blockade: U.S.S.R. cuts off West Berlin in an attempt to force it to join Eastern bloc. The blockade is broken by an Anglo-American airlift of supplies.

1949 East and West Germany are established as separate states.

Barbed wire and soldiers guarded the borders between East and West Germany.

The Americas

1941 Japanese attack U.S. naval base at Pearl Harbor, Hawaii. U.S.A. enters Second World War.

The Japanese attack on Pearl Harbor

1942 First nuclear reactor is built by Enrico Fermi in the U.S.A.

1942 Mexico and Brazil declare war on Germany and Japan.

1943 Revolution in Argentina: Juan Perón rises to power as virtual military dictator. He becomes President in **1946**.

1945 U.S. explodes first atom bomb in New Mexico.

1945 United Nations (UN) is set up in San Francisco, U.S.A.

UN symbol

1947 U.S. introduces the Marshall Plan, to give economic aid to non-communist countries.

German poster advertizing the Marshall Plan

1947 U.S. President Harry Truman introduces Cold War doctrine: the U.S. offers to support groups fighting communism.

1948 The invention of the transistor miniaturizes electronic circuitry.

1949 North Atlantic Treaty Organization (NATO) is formed: a military alliance to counter the communist threat.

Asia and Australasia

1950-1953 The Korean War: North Korea, backed by the U.S.S.R., invades South Korea. UN forces (mainly U.S.) support South Korea. China supports North Korea. Communists make gains at first, but in **1951** UN forces counterattack. Treaty of Panmunjon (**1953**) establishes the border between North and South Korea.

Map of Korea 1953

U.S. tank from Korean War

1950 China invades Tibet.

1951 Mussadeq, Prime Minister of Iran, nationalizes the Anglo-Iranian Oil Company. Tension with Britain follows.

1951 Australia, New Zealand and U.S.A. sign ANZUS pact.

1951 Peace treaty gives Japan full independence. Rapid economic growth begins. U.S. occupation ends in **1952**.

1953 Edmund Hillary (New Zealand) and Sherpa Tensing (Nepal) reach the summit of Mount Everest, the world's highest mountain.

The world's highest mountains

Everest, Himalayas 8,846m (29,022 ft)
K2, Himalayas
Mont Blanc, Alps
Fujiyama, Japan
McKinley, Alaska Range
Kilimanjaro, Africa
Aconcagua, Andes

1954 Southeast Asia Treaty Organization (SEATO) is set up to check the spread of communism. It is signed by Australia, France, New Zealand, Britain, Pakistan, Philippines, Thailand and the U.S.A.

1954 Major French defeat by Vietnamese nationalists at Dien Bien Phu. North Vietnam sets up an independent state, based in Hanoi.

1954 Geneva Conference: Cambodia, Laos and South Vietnam become independent states.

1954-1973 The Vietnam War (see page 169).

A military parade in Malaya in 1957

1957 Malaya wins independence.

1959 Unsuccessful uprising in Tibet against the Chinese. The Dalai Lama flees to India.

1958 Mao Zedong announces the Great Leap Forward, a plan for rapid industrial growth.

Africa and the Middle East

1951 King Abdullah of Jordan is assassinated.

1952 Revolution in Egypt: King Farouk abdicates. A republic is proclaimed in **1953**.

1952-1955 Risings by the Mau Mau in Kenya, a secret society opposed to British rule.

Kenyan shields

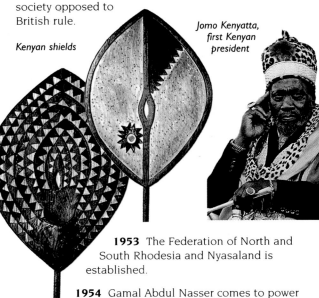

Jomo Kenyatta, first Kenyan president

1953 The Federation of North and South Rhodesia and Nyasaland is established.

1954 Gamal Abdul Nasser comes to power in Egypt.

1954-1962 Nationalist revolt in Algeria against French rule ends with independence.

1956 Second Arab-Israeli War.

1956 Oil is discovered in Nigeria.

1956 Sudan and Morocco become independent.

1956 Suez Crisis: President Nasser of Egypt nationalizes the Suez Canal. This is opposed by Britain and France. Israel invades Egypt, and Britain and France occupy the Canal Zone. U.S. opposition and world opinion force them to withdraw.

1957 Gold Coast (renamed Ghana) becomes independent under Kwame Nkrumah. An important step in the decolonization of Africa.

The flag of Ghana

1957 Tunisia is made a republic.

1957 King Feisal of Iraq is assassinated and a republic is proclaimed.

1958 United Arab Republic (U.A.R.) is set up between Egypt and Syria, later joined by Yemen. Syria leaves in **1960**.

Yemeni hats

Southern and Western Europe

1951 European Coal and Steel Treaty between Belgium, France, Holland, Italy, Luxembourg and West Germany.

1952 Elizabeth II becomes Queen of Great Britain and Northern Ireland.

1953 DNA structure is discovered by Francis Crick (U.K.) and James Watson (U.S.).

Model of a DNA molecule in the shape of a double helix

1954 Roger Bannister (U.K.) runs first 4 minute mile.

1957 Treaty of Rome establishes the European Economic Community (EEC). Members: France, Germany, Italy, Belgium, Netherlands and Luxembourg.

1958 De Gaulle becomes Prime Minister, then President, of France. The Fifth Republic is established.

1959 The first air cushioned vehicle (ACV), designed by Christopher Cockerell (U.K.), is publicly demonstrated.

A modern air cushioned vehicle

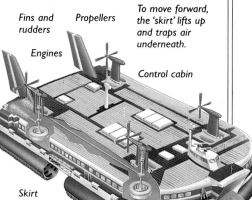

Fins and rudders

Propellers

Engines

To move forward, the 'skirt' lifts up and traps air underneath.

Control cabin

Skirt

Northern and Eastern Europe

1951 U.S.S.R. explodes its first atom bomb.

1953 Death of Stalin. Nikita Khrushchev becomes party leader in U.S.S.R.

Stalin

1953 Imre Nagy, liberal Communist Party leader, introduces reforms in Hungary.

1953 Soviet tanks crush anti-communist uprising in East Berlin.

1954 EOKA movement in Cyprus for union with Greece. Anti-British unrest till **1959**.

1956 Anti-communist uprising in Hungary is crushed by the U.S.S.R. Imre Nagy is executed.

Soviet tanks putting down the anti-communist revolt in Hungary in 1956

1955 The Warsaw Pact is signed: a military treaty and association between the communist states of Eastern Europe.

1957 U.S.S.R. launches the first Space satellite, *Sputnik* 1. Laika, a small dog, becomes first living creature in Space.

The rocket used to propel Sputnik into Space

The Americas

1950 Death of Eva Perón, popular and influential wife of President Juan Perón of Argentina.

1950 U.S. President Truman allows development of hydrogen bomb.

1950-1954 Senator McCarthy leads drive against communism in U.S.A.

Poster warning of the dangers of communism

1952 Civil war in Cuba: General Batista seizes power, opposed by communists led by Fidel Castro.

1955 Revolution in Argentina overthrows Juan Perón.

1958 The integrated circuit, or silicon chip, is demonstrated by Jack Kilby of Texas Instruments, U.S.A.

A silicon chip

1958 Alaska is 49th state of U.S.A.

1958-1967 Growing demands for civil rights for African Americans in U.S.A.

1959 Cuba: Fidel Castro overthrows Batista, with the help of Che Guevara, an Argentinian Marxist experienced in guerilla warfare.

Images of Che Guevara became a symbol of revolution all over the world.

1959 Failed invasion of Cuba by a small band of Cuban exiles trained by the American C.I.A.

1959 Hawaii is 50th state of U.S.A.

Decolonization

In **1939**, many European countries had widespread colonial empires. Virtually the whole of Africa was divided between Britain, France, Italy, Belgium and Portugal, as well as large parts of Asia, the Pacific and the Caribbean. But, between **1947** and **1975**, most of these colonies disappeared forever. Today, only a handful of colonies (mainly small islands) still exists.

The Second World War had the effect of weakening the European powers, and speeding up the break-up of their empires. Many of the Asian colonies had been occupied by Japan. Once the War was over, struggles against the Japanese developed into independence movements. Public opinion in Europe was also changing. It was no longer seen as justifiable or practicable that a nation should rule over people in a distant continent.

INDEPENDENCE FOR INDIA

The independence of India and Pakistan in **1947** was an important landmark, beginning the break-up of the largest of the empires, the British empire.

Indian soldier in the British army

Hindus and Muslims had been campaigning separately for independence in India since the late 19th century. After **1920**, the largest group, the Indian National Congress, was led by Mohandas Gandhi, who became known as the Mahatma ("the great soul"). Gandhi encouraged the Hindus and Muslims to work together and attracted great support for his campaign of non-violent resistance to British rule.

But a number of Muslims, led by Mohammed Ali Jinnah, wanted a separate state. Faced with an Indian civil war, Britain decided to partition the subcontinent between Hindu India (the major part) and Muslim Pakistan, But millions were uprooted as they migrated to join their religious groups, and there were terrible massacres and riots. In **1948**, Gandhi himself was murdered by an extremist Hindu.

Jawaharlal Nehru, first Indian Prime Minister

After Indian independence, it was harder to resist demands from colonies elsewhere. Britain withdrew from Ceylon (Sri Lanka) in **1947** and Burma in **1948**, and in **1949**, the Dutch were forced to give up Indonesia. In Indochina, there was a struggle against French rule, between **1946** and **1954**, when they suffered a crushing defeat at Dien Bien Phu. This led to the independence of North and South Vietnam, Cambodia and Laos.

A spinning wheel, the symbol of the Indian National Congress

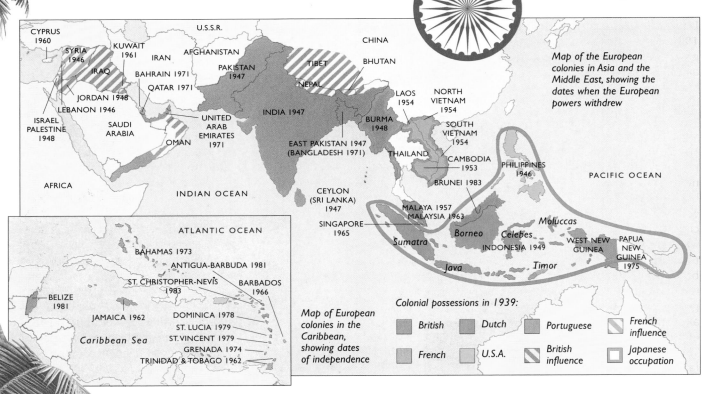

Map of the European colonies in Asia and the Middle East, showing the dates when the European powers withdrew

Map of European colonies in the Caribbean, showing dates of independence

Colonial possessions in 1939:

- British
- French
- Dutch
- U.S.A.
- Portuguese
- British influence
- French influence
- Japanese occupation

THE WINDS OF CHANGE

In **1957**, the Gold Coast (Ghana) became the first of many African countries to win independence from Britain. The British Prime Minister Harold Macmillan spoke of "winds of change" blowing through the continent. The independence of Kenya in **1963** was also significant, as Kenya had a large white settler population who resisted change.

WHITE SETTLER RULE

The situation was more difficult in Southern Rhodesia, which had even more white settlers. A white minority government, led by Ian Smith, broke away from British rule in **1965** and declared independence. This was called UDI (Unilateral Declaration of Independence). In **1980**, after years of guerilla warfare, power was given to a black majority, and Rhodesia became Zimbabwe.

CIVIL WARS, COUPS AND DICTATORSHIPS

Decolonization was neither quick nor easy. There were many terrible wars, both against the colonial rulers and civil wars to decide who should rule in their place. Fighting broke out between the different ethnic groups in the Congo, after the withdrawal of Belgium in **1960**. The "Congo Crisis" lasted until **1965**, when the United Nations sent forces to restore order. Especially bad were the wars against the French in Algeria (**1954-1962**), the Portuguese in Angola and Mozambique (**1961-1975**), and a civil war in Nigeria (**1967-1970**), when the eastern part (Biafra) attempted to break away. Algeria had a huge number of colonists, which influenced the French to resist independence. Their attempts to crush a revolt by the nationalist FLN led to over a million deaths.

Algerian independence day in 1962 and the Algerian flag

Portugal, ruled by dictator until **1974**, was the last to give up its African colonies.

Map of Africa with independence dates and names

Colonial possessions in 1939:

- British
- French
- Belgian
- Italian
- Spanish
- Portuguese
- British influence

TUNISIA 1956
MOROCCO 1956
WESTERN SAHARA 1975
ALGERIA 1962
LIBYA 1951
EGYPT
UPPER VOLTA 1960 (BURKINA FASO 1984)
MAURITANIA 1960
MALI 1960
NIGER 1960
SUDAN 1956
DIJBOUTI 1977
SENEGAL 1960
THE GAMBIA 1965
DAHOMEY 1960 (BENIN 1975)
UPPER VOLTA 1960
CHAD 1960
SOMALIA 1960
GUINEA-BISSAU 1965
GUINEA 1958
NIGERIA 1960
ETHIOPIA 1941
IVORY COAST 1960
LIBERIA
CENTRAL AFRICAN REPUBLIC 1960
UGANDA 1962
SIERRA LEONE 1961
TOGO 1960
CAMEROON 1960-1
ZAIRE 1960
KENYA 1963
GHANA 1957
CONGO 1960
GABON 1960
RWANDA 1962
EQUATORIAL GUINEA 1968
BURUNDI 1962
TANZANIA 1964
CABINDA 1975
ANGOLA 1975
ZAMBIA 1964
MALAWI 1964
MADAGASCAR 1960
ZIMBABWE 1980
MOZAMBIQUE 1975
NAMIBIA 1990
BOTSWANA 1966
SWAZILAND 1968
LESOTHO 1966
REPUBLIC OF SOUTH AFRICA

Flags of Ghana, Botswana, Uganda, Ivory Coast, Swaziland and Togo

President Mobutu of Zaire

But they became independent in **1975**, as soon as the dictatorship was overthrown.

In spite of the introduction of democracies at the outset of independence, many ex-colonies (especially in Africa) have been subject to coups, dictatorships, and frequent changes of government. The most notorious dictators include Jean-Bedel Bokassa of the Central African Republic (**1965-1979**), who made himself emperor in **1976**, and President Mobutu Sese Seko of Zaire (**1960-1997**).

Asia and Australasia

1960 War between China and India over disputed border.

1960 Worsening relations between China and U.S.S.R.

1960 Mrs. Bandaranaike of Sri Lanka becomes first elected woman prime minister in the world.

1961 U.S. starts sending troops to South Vietnam, to fight attacks by communist North Vietnamese, the Vietminh. They begin bombing North Vietnam in **1965**.

1964 State of emergency in Malaya after attacks by Indonesian guerillas.

1965 India and Pakistan fight over the Kashmir region on the border between them.

1965 Singapore becomes independent from Malaya.

1966 Indira Gandhi becomes Prime Minister of India.

Indira Gandhi

1966 Mao Zedong starts the Cultural Revolution in China: a two year period of terror in which supposed capitalist influences are crushed.

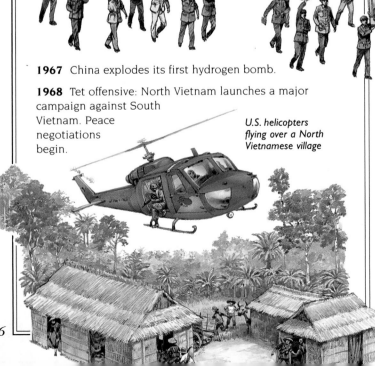

A demonstration in support of Mao during the Cultural Revolution

1967 China explodes its first hydrogen bomb.

1968 Tet offensive: North Vietnam launches a major campaign against South Vietnam. Peace negotiations begin.

U.S. helicopters flying over a North Vietnamese village

Africa and the Middle East

1960 Organization of Petroleum Exporting Countries (OPEC) is set up in Baghdad, Iraq.

1960 Many African countries become independent.

Stamps from Ghana, Congo, Gambia and Nigeria

1960 Sharpeville massacre in South Africa. 67 black Africans are killed when troops fire on a demonstration.

1960-1965 Chaos and civil war in the Congo following independence from Belgium. A military coup in the Congo brings President Mobutu to power. Katanga province declares independence.

1961 South Africa leaves the Commonwealth.

1962 Revolution in Yemen. The monarchy is abolished.

1963 Organization for African Unity (OAU) is formed in Addis Ababa, Ethiopia, by 30 African countries.

1964 Tanganyika and Zanzibar unite to become Tanzania.

1964 Rebel activity against the Portuguese in Mozambique.

1964 The last French forces leave Algeria.

Ian Smith

1965 UDI (Unilateral Declaration of Independence): Ian Smith, leader of the Rhodesian Front Party, declares Southern Rhodesia independent under white minority rule. Civil war follows.

1966 Jean Bokassa seizes power in the Central African Republic.

1966 Milton Obote seizes power in Uganda.

1966 Nkrumah is overthrown in Ghana.

1966 South African Prime Minister Verwoerd is assassinated.

1966 Revolution in Nigeria.

1967 Six Days' War between Israel and Arab states. Israel occupies Sinai.

Israeli flag

1967-1970 Nigerian Civil War: Eastern Nigeria breaks away and declares independence as Biafra.

1968 Guerilla warfare increases in Rhodesia.

1969 A revolution in Libya overthrows King Idris I and puts Colonel Gadaffi in power.

Southern and Western Europe

1961 Amnesty International is founded in London, to fight for human rights.

1962 Britain applies to join the EEC, but is rejected.

Flags of EEC countries: France, West Germany, Netherlands, Belgium, Italy, and Luxembourg

1965 Death of Winston Churchill.

1968-1969 Civil rights riots in Northern Ireland. Period of violence and clashes between Protestant Unionists (who want to maintain union with Britain) and Republicans (who want separation).

May 1968 Student unrest breaks out in Paris, and spreads to other parts of France. Demonstrations are suppressed by the police, which causes riots. Workers join forces with the students, which leads to a general strike against policies of President De Gaulle.

MAI68

President de Gaulle (left) Banner used by French students in May 1968 (right)

1969 Resignation of General de Gaulle as President of France.

Northern and Eastern Europe

1960 Cyprus gains independence from Britain, Greece and Turkey.

1961 Yuri Gagarin (U.S.S.R.) makes the first manned spaceflight. He completes an entire orbit of the Earth in *Vostok* 1.

Yuri Gagarin and medal of a Pilot-Cosmonaut

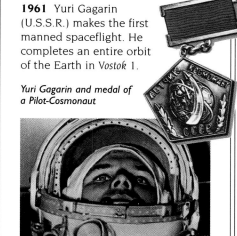

1961 East Germans and Russians build the Berlin Wall to stop East Germans fleeing to the West.

1963 Valentina Tereshkova (U.S.S.R.) is first woman in space.

Valentina in the command module of Vostok 6

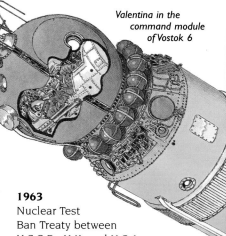

1963 Nuclear Test Ban Treaty between U.S.S.R., U.K. and U.S.A.

1964 Fighting between Greeks and Turks in Cyprus.

1964 Leonid Brezhnev succeeds Khrushchev as leader in U.S.S.R.

1965 Alexei Leonov (U.S.S.R.) is the first person to "walk in space".

1967 Greek monarchy is abolished.

October 1968 U.S.S.R. crushes the Prague Spring, a liberal movement in the Czech Communist Party.

The Americas

1960 Brasilia is capital of Brazil.

1961 Bay of Pigs: an invasion of Cuba, backed by the U.S.A. to overthrow Fidel Castro, fails.

1962 Jamaica, Trinidad and Tobago gain independence.

1962 The U.S. launches *Telstar*, the first satellite to relay live television and telephone calls.

Telstar satellite

1962 Cuban missile crisis: U.S.S.R. establishes nuclear bases in Cuba. U.S. threatens war unless they are dismantled. U.S.S.R. gives in.

1963 U.S. President Kennedy is assassinated in Dallas, Texas.

Seal of U.S. President

1964 President Johnson signs U.S. Civil Rights Bill.

1965 First U.S. spacecraft lands on the Moon.

Saturn 5, the first rocket to take people to the Moon

1966 British Guiana (Guyana) and Barbados become independent.

1967 Che Guevara, leader of guerillas in Bolivia, is killed.

1968 Martin Luther King, an African American civil rights leader, is assassinated.

1968 Senator Robert Kennedy is assassinated.

1969 Anti-Vietnam War demonstrations grow.

1969 Woodstock pop festival.

1969 July 21: U.S. astronaut Neil Armstrong is first man on the Moon.

Neil Armstrong on the Moon

The Cold War

After World War Two, the two superpowers, the U.S.S.R. and the U.S.A., were driven apart by political differences and mutual suspicion. Both sides built up their nuclear forces, and engaged in a war of propaganda and threats. This state, which existed between them from **1948** until the fall of the Soviet Union in **1991**, is known as the Cold War.

A U.S. nuclear missile

Map of divided Europe in 1946:
- Communist countries
- The Iron Curtain

WESTERN EUROPE
Berlin • EAST GERMANY, POLAND, U.S.S.R., CZECHOSLOVAKIA, HUNGARY, ROMANIA, YUGOSLAVIA, BULGARIA, ALBANIA

Map of divided Europe in 1946

THE IRON CURTAIN

After **1945**, Soviet troops settled in many of the German-occupied countries of Eastern Europe, and communist governments were set up. In **1946**, as these countries were cut off from the rest of the continent, the former British Prime Minister Winston Churchill spoke of an "iron curtain" descending across Europe. Increased tensions led to the building of military alliances. In **1949**, non-communist countries formed NATO (the North Atlantic Treaty Organization). In **1955**, the communist countries, or Eastern Bloc, responded with Warsaw Pact.

The Berlin blockade was beaten by the Berlin airlift: U.S. planes flying in regular supplies. After almost a year, the blockade was lifted, and in **1949**, the country was officially divided.

A DIVIDED GERMANY

After the War, the city of Berlin and Germany itself was divided into British, French, U.S. and Soviet sectors. By **1947**, Germany was functioning as two countries: East (the Soviet zone) and West (the rest). In **1948**, the Soviets tried to force West Berlin to join the East by closing all links to the city.

Soviet tanks patrolling the border zone

The Berlin Wall by the Brandenburg Gate

THE BERLIN WALL

Probably the most potent symbol of the Cold War was the Berlin Wall. It was constructed by the Soviets in **1961**, to prevent the steady flow of people fleeing the communist East for the capitalist West. By the time it was built, some 20,000 people a month were escaping via East Berlin.

Although the Wall was patrolled by tanks and guards armed with machine guns, it didn't stop the most determined . Between **1961** and **1989**, over 170 people were killed trying to get over the Wall.

Waiting for supplies during the Berlin airlift

CUBA

The Cold War reached its most dangerous moment with the Cuban Missile Crisis in **1962**. The U.S.S.R. planned to use Cuba (led by the pro-communist Fidel Castro) as a base for its nuclear missiles. The U.S.A., seeing its security at risk, began a naval blockade of the island, refusing to let in Soviet ships. For days, the world teetered on the brink of nuclear war, until the U.S.S.R. was persuaded to back down.

THE KOREAN AND VIETNAM WARS

Although there was no direct fighting between them, the two superpowers supported armed struggles between communists and anti-communists in the Third World.

U.S. soldier in Vietnam

The two main examples of this were the Korean War (**1950-1953**) and the Vietnam War (**1954-1973**). After World War Two, Korea was divided into Soviet-occupied North and U.S.-occupied South. In **1950**, after the superpowers had left, the North Koreans invaded

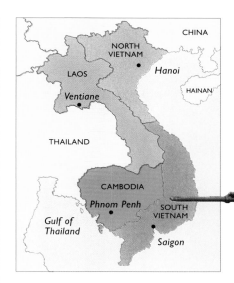

Map of Indochina in 1945
Anti-war poster (below)

the South and attempted to unify the country. The UN and U.S. occupied Korea, and China sent troops to back the North Koreans. This led to a long and bloody war, which left the country divided.

Civil war also broke out in Vietnam because the communist regime in North Vietnam, led by Ho Chi Minh, did not accept the division of the country into North and South. North Vietnam backed the Viet Cong, the communist rebels in the South, while the U.S. supported the South Vietnamese government. From **1961**, the Americans became more actively involved, and in **1965** U.S. planes began bombing the North.

Despite a huge U.S. presence (half a million troops by **1968**), the Viet Cong were masters of jungle warfare. With demoralized troops, and anti-war feeling at home, the Americans withdrew in **1973**, after a ceasefire. But the North was determined to unite the country, and in **1975** they took Saigon (now Ho Chi Minh city). Laos fell under Vietnamese control in **1975**, and Cambodia in **1978**.

THE CULTURAL REVOLUTION

Communism in China developed independently of the Soviet Union.

A young Chinese Red Guard during the Cultural Revolution

In **1967**, the Chinese leader Mao Zedong launched the Cultural Revolution, in an attempt to keep to pure communist ideals. He encouraged young people to join a group called the Red Guards, who used spying, violence and intimidation to seek out supposed anti-revolutionaries. During this time, schools were closed and work disrupted, and millions were killed or imprisoned.

By **1973**, Mao was old and ill and day-to-day governing was taken over by Deng Xiaoping. After Mao's death in **1976**, the Cultural Revolution was finally over.

Chinese flag

DETENTE

From the **1970s**, there was an easing of tension between the two sides in the Cold War, known as *détente*. This was encouraged by the appointment of Mikhail Gorbachev as Soviet leader in **1985**. His policies of *glasnost* (openness) and *perestroika* (restructuring) led swiftly and unexpectedly to the dissolution of the Soviet Union itself in **1991**.

Asia and Australasia

1970 Khmer Republic is set up in Cambodia.

1971 Pakistan attacks India, but is defeated.

1972 Pakistan is forced to give up East Pakistan, which forms the independent state of Bangladesh.

1972 Ceylon changes its name to Sri Lanka.

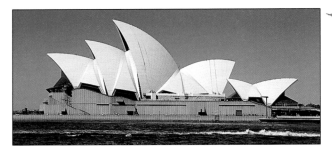

Sydney Opera House, Australia

1973 Australia: opening of the Sydney Opera House.

1973 The last American troops leave Vietnam.

1973 King of Afghanistan is overthrown.

1974 Largest ever tomb is discovered, belonging to Chinese emperor Shi Huangdi, containing 7,500 pottery soldiers, horses and chariots.

Terracotta army from the tomb of Shi Huangdi

1975 North and South Vietnam are united under communist rule.

1975 Communists seize power in Cambodia and Laos. Cambodia is ruled by Khmer Rouge dictator Pol Pot. Millions die under his rule: mass graves found in **1979**.

1976 Death of Mao Zedong. The fall of the "Gang of Four", Mao's closest associates, including his widow.

1977 A military coup in Pakistan by General Zia al-Haq. Former President Bhutto is overthrown and later hanged.

1978 Vietnamese invade Cambodia to help rebels overthrow the Khmer Rouge government. A pro-Vietnamese regime is set up.

1979 The Shah of Iran is overthrown, and an Islamic republic is set up, led by Ayatollah Khomeini.

1979 Civil war against the pro-Soviet regime in Afghanistan. Soviet troops invade in support of the government. A period of guerilla war follows.

Zimbabwe flag

Africa and the Middle East

1970 Military coup in Uganda brings Idi Amin to power.

1970 Israel and Egypt fight over Sinai.

1972 President Idi Amin expels many of the 40,000 Asians living in Uganda.

1973 Yom Kippur War between Israel and the Arab states, who achieve some success. Israel is attacked by Egypt and Syria. OPEC restricts oil supplies. Leads to huge increases in oil prices and a worldwide economic crisis.

Israeli F4E fighter plane

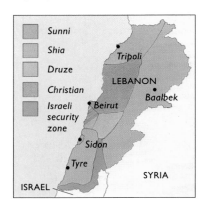

Oil rig and oil tanker

1974 Ethiopia: Haile Selassie is deposed and a Marxist government is established.

1974 Civil war begins between rival religious (Christian and Muslim) and political groups in Lebanon.

Map of Lebanon, showing the majority religious group in each area

	Sunni
	Shia
	Druze
	Christian
	Israeli security zone

Tripoli

LEBANON

Baalbek

Beirut

Sidon

Tyre

SYRIA

ISRAEL

1975 Angola and Mozambique become independent.

1975 King Faisal of Saudi Arabia is assassinated.

1976 Serious rioting in Soweto, near Johannesburg.

1977 Jean Bokassa crowns himself emperor of the Central African Empire.

1977 President Sadat of Egypt visits Israel for peace talks.

1978 UN peace troops sent to Israel/Lebanon border.

1979 Peace treaty between Israel and Egypt. Israel agrees to withdraw from Sinai.

1979 Uganda: civil war and military invasion by Tanzania leads to the overthrow of Idi Amin.

1979 Lancaster House Conference in London draws up a constitution for majority rule in Rhodesia, to be renamed Zimbabwe.

Southern and Western Europe

1970 British find oil in North Sea.

1970 Death of President de Gaulle of France.

1970 Spain: serious unrest among Basque separatists (people from the Basque region who want separation from Spain).

Juan Carlos, King of Spain from 1975

1971 Decimal currency is adopted in Britain.

1972 The situation in Northern Ireland worsens. Britain imposes direct rule from Westminster.

1973 Eire, Denmark and U.K. join the EEC.

1974 Revolution in Portugal. The military dictatorship is overthrown and replaced by democracy.

1975 Death of General Franco in Spain. The monarchy is restored under King Juan Carlos.

1976 Concorde, the first supersonic passenger plane, designed by Britain and France, begins a service flying across the Atlantic.

1977 King Juan Carlos restores democracy in Spain.

Concorde

1978 First test-tube baby, Louise Brown, born in U.K.

1979 Lord Mountbatten is killed by an IRA bomb.

1979 Margaret Thatcher becomes the first woman prime minister in U.K.

Conservative Party symbol

Northern and Eastern Europe

1971 Former Soviet leader Nikita Khrushchev dies.

1971 Women are given the vote in Switzerland.

1972 Munich Olympic Games: Israeli athletes are murdered by *Black September*, an Arab terrorist organization.

The Olympic logo

1973 Greece becomes a republic. President Papadopoulos is overthrown in a military coup.

1974 Turks invade Cyprus and split the island into northern Turkish sector and southern Greek sector.

Map of divided Cyprus

Kyrenia
Lefka · Nikosia · Famagusta
Paphos (Ktima) · Larnaca · Dh
eklia
Limassol
Akrotiri

	Turkish sector
	Greek sector
→	Turkish invasion

1975 West Germany: trial of the Baader-Meinhof terrorist gang.

1976 Helsinki Convention on Human Rights is adopted.

1977 *Charter* 77, a human rights organization, is formed, led by Czech playwright Vaclav Havel.

The Americas

1970 National guardsmen shoot four students dead at a demonstration at Kent State University, Ohio.

1971 Death of François "Papa Doc" Duvalier, President of Haiti since **1957**.

1973 U.S.-backed military coup in Chile, led by General Pinochet. Marxist President Allende is killed.

Chilean flag

1973 Juan Perón becomes President of Argentina again.

1973 Civil war in Nicaragua, between the *Sandinistas* (nationalist and communist guerillas) and the government (ruled by the Somoza family since **1933**).

1973-1974 Watergate scandal: U.S. President Nixon resigns.

1977 Space shuttle, the first reusable spacecraft, is tested.

The space shuttle

Parachutes slow the descent of the rockets.

Flight deck

Cargo bay

Cocoon for carrying satellites

Steering engine

Three main engines

1978 Agreement between Israel and Egypt at Camp David, U.S.A.

1978 U.S. begins diplomatic relations with China.

1978 900 members of a religious cult die in a mass suicide in Guyana.

1979 Nicaragua: Somoza is overthrown. Sandinista government comes to power.

Asia and Australasia

Compact disc **1982** First compact disc (CD) introduced by Sony (Japan) and Philips (Holland).

1982 Scientists first spot a hole in the ozone layer over Antarctica.

1983 Unrest between Tamil separatists and Singhalese majority in Sri Lanka.

1984 Britain and China agree on terms for the independence of Hong Kong.

A view of Hong Kong

1984 Assassination of Indian Prime Minister Indira Gandhi by a Sikh bodyguard, following repressive government measures against Sikh unrest in the Punjab. She is succeeded by her son, Rajiv.

1984 Fatal chemical leak at factory in Bhopal, India.

1985 French sink Greenpeace boat *Rainbow Warrior* in New Zealand. Greenpeace had been trying to stop French nuclear testing in the Pacific.

The Rainbow Warrior, and a blue whale, one of the endangered species, Greenpeace is trying to protect

1986 President Marcos is ousted after 20 years in power in the Philippines. He is succeeded by Corazon Aquino.

1987 India sends troops to Sri Lanka to control Tamil rebels.

1987 China: Chairman Deng Xiaoping resigns from all posts, except control of the army.

1988 Benazir Bhutto becomes Prime Minister of Pakistan.

1989 Soviet army completes withdrawal from Afghanistan.

1989 China: massacre of peaceful protesters by the Chinese army at Tiananmen Square, Beijing.

Africa and the Middle East

1980 Rhodesia becomes independent as Zimbabwe, with Robert Mugabe as Prime Minister.

1980 War between Iran and Iraq.

Flags of Iran (top) and Iraq (bottom)

1981 President Sadat of Egypt is assassinated.

1982 Israel invades Lebanon, in an attempt to drive out the PLO and establish a strong Christian government in Beirut. Syria opposes Israel. Civil war follows. Hundreds of Palestinians are massacred in Shabra and Shatila refugee camps.

PLO poster

1984–1985 A ten-year drought and civil war lead to famine in Ethiopia, Sudan and Chad. Thousands die.

1985 War between Iran and Iraq intensifies.

1985 Israeli troops withdraw from Lebanon.

1985 Riots in Eastern Cape, South Africa.

1986 State of Emergency declared in South Africa. Serious rioting and hundreds of deaths follow police violence.

1986 U.S. bombs Libya, after Libyans carry out acts of terrorism in Europe.

1986 Commonwealth and U.S. agree to economic sanctions against South Africa.

1986 A new constitution is adopted in Ethiopia. Colonel Mengistu Mariam becomes first president.

1987 Mohammed Barre is re-elected President of Somalia.

Ethiopian refugees were fed a mixture of oats, powdered milk and sugar.

1988 Refugees flee to Ethiopia from Sudan.

1988 South Africa signs peace agreement with Angola and Cuba.

1988 Refugees flee to Rwanda after massacres in Burundi.

1989 F. W. de Klerk becomes President of South Africa.

1989 Death of Iranian leader, Ayatollah Khomeini.

Southern and Western Europe

1980 Terrorist bomb kills 84 at Bologna railway station, Italy.

1981 François Mitterand becomes first Socialist President of France.

1981 Prince of Wales marries Lady Diana Spencer.

1982 AIDS virus is identified in France.

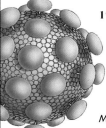

Model of AIDS virus

1984 U.K.: IRA bomb hits Conservative Conference.

1984-1985 Irish singer Bob Geldof organizes Band Aid and Live Aid, raising millions for Ethiopia.

Backstage pass for the Live Aid concert

1986 Spain and Portugal join EEC.

1986 Lloyds building is completed.

The Lloyds building, London

1987 Hurricane hits southern Britain and northern France.

1989 British writer Salman Rushdie is condemned to death by Ayatollah Khomeini for his book *Satanic Verses*.

Northern and Eastern Europe

1980 Death of President Tito, ruler in Yugoslavia since **1945**.

1980 Serious unrest in Poland, as the independent trade union movement *Solidarnosc* (Solidarity), led by Lech Walesa, gains support. Polish government declares martial law, bans Solidarity, and imprisons many of its leaders.

Solidarity logo

1981 Greece joins the EEC.

1985 Mikhail Gorbachev becomes leader in the U.S.S.R.

1985 Summit between Reagan and Gorbachev in Geneva.

1986 The Reykjavik summit between Reagan and Gorbachev fails.

1986 Major nuclear power disaster at Chernobyl, U.S.S.R.

After the disaster, radiation levels were too high for instruments to record.

1987 Gorbachev encourages *glasnost* ("openness") and *perestroika* ("restructuring") in the U.S.S.R.

1989 Tadeusz Mazowiecki is elected Prime Minister of a Solidarity-led government in Poland.

1989 End of communist rule in Czechoslovakia.

1989 Civil war in Romania. President Ceausescu is executed.

1989 Germany: the Berlin Wall is knocked down.

Berliners celebrating the opening up of the Wall

The Americas

1980 Archbishop Romero is shot in church in El Salvador.

1981 Ronald Reagan becomes U.S. President.

1981 The space shuttle makes its first spaceflight.

The space shuttle provided the first reusable method of launching spacecraft.

1982 British Honduras becomes independent Belize.

1982 Falklands War: Argentina invades the Falkland Islands. British naval taskforce retakes the islands.

1983 Left-wing coup in Grenada is put down with U.S. intervention.

1983 Military regime falls and democracy is restored in Argentina.

1985 Democracy is restored in Brazil and Uruguay.

1985 U.S. supplies aid to the Contra rebels in Nicaragua.

1985 Colombian volcano erupts.

1986 Spacecraft *Voyager* 2 sends pictures of Uranus. *Uranus*

1986 *Challenger* space shuttle explodes on lift-off.

1986 Iran-Contra scandal in U.S.A.

1987 Washington treaty eliminates medium range nuclear missiles.

1987 International Stock Market crash begins in Wall St., New York.

1989 Stealth bomber B2 developed by Northrop and U.S. air force.

1989 U.S. invades Panama. Dictator Noriega is removed from power.

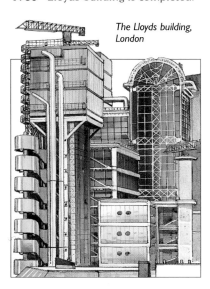

The end of the century

Dramatic, and often unexpected, changes swept the international political scene in the last decade of the 20th century. Communism, which did so much to shape politics earlier in the century, began to crumble irretrievably from the late **1980s**. This led to the most remarkable change of all: the break-up of one of the two great superpowers of the 20th century, the Soviet Union, and with it changes in the balance of world power.

THE IRON CURTAIN RISES

Resistance from inside the Eastern bloc came first from Poland. Strikes by the non-communist trade union, Solidarity, led by Lech Walesa, brought the economy to a standstill

in **1988**, and the government was forced to hold talks. In **1989**, the Poles were given free elections, and in **1990**, communist power ended.

The Polish example had a liberating influence on the other countries of Eastern Europe. In Czechoslovakia, Bulgaria, Hungary and communist regimes were forced to tolerate new political parties. Only Romania and Albania held out against change. When Hungary opened its borders to Austria in **1989**, it allowed the free flow of people between East and West for the first time since the Berlin Wall was built in **1961**. The lifting of the Iron Curtain was now inevitable. All over East Germany,

Wenceslas Square, in Prague, which became a meeting place for reformers

People waved the Romanian flag with the communist symbol ripped from the middle.

people took to the streets demanding change. In **November 1989**, the government gave in. The Wall was dismantled, and on **October 23, 1990**, East and West Germany were reunited.

THE END OF THE SOVIET UNION

Meanwhile, the Soviet Union was itself in turmoil, with economic decline, made worse by its long, unpopular war in Afghanistan. It no longer had the power nor, since the rise in **1985** of the reforming leader Gorbachev, the will to put a stop to events in Eastern Europe.

Mikhail Gorbachev

In **1989**, Gorbachev introduced elections for a council of deputies (representatives) from each Soviet republic. Leading communists were defeated by reformers, such as Boris Yeltsin. But these reforms weakened Soviet unity, as nationalists won support, especially in Latvia, Lithuania and Estonia, which claimed independence in **1990**.

Political and military leaders were split between hardline communists and radical reformers. In **August 1991**, the hardliners seized power in a coup, but it was overthrown by a mass protest led by Yeltsin, who eventually won over the troops. On **December 31, 1991**, the U.S.S.R. officially ceased to exist. Gorbachev, as President, was out of a job, while Yeltsin, as President of Russia, was in control of the largest republic. Most of the Soviet republics were granted independence, while others, like Azerbaijan, continue to fight for it.

Map of former Soviet Union and new republics of Eastern Europe

- Republics of former Soviet Union
- Eastern European Republics

Part of Russian Federation

RUSSIAN FEDERATION

Tallinn
St Petersburg
LATVIA
Riga
ESTONIA
Kaliningrad
Moscow
Vilnius
LITHUANIA
EAST GERMANY
Minsk
POLAND
BELARUS
CZECH REPUBLIC
Kiev
SLOVAKIA
UKRAINE
HUNGARY
MOLDOVA
See p.175
Chisinau
ROMANIA
BULGARIA
Black Sea
ALBANIA
GEORGIA
Tblisi
ARMENIA
Yerevan
Baku
AZERBAIJAN
Caspian Sea
Aral Sea
KAZAKHSTAN
Almaty
Dishkek
KYRGYZSTAN
Tashkent
UZBEKISTAN
TAJIKISTAN
Dushanbe
TURKMENISTAN
Ashgabat

Pulling down the statue of Dzerzhinsky, founder of the Soviet secret police

YUGOSLAVIA

Yugoslavia, united since World War Two largely by the will of its leader, Marshall Tito, was made up of states containing people from different linguistic and religious (Muslim, Catholic and Orthodox) groups. After Tito's death in **1980**, these states began to pull apart. In **1991**, Croatia and Slovenia declared independence. Serbia tried to stop them, and civil war broke out. It spread to Bosnia and Herzegovina, and the scale of atrocities and bloodshed intensified.

United Nations peacekeepers in Yugoslavia

Map of the fomer Yugoslavia in the 1990s

SOUTH AFRICA

By the **1980s**, the white regime in South Africa became increasingly isolated from the rest of the world, economically and diplomatically, because of its policy of *apartheid*. By **1990**, President F. W. de Klerk had become convinced that the only way forward was to end *apartheid*.

There was resistance from some white extremists, as well as tensions between the two main black parties: the ANC (African National Congress), led by Nelson Mandela, and the Zulu Inkatha Party, led by Chief Mangosouthu Gatsha Buthelezi. Free elections were held in **1994,** and Mandela became the country's first black president.

THE GULF WAR

In the **1990s**, tensions continued in the Middle East, where the dispute between Israelis and Palestinians remained unresolved. The invasion of Kuwait by Iraq, under Sadam Hussein, led to the Gulf War (**1990-1991**). Despite Iraq's defeat, there is still wide concern about its development of chemical and nuclear weapons.

Burning oil wells after the Gulf War

CHINA AND HONG KONG

There were also calls for democracy in China. In **April 1989**, 100,000 students occupied Tiananmen Square, Beijing. The army moved in to break up the protest, and thousands were killed. Despite economic reforms and some liberalization, the government has stood firm against any fundamental political changes.

Hong Kong flag

On **July 1,1997**, in spite of misgivings on the part of some of the population, the capitalist colony of Hong Kong was transferred to communist China, following the expiry of its 99 year lease to Britain.

IMPORTANT DATES

1980 Solidarity wins new rights in Poland.

1985 *Perestroika* in the U.S.S.R.

November 27, 1988 Communist government in Czechoslovakia is forced to resign after peaceful pro-democracy demonstrations sweep the country. Vaclav Havel, leader of Civic Forum, is elected President.

1988 INF treaty between U.S.A. and U.S.S.R.: agreement to reduce production of nuclear weapons.

May 1989 Hungary opens its border with Austria.

November 1989 Berlin Wall falls.

December 25, 1989 President Ceausescu of Romania executed.

1990 Communist Party is defeated in Polish elections. Tadeusz Mazowiecki is first non-communist prime minister in Soviet bloc.

March 1990 Free elections are held in Hungary, won by non-communist Democratic Forum.

May 1990 Communist and non-communist coalition elected in Romania.

1990 Nelson Mandela freed from prison after 27 years.

1991- Civil War in Yugoslavia.

December 31, 1991 The Soviet Union is dissolved. Its former republics become independent.

1992 Earth Summit Conference: world leaders agree on steps to try to tackle air pollution and global warming.

1994 Nelson Mandela is President of South Africa.

1997 Hong Kong is restored to China.

Dolphin and globe, environmental symbols

Asia and Australasia

1990 Benazir Bhutto, Prime Minister of Pakistan, is dismissed by the President.

Benazir Bhutto

1991 Paul Keating becomes Australian Prime Minister.

1991 Rajiv Gandhi, former Prime Minister of India, is murdered by a suicide bomber.

1991 A military junta, led by General Sunthorn Kongsompong, takes power in Thailand.

Aboriginal clapsticks

1993 Native Titles Bill is passed in Australia. A tribunal is set up to try to restore land rights to native Aboriginals.

1995 Meeting of APEC (Asia-Pacific Economic Co-operation): mutual opening of markets planned for **2020**.

1995 Earthquake destroys much of Kobe, Japan.

1995 Religious sect releases poison gas on trains in Tokyo, Japan.

1995-1996 France carries out nuclear testing at Mururoa, South Pacific.

1996 China signs a nuclear test ban treaty.

1996 Bombing campaign in Sri Lanka by the Tamil Tigers. State of emergency extended.

1996 China and Russia sign a strategic partnership.

1997 Death of former Chairman Deng Xiaoping in China.

1997 Demonstrations in Seoul, South Korea.

1997 Fires caused by forest clearance in Indonesia grow out of control, spreading pollution through Southeast Asia.

1997 Hong Kong: 99-year lease to Britain expires on **June 30**. Britain returns Hong Kong to China on **July 1**.

Street scene in Hong Kong

Africa and the Middle East

1990 Rwanda invaded by Tutsi-led rebels. The invasion is contained, and multiparty democracy is established.

1990 Namibia becomes independent from South Africa.

1990 Iraq, led by Saddam Hussein, invades Kuwait. Leads to worldwide protest and a rise in oil prices.

1990 ANC (African National Congress) ban is lifted in South Africa. *Apartheid* begins to break up. Nelson Mandela is released after 27 years in prison.

1990-1991 Gulf War: UN operation "Desert Storm" forces Iraq to withdraw from Kuwait. Iraqi forces leak 2 million barrels of oil into the Persian Gulf, causing worst oil pollution in history.

A sea bird suffering the ill effects of the oil spill

1991 Mogadishu, Somali capital, is captured by rebel forces and President Barre is overthrown.

1992-1995 UN peacekeepers intervene in Somalia, but fail to maintain peace.

1992 Civil war in Algeria.

1993 Peace agreement between Yasser Arafat, PLO leader, and Israeli Prime Minister Yitzhak Rabin. Some self-rule for Palestinians on Gaza Strip and West Bank of River Jordan.

1993 Ethiopia recognizes Eritrea's independence.

1994 Nigeria executes 9 minority rights activists.

1994 Nelson Mandela becomes President of South Africa, after first multiracial elections.

Nelson Mandela

1994 Civil war in Rwanda, between Hutu people and the Tutsi government. Thousands die.

1995 Israel: Rabin is assassinated by a Jewish extremist.

1996 Ethiopian forces attack Muslim fundamentalist militia in northern Somalia.

1997 President Mobutu Sese Seko of Zaire is deposed and dies soon after. Replaced by Laurent Kabila, leader of the rebel forces. Zaire renamed Democratic Republic of Congo.

1997 Israel hands over Hebron and other Palestinian land.

1997 Atrocities in Algeria by anti-government forces.

1997 Massacre of over 60 tourists near Luxor, Egypt.

Giraffe and lion, found in southern Africa

Southern and Western Europe

1990 Margaret Thatcher resigns as British Prime Minister.

1990 Mary Robinson becomes first woman President of Eire.

An Ecu, a design for a possible future European coin

1993 The Single European Market is established.

1993 Downing Street Declaration: British and Irish prime ministers work for peace in Northern Ireland.

1994 Channel Tunnel opens between Britain and France.

Digging the Channel Tunnel

1994-1996 IRA ceasefire.

1995 EU summit in Madrid: single currency, the Euro, planned for **1999**.

1995 Jacques Chirac is elected President of France.

1995 London: collapse of Barings Bank, after trader Nick Leeson makes huge losses in Singapore.

1997 U.K.: Tony Blair becomes Labour Prime Minister in a landslide victory, after 18 years of Tory rule.

1997 Diana, Princess of Wales, is killed in a car crash in Paris.

1997 Scotland and Wales vote for devolution. They are given their own elected parliaments.

Diana, Princess of Wales

Northern and Eastern Europe

1990 Germany is reunified.

1990 Lech Walesa, becomes President of Poland.

1990 Boris Yeltsin is elected President of the Republic of Russia.

1991 Soviet leader, Mikhail Gorbachev, is ousted in a coup led by military and KGB leaders. Gorbachev is restored, but later resigns. U.S.S.R. is dissolved, and renamed Commonwealth of Independent States (C.I.S.).

Flags of U.S.S.R. and Russia

Soviet peace poster

1991 Latvia, Lithuania and Estonia become independent.

1991 Civil war begins in Yugoslavia. Croatia, Macedonia and Slovenia become independent. Bosnia-Herzegovina follows in **1992**.

1993 Czechoslovakia splits into Czech and Slovak republics.

1994 Ferry *Estonia* sinks in the Baltic Sea. Over 900 are drowned.

1994 Russian tanks invade breakaway region of Chechenia.

1995 End of fighting between government and Bosnian Serbs.

1995 Scientists in Geneva create antimatter for the first time.

1995 Austria, Finland and Sweden join the EU.

1996 Croatia and former Yugoslavia establish diplomatic relations.

1996 Ceasefire in Chechenia.

1997 Collapse of the economy leads to popular uprising in Albania and fall of the government.

The Americas

1990 Sandinista government is defeated in Nicaraguan elections.

1992 Virtual Reality is developed by Gilman Louie in U.S.A.

1992 Boutros Boutros-Ghali becomes UN secretary-general.

1992 The first UN summit on the environment is held in Brazil.

Rainforest wildlife

1992 Mass riots in Los Angeles, U.S.A., after four white policemen are acquitted of beating a black motorist.

1993 Bill Clinton becomes U.S. president.

1993 Huge bomb damages the World Trade Center in New York.

1993 51-day siege in Waco, Texas. 80 cult members commit suicide.

1994-1995 Trial of football star O.J. Simpson, for the murder of his ex-wife, is seen by millions on TV, and drags on for months.

1994 U.S. forces occupy Haiti and restore elected President Aristide to power after military coup.

1995 Bomb wrecks federal building in Oklahoma City: the worst terrorist attack in U.S. history.

1995 Quebec votes to remain part of Canada.

1997 4-month siege of Japanese embassy, Lima, Peru by Tupac Amaru guerillas.

Quebec flag

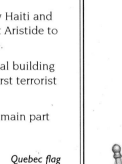

1997 Climatic change due to El Niño phenomenon causes extensive damage in South America and southern U.S.A.

1997 Pathfinder probe lands on Mars.

Mars

World history map

This map shows modern country names, with scenes from world history, and things from around the world today.

Arctic tern

ARCTIC OCEAN

Inuit fisherman from Greenland

First flight of Concorde, the world's only supersonic airliner, 1969 (Anglo-French)

Bering Strait

Alaska

Bear Lake

Baffin Bay

GREENLAND

ICELAND

NORWAY

Gulf of Alaska

CANADA

Canadian flag, adopted in 1965

Hudson Bay

NORTH ATLANTIC OCEAN

UNITED KINGDOM

SCOTLAND

IRELAND

ENGLAND

WALES

NORTH AMERICA

Quebec

Newfoundland

Vancouver Island

Native North Americans

Great Lakes

Bay of Biscay

FRANCE

UNITED STATES OF AMERICA

SPAIN

PORTUGAL

TUNISIA

The United States has sent many people into space, including the first man on the Moon in 1969.

In 1492 Christopher Columbus sailed from Spain to the Caribbean in the Santa Maria.

Canary Islands

MOROCCO

ALGERIA

Baja California

MEXICO

Gulf of Mexico

CUBA

BAHAMAS

HAITI

WESTERN SAHARA

SENEGAL

Sahara

DOMINICAN REPUBLIC

JAMAICA

GAMBIA

MAURITANIA

PACIFIC OCEAN

BELIZE

West Indies

PUERTO RICO

Leeward Islands

Cape Verde Islands

GUINEA

MALI

NIGER

GUATEMALA

Caribbean Sea

BURKINA FASO

NIGERIA

EL SALVADOR

HONDURAS

TRINIDAD AND TOBAGO

SIERRA LEONE

NICARAGUA

VENEZUELA

GUYANA

GUINEA-BISSAU

LIBERIA

GHANA

TOGO

COSTA RICA

COLOMBIA

SURINAM

IVORY COAST

BENIN

PANAMA

FRENCH GUIANA

An American clipper, a fast cargo ship built in the mid-19th century

Galápagos

ECUADOR

Gold cockerel, Ashanti kingdom, Ghana, 18th-19th centuries

EQUATORIAL GUINEA

GABON

SOUTH AMERICA

PERU

BRAZIL

SOUTH ATLANTIC OCEAN

Aztec warrior, 13th-16th centuries, Mexico

BOLIVIA

PARAGUAY

South American wildlife is unique, and much of it is now endangered.

Head from 12th century kingdom of Ife, Nigeria

CHILE

URUGUAY

ARGENTINA

The 15th century Inca city of Machu Picchu, Peru

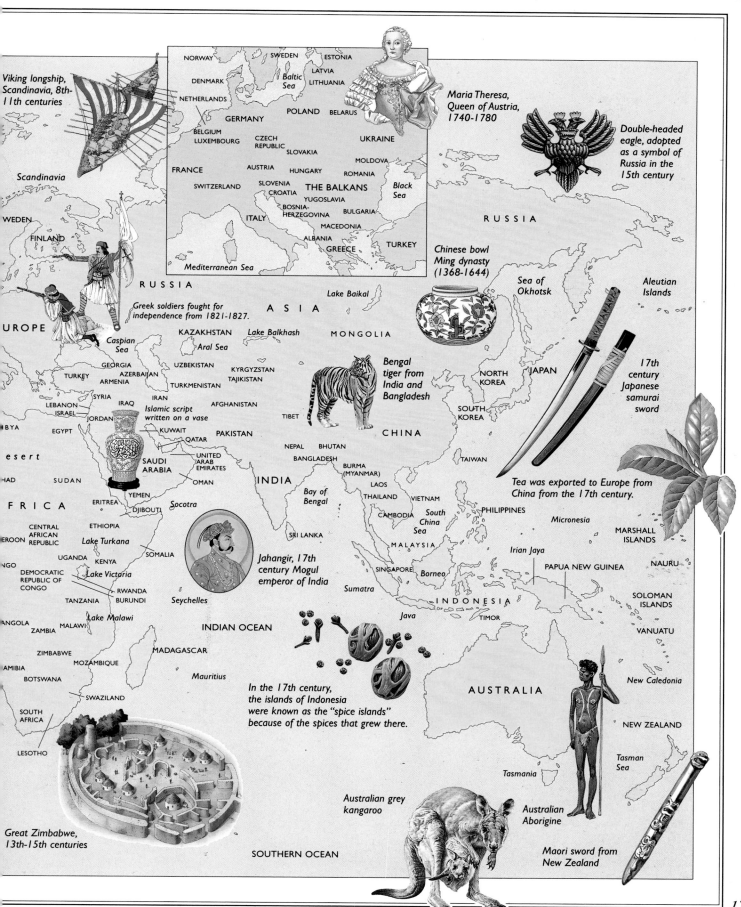

Viking longship, Scandinavia, 8th-11th centuries

Scandinavia

Maria Theresa, Queen of Austria, 1740-1780

Double-headed eagle, adopted as a symbol of Russia in the 15th century

NORWAY
SWEDEN
ESTONIA
LATVIA
LITHUANIA
DENMARK
Baltic Sea
NETHERLANDS
GERMANY
POLAND
BELARUS
BELGIUM
LUXEMBOURG
CZECH REPUBLIC
SLOVAKIA
UKRAINE
FRANCE
AUSTRIA
HUNGARY
MOLDOVA
SWITZERLAND
SLOVENIA
CROATIA
THE BALKANS
ROMANIA
Black Sea
BOSNIA-HERZEGOVINA
YUGOSLAVIA
BULGARIA
ITALY
MACEDONIA
ALBANIA
GREECE
TURKEY
Mediterranean Sea

WEDEN

FINLAND

Greek soldiers fought for independence from 1821-1827.

R U S S I A

A S I A

Lake Baikal

Chinese bowl Ming dynasty (1368-1644)

Sea of Okhotsk

Aleutian Islands

Caspian Sea

KAZAKHSTAN
Lake Balkhash
MONGOLIA
Aral Sea

UROPE

TURKEY
GEORGIA
AZERBAIJAN
ARMENIA
UZBEKISTAN
KYRGYZSTAN
TAJIKISTAN
TURKMENISTAN

NORTH KOREA
JAPAN

17th century Japanese samurai sword

SYRIA
LEBANON
ISRAEL
IRAQ
IRAN
AFGHANISTAN

Islamic script written on a vase

SOUTH KOREA

BYA

JORDAN
EGYPT
KUWAIT
QATAR
UNITED ARAB EMIRATES

Bengal tiger from India and Bangladesh

TIBET

PAKISTAN
NEPAL
BHUTAN
BANGLADESH
BURMA (MYANMAR)

CHINA

TAIWAN

esert

HAD
SUDAN
SAUDI ARABIA
OMAN
YEMEN

INDIA

LAOS
THAILAND
VIETNAM

Bay of Bengal

Tea was exported to Europe from China from the 17th century.

FRICA

ERITREA
DJIBOUTI
Socotra

CAMBODIA
South China Sea
PHILIPPINES

Micronesia

MARSHALL ISLANDS

CENTRAL AFRICAN REPUBLIC
EROON
ETHIOPIA
Lake Turkana
SRI LANKA

MALAYSIA

Irian Jaya

NAURU

NGO
UGANDA
KENYA
SOMALIA
DEMOCRATIC REPUBLIC OF CONGO
Lake Victoria
RWANDA
BURUNDI
TANZANIA

SINGAPORE
Borneo

PAPUA NEW GUINEA

SOLOMAN ISLANDS

Jahangir, 17th century Mogul emperor of India

Seychelles

Sumatra

I N D O N E S I A

VANUATU

ANGOLA
ZAMBIA
MALAWI
Lake Malawi

INDIAN OCEAN

Java

TIMOR

ZIMBABWE
MOZAMBIQUE
MADAGASCAR

Mauritius

AMIBIA
BOTSWANA

In the 17th century, the islands of Indonesia were known as the "spice islands" because of the spices that grew there.

AUSTRALIA

New Caledonia

SWAZILAND

SOUTH AFRICA

NEW ZEALAND

LESOTHO

Tasman Sea

Tasmania

Great Zimbabwe, 13th-15th centuries

Australian grey kangaroo

Australian Aborigine

Maori sword from New Zealand

SOUTHERN OCEAN

Monarchs and political leaders

KINGS AND QUEENS OF ENGLAND

Saxons	**802-106**
Normans	**1066-1154**
Plantagenets	**1154-1399**
Lancastrians	**1399-1461**
Yorkists	**1461-1485**
Tudors	**1485-1603**
Stuarts	**1603-1714**
Hanoverians	**1714-1910**
Windsors	**1910-**

802-839	Egbert
839-858	Ethelwulf
858-860	Ethelbald
860-866	Ethelbert
866-871	St. Ethelred I
871-899	Alfred the Great
899-925	Edward the Elder
925-939	Athelstan
939-946	Edmund I
946-955	Eadred
955-959	Edwy
959-975	Edgar
975-978	Edward the Martyr
978-1016	Ethelred II "The Unready"
1016	Edmund II "Ironside"
1016-1035	Canute (or Cnut)
1037-1040	Harold I
1040-1042	Harthacnut
1042-1066	Edward the Confessor
1066	Harold II
1066-1087	William I "The Conqueror"
1087-1100	William II
1100-1135	Henry I
1135-1154	Stephen
1135	Matilda declared Queen
1154-1189	Henry II
1189-1199	Richard I
1199-1216	John
1216-1272	Henry III
1272-1307	Edward I
1307-1327	Edward II
1327-1377	Edward III
1377-1399	Richard II
1399-1413	Henry IV
1413-1422	Henry V
1422-1461	Henry VI
1461-1470	Edward IV
1470-1471	Henry VI regained crown
1471-1483	Edward IV regained crown
1483	Edward V
1483-1485	Richard III
1485-1509	Henry VII
1509-1547	Henry VIII
1547-1553	Edward VI
1553	Lady Jane Grey
1553-1558	Mary I
1558-1603	Elizabeth I

KINGS AND QUEENS OF ENGLAND AND SCOTLAND

1603-1625	James I
1625-1649	Charles I
1649-1660	Britain is ruled as a commonwealth
(1653-1658	Oliver Cromwell is Lord Protector)
1660-1685	Charles II
1685-1688	James II
1689-1694	William III and Mary II
1694-1702	William III reigned alone
1702-1714	Anne

KINGS AND QUEENS OF UNITED KINGDOM

1714-1727	George I
1727-1760	George II
1760-1820	George III
1820-1830	George IV
1830-1837	William IV
1837-1901	Victoria
1901-1910	Edward VII
1910-1936	George V
1936	Edward VIII
1936-1952	George VI
1952-	Elizabeth II

KINGS AND QUEENS OF SCOTLAND

843-860	Kenneth MacAlpin
1005-1034	Malcolm II
1057-1093	Malcolm III
1124-1153	David I
1153-1165	Malcolm IV
1214-1249	Alexander II
1249-1286	Alexander III
1286-1290	Margaret of Norway
1292-1296	John Balliol (removed by Edward I of England)
1306-1329	Robert I "the Bruce"
1329-1371	David II
1371-1390	Robert II
1390-1406	Robert III
1406-1437	James I
1437-1460	James II
1460-1488	James III
1488-1513	James IV
1513-1542	James V
1542-1567	Mary Stuart
1567-1603	James VI (who becomes James I of England, Scotland and Ireland)

PRIME MINISTERS OF CANADA

In **1867** Lower Canada (Quebec), Upper Canada (Ontario), Nova Scotia, and New Brunswick united to form the Dominion of Canada.
Party: Conservative (C), Progressive Conservative (Prog.C), Liberal (Lib), Unionist (UN)

1867-1873	(C) Sir John A. Macdonald
1873-1878	(Lib) Alexander Mackenzie
1878-1891	(C) Sir John A. Macdonald
1891-1892	(C) Sir John J. Abbott
1892-1894	(C) Sir John S. D. Thompson
1894-1896	(C) Sir MacKenzie Bowell
1896	(C) Sir Charles Tupper
1896-1911	(Lib) Sir Wilfred Laurier
1911-1920	(C/UN) Sir Robert L. Borden
1920-1921	(UN) Arthur Meighen
1921-1926	(Lib) W. L. Mackenzie King
1926	(C) Arthur Meighen
1926-1930	(Lib) W. L. Mackenzie King
1930-1935	(C) Richard Bedford Bennett
1935-1948	(Lib) W. L. Mackenzie King
1948-1957	(Lib) Louis St. Laurent
1957-1963	(Prog.C) John G. Diefenbaker
1963-1968	(Lib) Lester B. Pearson
1968-1979	(Lib) Pierre Elliott Trudeau
1979-1980	(Prog.C) Joe Clark
1980-1984	(Lib) Pierre Elliott Trudeau
1984	(Lib) John Turner
1984-1993	(C) Brian Mulroney
1993	(Prog.C) Kim Campbell
1993-	(Lib) Jean Chrétien

PRIME MINISTERS OF NEW ZEALAND

From **1856-1907** self-government was granted in New Zealand. In **1907** the country became a dominion.
Party: Liberal (Lib), Labour (Lab), Reform (Ref), United (U), National (Nat)

1906-1912	(Lib) Sir G. Joseph Ward
1912	(Lib) Thomas MacKenzie
1912-1925	(Ref) William F. Massey
1925	(Ref) Sir Francis Bell
1925-1928	(Ref) Joseph G. Coates
1928-1930	(U) Sir Joseph G. Ward
1930-1935	(U) George W. Forbes
1935-1940	(Lab) Michael J. Savage
1940-1949	(Lab) Peter Fraser
1949-1957	(Nat) Sir Sidney G. Holland
1957	(Nat) Sir Keith J. Holyoake
1957-1960	(Lab) Sir Walter Nash
1960-1972	(Nat) Sir Keith J. Holyoake
1972	(Nat) John Ross Marshall
1972-1974	(Lab) Norman E. Kirk
1974	(Lab) Hugh Watt (acting)
1974-1975	(Lab) Sir Wallace Rowling
1975-1984	(Nat) Robert D. Muldoon
1984-1989	(Lab) David R. Lange
1989-1990	(Lab) Geoffrey Palmer
1990	(Lab) Mike Moore
1990-1997	(Nat) Jim Bolger
1997-	(Nat) Jenny Shipley

PRIME MINISTERS OF AUSTRALIA

In **1901**, the separate British colonies in Australia joined the Commonwealth and became states with a central government. Party: Free Trade/Protectionist (FT/P), Protectionist (Pro), Labour (Lab), Liberal (Lib), United Australian (UAus), United Country (UC), Nationalist (Nat), Nationalist Country (N/C), Country (Co)

1901-1903	(Pro) Edmund Barton
1903-1904	(Pro) Alfred Deakin
1904	(Lab) John Christian Watson
1904-1905	(FT/P) Sir George H. Reid
1905-1908	(Pro) Alfred Deakin
1908-1909	(Lab) Andrew Fisher
1909-1910	(Pro) Alfred Deakin
1910-1913	(Lab) Andrew Fisher
1913-1914	(Lib) Joseph Cook
1914-1915	(Lab) Andrew Fisher
1915-1923	(Lab/Nat) William M. Hughes
1923-1929	(Nat/Co) Stanley M. Bruce
1929-1932	(Lab) James Henry Scullin
1932-1939	(UAus/Co) Joseph A. Lyons
1939	(April)(UC) Sir Earle Page
1939-1941	(UAus) Sir Robert G. Menzies
1941	(Co) Sir Arthur Wm. Fadden
1941-1945	(Lab) John Joseph Curtin
1945	(Lab) Francis Michael Forde
1945-1949	(Lab) Joseph B. Chifley
1949-1966	(Lib) Robert G. Menzies
1966-1967	(Lib) Harold E. Holt
1967-1968	(Co) John McEwen
1968-1971	(Lib) Sir John Grey Gorton
1971-1972	(Lib) Sir William McMahon
1972-1975	(Lib) Gough Whitlam
1975-1983	(Lab) John Malcom Fraser
1983-1991	(Lab) Bob Hawke
1991-1996	(Lab) Paul Keating
1996-	(Lib) John Howard

PRESIDENTS OF EIRE

Party: Fianna Foil (FF), Fine Gael (FG), Labour (Lab), United Ireland (UI)

1938-1945	(No party) Douglas Hyde
1945-1959	(FF) Sean O'Kelly
1959-1973	(FF) Eamon de Valera
1973-1974	(FF) Erskine Childers
1974-1976	(FF) Cearbhall O'Dalaigh
1976-1989	(FF) Patrick John Hillery
1989-1997	(Lab) Mary Robinson
1997-	(FF) Mary McAleese

PRIME MINISTERS OF EIRE

1922-1932	(UI) William Cosgrave
1932-1948	(FF) Eamon de Valera
1948-1951	(FG) John Aloysius Costello
1951-1954	(FF) Eamon de Valera
1954-1957	(FG) John Aloysius Costello
1957-1959	(FF) Eamon de Valera
1959-1966	(FF) Sean Lemass
1966-1973	(FF) Jack Lynch
1973-1977	(FG) Liam Cosgrave
1977-1979	(FF) Jack Lynch
1979-1981	(FF) Charles Haughey
1981-1982	(FG) Garrett Fitzgerald
1982	(FF) Charles Haughey
1982-1987	(FG) Garrett Fitzgerald
1987-1992	(FF) Charles Haughey
1992-1994	(FF) Albert Reynolds
1994-1997	(FG) John Bruton
1997-	(FF) Bertie Earhern

PRIME MINISTERS OF GREAT BRITAIN

Party: Conservative (C), Labour (Lab), Liberal (Lib), Conservative-Unionist (CU), Coalition (Coal), National (N), Tory (T), Whig (W)

1721-1742	(W) Sir Robert Walpole
1742-1743	(W) Sir Spencer Compton
1743-1754	(W) Henry Pelham
1754-1756	(W) Duke of Newcastle
1756-1757	(W) Duke of Devonshire
1757-1762	(W) Duke of Newcastle
1762-1763	(T) John Stuart, Earl of Bute
1763-1765	(W) George Grenville
1765-1766	(W) Marquis of Rockingham
1766-1768	(W) William Pitt the Elder
1768-1770	(W) Duke of Grafton
1770-1782	(T) Lord North
1782-1783	(W) Earl of Shelburne
1783	(Coal) Duke of Portland
1783-1801	(T) William Pitt (Younger)
1801-1804	(T) Henry Addington
1804-1806	(T) William Pitt (Younger)
1806-1807	(W) Lord Grenville
1807-1809	(T) Duke of Portland
1809-1812	(T) Spencer Perceval
1812-1827	(T) Earl of Liverpool
1827	(T) George Canning
1827-1828	(T) Viscount Goderich
1828-1830	(T) Duke of Wellington
1830-1834	(Lib) Earl Grey
1834	(Lib) Lord Melbourne
1834-1835	(C) Sir Robert Peel
1835-1841	(Lib) Lord Melbourne
1841-1846	(C) Sir Robert Peel
1846-1852	(Lib) Lord John Russell
1852	(C) Earl of Derby
1852-1855	(Lib-Coal) Earl of Aberdeen
1855-1858	(Lib) Lord Palmerston
1858-1859	(C) Earl of Derby
1859-1865	(Lib) Lord Palmerston
1865-1866	(Lib) Lord John Russell
1866-1868	(C) Earl of Derby
1868	(C) Benjamin Disraeli
1868-1874	(Lib) William Gladstone
1874-1880	(C) Benjamin Disraeli
1880-1885	(Lib) William Gladstone
1885-1886	(C) Marquess of Salisbury
1886	(Lib) William Gladstone
1886-1892	(CU) Marquess of Salisbury
1892-1894	(Lib) William Gladstone
1894-1895	(Lib) Earl of Rosebery
1895-1902	(CU) Marquess of Salisbury
1902-1905	(CU) Arthur James Balfour
1905-1908	(Lib) Sir H. Campbell-Bannerman
1908-1915	(Lib) Herbert Henry Asquith
1915-1916	(Coal) Herbert Henry Asquith
1916-1922	(Coal) David Lloyd George
1922-1923	(C) Andrew Bonar Law
1923-1924	(C) Stanley Baldwin
1924	(Lab) J. Ramsay MacDonald
1924-1929	(C) Stanley Baldwin
1929-1931	(Lab) J.Ramsay MacDonald
1931-1935	(Nat) J. Ramsay MacDonald
1935-1937	(Nat) Stanley Baldwin
1937-1940	(Nat) Neville Chamberlain
1940-1945	(Coal) Sir Winston Churchill
1945-1951	(Lab) Clement Attlee
1951-1955	(C) Sir Winston Churchill
1955-1957	(C) Sir Anthony Eden
1957-1963	(C) Sir Harold Macmillan
1963-1964	(C) Sir Alec Douglas-Home
1964-1970	(Lab) Sir Harold Wilson
1970-1974	(C) Sir Edward Heath
1974-1976	(Lab) Sir Harold Wilson
1976-1979	(Lab) James Callaghan
1979-1990	(C) Margaret Thatcher
1990-1997	(C) John Major
1997-	(Lab) Tony Blair

PRESIDENTS OF U.S.A.

Inauguration date followed by Party: Federation (F), Republican (R), Democrat (D), Whig (W)

1789	(F) George Washington	1732-1799
1797	(F) John Adams	1735-1826
1801	(R) Thomas Jefferson	1743-1826
1809	(R) James Madison	1751-1836
1817	(R) James Monroe	1758-1831
1825	(R) John Quincy Adams	1767-1848
1829	(D) Andrew Jackson	1767-1845
1837	(D) Martin Van Buren	1782-1862
1841	(W) William Harrison	1773-1841
1841	(W) John Tyler	1790-1862
1845	(D) James Knox Polk	1795-1849
1849	(W) Zachary Taylor	1784-1850
1850	(W) Millard Fillmore	1800-1874
1853	(D) Franklin Pierce	1804-1869
1857	(D) James Buchanan	1791-1868
1861	(R) Abraham Lincoln	1809-1865
1865	(R) Andrew Johnson	1808-1875
1869	(R) Ulysses S. Grant	1822-1885
1877	(R) Rutherford Hayes	1822-1893
1881	(R) James Garfield	1831-1881
1881	(R) Chester Arthur	1830-1886
1885	(D) Grover Cleveland	1837-1908
1889	(R) Benjamin Harrison	1833-1901
1893	(D) Grover Cleveland	1837-1908
1897	(R) William McKinley	1843-1901
1901	(R) Theodore Roosevelt	1858-1919
1909	(R) William Taft	1857-1930
1913	(D) Woodrow Wilson	1856-1924
1921	(R) Warren Harding	1865-1923
1923	(R) Calvin Coolidge	1872-1933
1929	(R) Herbert Hoover	1874-1964
1933	(D) Franklin Roosevelt	1882-1945
1945	(D) Harry S. Truman	1884-1972
1953	(D) Dwight Eisenhower	1890-1969
1961	(D) John F. Kennedy	1917-1963
1963	(D) Lyndon B. Johnson	1908-1973
1969	(R) Richard Nixon	1913-1994
1974	(R) Gerald Ford	1913-
1977	(D) Jimmy Carter	1924-
1981	(R) Ronald Reagan	1911-
1989	(R) George Bush	1924-
1993	(D) Bill Clinton	1946-

Glossary

amnesty General pardon given by a government for crimes committed. Sometimes granted in an attempt to reach a settlement during a civil war.

annex To join a territory to a larger one by conquering or occupying it.

apartheid South African policy of the separation of races.

aristocracy Government by nobles, or a privileged class.

autocracy Government by a person or group, with unrestricted authority, that does not allow opposition. Government of this kind is described as autocratic.

autonomy Self-government, often limited, granted to a nation or people by a more powerful nation.

Bantu African languages and peoples found between the equator and the Cape of Good Hope.

baptize To immerse a person in water, as part of the initiation ceremony into the Christian Church.

caliph Title of successors of Mohammed, as rulers of Islamic states. The office or state is called a caliphate.

canonize To declare a person a saint.

capitalism System in which the means of production (industries, businesses, etc.) are owned by a relatively small group, who provide the investment and take a major share of the profits.

cede To give up or surrender a territory, often as part of the terms of a peace treaty following a war.

charter Document issued by a government, granting certain rights, such as the right to found a colony.

Christendom The people and nations who belong to the Christian Church.

Christianity The religion founded by Jesus of Nazareth in Palestine, known as Jesus Christ.

city-state A state that is made up of a city and its surrounding territory, such as the city-states of Ancient Greece or Italy during the Renaissance.

civil rights Equality in social, economic and political matters.

coalition Temporary alliance between different groups or parties, such as in a government.

collectivization Organization of the ownership of the means of production (industries, agriculture etc.) into groups, or collectives.

colony A settlement in a country distant from the homeland. A Crown colony is one whose administration is controlled by the King or Queen.

Commonwealth Organization of former member countries of the British empire, with the purpose of mutual co-operation and aid.

communism An ideology mainly based on the ideas of Karl Marx, which advocates a society without social classes, in which private ownership has been abolished. A system in which the means of production (industries and businesses) are owned by the state.

Congress The government of the U.S.A., made up of the Senate and the House of Representatives.

coup d'état Sudden overthrow of an existing government by a small group, often army officers.

demilitarization The removal of any military presence (soldiers, weapons, etc.) from an area.

democracy An ideology which originated in Ancient Greece, meaning "rule by the people".

dependency Territory subject to a nation, to which it is not usually linked geographically.

despot An absolute or autocratic ruler, or tyrant.

dictator A non-royal autocratic ruler, who imposes his rule by force. The government is called a dictatorship.

dominion The name formerly used for a self-governing colony within the British empire, such as Canada.

ecclesiastical Relating to the Christian Church or clergy.

egalitarian System that promotes equality between people.

enlightened despot A despot who tries to govern in the interests of the people, according to the ideals of the Enlightenment.

excommunicate To expel a person from the Catholic Church. This is done by the Pope.

fascism An ideology first developed by Mussolini. A form of government which allows no rival political parties and which controls the lives of its citizens. Nazism is a form of fascism.

federal Relating to a type of government in which power is shared between central government and several regional governments

guerilla A fighter operating in secret, usually against the government. From the Spanish *guerra*, meaning war.

hegemony Domination of one power or state within a league or federation.

homage Public display of respect to someone, such as a feudal lord.

infallibility Being incapable of error. A principle applied to certain pronouncements of the papacy.

Islam The religion of Muslims, based around the holy book the *Koran*, which teaches that there is only one God and Mohammed is his prophet.

Judaism The religion of the Jewish people, based on the *Old Testament* of the *Bible* and the *Talmud*, with a central belief in one God.

junta Goverment by a group of army officers, often after a coup d'état.

left-wing Term used to describe any ideology that tends towards socialism or communism.

liberalism Ideology advocating individual freedom and the idea that governments should interfere as little as possible in people's lives.

mandate Authority given to a country by the League of Nations, which met between 1920 and 1946, to administer another country under its trusteeship.

martial law Rule of law established by military courts, and maintained by the army, in the absence of civil authority.

Marxist Person or government following the teachings of Karl Marx. The belief that actions and institutions are determined by economics, that the class struggle is the instrument of change and that capitalism will eventually be overcome by communism.

medieval Relating to the Middle Ages, a period in European history dating loosely from **c.1000-1500.**

minority rule Government by a group of people who are different, politically or racially, from a larger group over whom they rule.

monopoly Sole right to trade in a specific product or a specific area.

nationalism Common cultural characteristics that link groups of people together. It sometimes leads to a movement for national independence, or separation from another ruling state.

nepotism Granting of an official position, or other privilege, to a member of the family, or friend.

nomads People who move continually from place to place.

oligarchy Government by a small group of people, such as in Ancient Greece.

one-party-state Nation that is dominated by the one and only party that is allowed to exist.

papal bull Formal document issued by the Pope.

parliamentary democracy Modern form of democracy, in which representatives elected by the people make decisions on their behalf.

patent Document issued by a government, granting specific rights.

plebiscite Direct vote by the people on an issue of particular importance, such as unification with another state.

pretender Someone who makes a claim to a throne or a title.

privateer Privately-employed soldier, sailor or vessel commissioned for service by a government.

protector Someone who exercises royal authority during the reign of a child, or an ill or unfit monarch.

protectorate Territory largely controlled by, but not annexed to, a more powerful nation.

radical Tending towards extreme or fundamental social, political or economic changes.

regent Ruler of a country during the reign of a child or the absence or incapacity of the monarch.

republic State governed by the representatives of the people, without a king or queen.

residency Official house of a British governor in an Indian princedom.

sack Plunder or destruction of a place by an army or mob.

secular Relating to worldly, as opposed to religious matters.

serf A person with no freedom, who is bound to the land. Found in medieval Europe and pre-revolutionary Russia.

separatist Person or organisation that advocates separation from a larger unit.

socialism Ideology that stresses equality of income and wealth, and public (state) ownership of industries (the means of production).

sovereignty Supreme authority or power of a sovereign or state.

state of emergency Crisis during which a government temporarily suspends all the usual rights and liberties of a people.

suffragette A woman who fought a militant campaign for votes for women, especially in Britain at the start of the 20th century.

sultan Supreme ruler of a Muslim state, such as the Ottoman empire.

suzerainty Position of a state exercising a degree of domination over a dependent state.

temporal See **secular**.

terrorist Someone who uses terror (bombing, assassinations, etc.) as a means of political persuasion.

Third World The relatively underdeveloped, unindustrialized countries of Africa, Asia and South America, outside the Eastern and Western blocs.

tribute Payment made by one nation or people to another, more dominant one, acknowledging submission.

triumvirate Coalition of three rulers, such as Caesar, Crassus and Pompey in Ancient Rome.

tyranny Oppressive and unjust government by a despotic ruler.

ultimatum A final offer by a government or party, in which it insists on certain conditions.

vassal A person or nation in a subordinate relationship to another person or nation.

Index

Picture credits

First published in 1998 by Usborne Publishing Ltd, Usborne House, 83-85 Saffron Hill, London EC1N 8RT, England. Copyright ©1998 Usborne Publishing Ltd.
First published in America August 1998 UE